GOD·FAMILY·COUNTRY

Our Three Great Loyalties

GOD·FAMILY· COUNTRY

Our Three Great Loyalties

Ezra Taft Benson

Published by Deseret Book Company, Salt Lake City, Utah, 1975

Library of Congress Catalog Card No. 74-84477
ISBN 0-87747-539-3

Frontispiece Picture (Opposite)
Photograph of an oil painting by Dean
Fawcett, hung in the U.S. Department of
Agriculture Administration Building following
President Benson's eight years as Secretary
of Agriculture, 1953-61.

Lithographed by

DESERET PRESS

in the United States of America

Foreword

This is a great book. It comes from a great man, and carries a message of inestimable value.

In it President Ezra Taft Benson discusses the Deity, the family, and the nation, doing so truly as one having the knowledge, authority, experience, and understanding to do so.

This remarkable volume also gives the reader an intimate glimpse into the deep and devout spiritual nature of the author. His is a spirituality that was born with him and has been evident throughout his long and brilliant career, easily recognized by people in other walks of life and in various religious faiths.

As a member of the Council of the Twelve, and as president of that unique body, President Benson in this book fully magnifies his calling as a special witness for Christ, for here he bears testimony of the Savior in language that no one can doubt or misunderstand.

He speaks in the fearless manner so characteristic of him, for he fears no man—only God—and not only strengthens the faithful with his testimony, but gives heart and courage to the weak and the doubting.

He gives strong reassurance to those who need a bolstering hand in defending true Christianity against avowed atheists, unbelieving intellectuals, and those who have political reasons for crushing true religion.

President Benson loves the Lord as only a special witness can, and gives of himself wholly and completely to His service.

To President Benson, love of Christ means service to Him with full heart and mind and soul. It is all encompassing. It embraces unquestioning faith, complete obedience, our day-to-day living habits, our family, and our civic life.

He knows that the whole duty of man is to serve God and keep His commandments. But he knows, too, that one cannot be a good Christian and be a careless or inactive church member. One cannot be a wholehearted Christian and not be a good family man, for a good family is indispensable to the highest kind of living.

And he understands fully, too, that no man can be a good Christian and at the same time be a bad citizen, a law breaker, one who incites to riot or arson, or one guilty of theft or duplicity or dishonesty in any form.

President Benson knows and teaches that we are the offspring of God, that our Heavenly Father is indeed our eternal progenitor, and that every man has in him the spark of divinity.

This is what gives meaning to life. It is what opens a view to our eternal destiny.

In this volume President Benson points out the true pathway to the Lord, which is traversed only through faith in God and sincere application of His principles to daily life, including home and nation.

Mark E. Petersen

Contents

Foreword - v

SECTION ONE: GOD

1. *The Perfect Example*
   In His Steps -   1
2. *The Son of God*
   Our Lord and Master - - - - - - - - - - - - - - - - - - 11
3. *A Spark of Divinity*
   Life Is Eternal - 19
4. *A Modern Prophet*
   Joseph Smith—Man of Destiny - - - - - - - - - - - 27
5. *The Worth of Souls*
   Missionary Work—A Major Responsibility - - - 43
6. *Answering the Call*
   Missionary Memories - - - - - - - - - - - - - - - - - - 51
7. *Helps for Missionaries*
   Essentials for Missionary Success - - - - - - - - - 57
8. *Faith-Promoting Experiences*
   A Love for the Work - - - - - - - - - - - - - - - - - - 69

9. *Eternal Verities*
   The Things That Endure ---------------- 77
10. *A Message for All Mankind*
   The Latter-day Saints and the World-------- 89
11. *Guides for Sunday*
   Keeping the Sabbath Day Holy ----------- 97
12. *An Anchor*
   The Power of Prayer ------------------ 109
13. *Talking to the Father*
   How to Improve Prayers, Public and Private -- 113
14. *Leadership Principles*
   How to Delegate Wisely ---------------- 129
15. *An Important Guide*
   Suggestions on Making Decisions ---------- 143
16. *Heeding Counsel*
   Listen to a Prophet's Voice --------------- 155

SECTION TWO: FAMILY

17. *Our Homes*
   The Family—A Sacred Institution ---------- 167
18. *Memories of Home*
   Family Joys ------------------------- 173
19. *The Patriarchal Order*
   Putting Father at the Head of the Family ---- 179
20. *How to Measure Up*
   A Challenge to Youth ----------------- 189
21. *Gratitude*
   Receive All Things with Thankfulness ------- 199
22. *Character Building*
   Scouting: Builder of Men ---------------- 207
23. *Guidelines for Health*
   Fitness—A Total Concept ---------------- 217
24. *Families Under Attack*
   Strengthening the Family ---------------- 223
25. *Dangers Within*
   Three Threatening Dangers -------------- 233
26. *Evil Effects of Rock Music*
   Satan's Thrust—Youth ----------------- 243

27. *Worldliness*
       Destructive Precepts of Men - - - - - - - - - - - - - - 253
28. *Preparedness*
       Prepare Ye - 265

SECTION THREE: COUNTRY

29. *Our Beliefs*
       The Twelfth Article of Faith - - - - - - - - - - - - - - 277
30. *Basic Political Principles*
       The Proper Role of Government - - - - - - - - - - - 281
31. *Free Enterprise*
       Survival of the American Way of Life - - - - - - - 305
32. *Citizenship*
       Civic Standards for the Faithful Saints - - - - - - 317
33. *The Fight for Freedom*
       Christ and the Constitution - - - - - - - - - - - - - 325
34. *A Path of Safety*
       Be Not Deceived - 335
35. *A Free People*
       The American Heritage of Freedom - - - - - - - 343
36. *Lessons of History*
       Watchman, Warn the Wicked - - - - - - - - - - - - 357
37. *Devotion to Sound Principles*
       America's Challenge - - - - - - - - - - - - - - - - - - 367
38. *Neutralizers*
       Not Commanded in All Things - - - - - - - - - - - 381
39. *A Nation Under God*
       Righteousness Exalteth a Nation - - - - - - - - - - 391
40. *Three Great Loyalties*
       God, Family, and Country - - - - - - - - - - - - - - 401

Appendix: Sources of Material Used - - - - - - - - - - - - - - - - - - 409

Index - 413

GOD

"Yes, knowledge is power, but the most vital and important knowledge is a knowledge of God—that he lives, that we are his children, that he loves us, that we are created in his image, that we can in faith pray to him and receive strength and inspiration in time of need.

"Such knowledge is priceless. True, man is saved no faster than he gains knowledge. Knowledge of what? Knowledge of God! Knowledge of his purpose and plans for the welfare, blessing, and eternal exaltation of us, his children. All useful knowledge is of value. The seeking of such knowledge is, therefore, commendable and rewarding. But in all of our searching for truth, we must remember that the knowledge of God, our Father, and his plans for us his children is of supreme importance."

—CHURCHWIDE YOUTH FIRESIDE ADDRESS
May 14, 1961

1

In His Steps

As a great Christian nation—a nation with a spiritual foundation—we join the Christian world in commemoration of that all-important and glorious event, the resurrection of the Lord Jesus Christ.

I bear witness that Jesus is the Christ, the Savior and Redeemer of the world, the very Son of God.

He was born the Babe of Bethlehem.

He lived and ministered among men.

He was crucified on Calvary.

He is risen—really resurrected.

He has appeared to men as a glorified Eternal King, in Palestine and also in America.

I bear this witness to all, but direct my remarks especially to our youth of the free world, for whom I have great hope and a fervent prayer.

My text, from Luke in the New Testament, stands out boldly in its impressive beauty. It covers a period of eighteen years following the return of Jesus from Jerusalem to Nazareth. Except for this one rich sentence of greatest import, the scriptures for this eighteen-year period are silent:

"And Jesus increased in wisdom and stature, and in favour with God and man." (Luke 2:52.)

Here, then, in one sentence—fourteen words—is the impressive, meaningful, and comprehensive account of eighteen years of preparation of the Son of God, the Savior and Redeemer of the world.

Here, in broad outline, in one succinct sentence—four points—are given the major fields of man's activity and striving: mental, physical, spiritual, and social.

Young men and women, remember, it is people, not things, that are all-important. Character is the one thing we make in this world and take with us into the next. God's purpose is to build people of character, not physical monuments to their material accumulations.

Point 1: "And Jesus increased in wisdom."

In the fourteenth chapter of John, Jesus is tenderly saying his farewell to his disciples after the Last Supper. He tells them that he goes to prepare a place for them in his Father's house, that where he is, they also may be. And Thomas says to him, "Lord, we know not whither thou goest; and how can we know the way?

"Jesus saith unto him, I am the way, the truth, and the life: no man cometh unto the Father, but by me." (John 14:5-6.)

The road lies before us. It is clearly marked.

In Proverbs we read: "Happy is the man that findeth wisdom, and the man that getteth understanding." (Proverbs 3:13.)

This same Jesus who increased in wisdom declared to a modern prophet: "Seek not for riches but for wisdom, and behold, the mysteries of God shall be unfolded unto you, and then shall you be rich." (D&C 6:7.)

It was once thought, and still is in some places, that when a young man sets out upon a quest for academic knowledge, his faith in God would soon be destroyed.

Our youth generally are living proof to the contrary. It is not the search for knowledge—nor the knowledge itself—that costs a man his faith. It is rather the conceit of small minds proving anew that a little knowledge can be a dangerous thing. It is intellectual pride that leads one to think he is self-sufficient in matters of mind and of spirit. Let us ever realize the vast difference that exists between discovery of the truth and the custodian of all truth. The one is human; the other is divine.

Religion and science have sometimes been in apparent conflict. Yet the conflict should only be apparent, not real, for science should seek truth, and true religion is truth. There can never be conflict between revealed religion and scientific fact. That they have often occupied different fields of truth is a mere detail. The gospel accepts and embraces all truth; science is slowly expanding her arms and reaching into the invisible domain in search of truth. The two are meeting daily —science as a child, revealed religion as the mother. Truth is truth, whether labeled science or religion. There can be no conflict. Time is on the side of truth, for truth is eternal.

Yes, truth is always consistent, whether it is revealed direct from God to man through his inspired prophets or comes from the laboratory through the diligent searching of his children and the influence of the Spirit of the Lord upon them.

Youth of the free nations, you face a changing world beset with many perplexities. But while change is and will continue to be all about us in the physical world, we must recognize that there are certain heaven-sent verities, principles, and values that are eternal. These never change.

As you travel life's highway, you will encounter theories, proposals, and programs that have wide appeal. You will be required to pass your judgment on them. Be not misled. Remember that ideas and theories are either sound or unsound; soundness does not depend upon which men hold them.

Our inability to explain a thing in terms of our materialism does not disprove its reality.

Opinions at variance with time-honored beliefs, although receiving considerable current acceptance, may not always rest on truth. It is the truth that endures. It is the truth that makes men courageous enough to become Christlike. It is the truth that makes men and nations free. Yes, be intelligent. Intelligence is the wise and judicious use of knowledge.

Continue to grow mentally—to grow in wisdom—to grow in truth. Desire it! Pray for it! Study it! Practice it!

Do all this and you will find truth; it cannot be denied you. Having found it, never forget its source, remembering always that "the glory of God is intelligence, or, in other words, light and truth." (D&C 93:36.)

"And Jesus increased in wisdom." Like the Master, in whose footsteps you should follow, may you constantly increase in wisdom.

Point 2: "And Jesus increased in . . . stature."

You, the youth of the free world, are the trustees of posterity. The future of your country will, sooner than you think, rest in your hands and those of your contemporaries.

Be worthy trustees. Continue to grow in stature.

Be cheerful in all that you do. Live joyfully. Live happily. Live enthusiastically, knowing that God does not dwell in gloom and melancholy, but in light and love.

A clean mind in a healthy body will enable you to render far more effective service to others. It will help you to provide more vigorous leadership. It will give your every experience in life more zest and meaning. Robust health is a noble and worthwhile attainment.

Possibly the best measure of the stature of men or

women is in their own homes, at their own firesides. Some of you have already established homes. Practically all of you will do so. As you look hopefully forward, what conclusions have you reached about marriage, the home, and family?

Are you planning for honorable parenthood even at the sacrifice perhaps of parties, clubs, and other social enticements? Parenthood carries with it peculiar responsibilities. Are you planning to accept these without quibbling? Are you willing to accept and enthrone motherhood as the highest calling of woman?

No nation rises above its homes. In building character, the Church, the school, and even the nation stand helpless when confronted with a weakened and degraded home. The good home is the rock foundation—the cornerstone of civilization. There can be no genuine happiness separate and apart from a good home, with the old-fashioned virtues at its base. If our nation is to endure, the home must be safeguarded, strengthened, and restored to its rightful importance.

Remember that moral purity is an eternal principle. Its violation destroys the noblest qualities and aspirations of man. Purity is life-giving; unchastity is deadly.

Moral purity is one of the greatest bulwarks of successful homemaking. Happy and successful homes—let alone individual lives—cannot be built on immorality.

Youthful sweethearts, be true to God's holy laws. Remember they cannot be broken with impunity. If you would be happy and successful in your early association, courtship, and homebuilding, conform your lives to the eternal laws of heaven. There is no other way.

And in so doing, you shall increase "in stature."

Point 3: "And Jesus increased . . . in favour with . . . man."

The formula for successful relationships with others

boils down to that divine code known as the Golden Rule:

"Therefore all things whatsoever ye would that men should do to you, do ye even so to them. . . ." (Matthew 7:12.)

It was the Master who said, ". . . whosoever will be chief among you, let him be your servant." (Matthew 20:27.)

Unselfish, willing service to others was the keynote of his relationship with men.

"For even the Son of man came not to be ministered unto, but to minister, and to give his life a ransom for many." (Mark 10:45.)

Love one another. Serve your fellowmen. The example has been given you. The road lies clearly before you.

If we would serve God through service to our brethren, we shall have need of a love for work. Energetic, purposeful work leads to vigorous health, praiseworthy achievement, a clear conscience, and refreshing sleep. It has always been a boon to man. Have a wholesome respect for labor, whether with head, heart, or hand. Accept the challenge given by one of America's eminent journalists, Edward W. Bok:

> When you are called to get into the game, get into it good and strong. There's no fun in going through life spoon-fed; in finding the soft seat. That makes a man soft, and a soft man is an abomination before God and man. And put everything you've got into it. Take hold and carry the biggest load your shoulders can carry, and then carry it right. Set the pace for others; don't let them set it for you.

May you ever enjoy the satisfaction of honest toil. The decree that by the sweat of his brow man should eat bread is still basic. You will never wish or dream yourself into heaven. You must pay the price in toil, in sacrifice, and in righteous living.

It is a truism that "security is achieved, not bestowed." It cannot be gained by self-pity or compromising principles. The world owes no man a living.

Youth of the world, as you strive to increase in favor
with man, be ever on your guard that you do not unwit-
tingly, in the name of tolerance, broadmindedness, and
so-called liberalism, encourage foreign "isms" and unsound
theories that strike at the very root of all we hold dear,
including our faith in God. Proposals will be offered and
programs will be sponsored that have wide, so-called "hu-
manitarian" appeal. Attractive labels are usually attached
to the most dangerous programs, often in the name of public welfare and personal security.

Have the courage to apply this standard of truth. Determine what the effect of the various issues at stake is upon
the character, the integrity, and the freedom of man. Which
increase his freedom? Which abrogate or destroy? Which
recognize and respect the individual dignity of man?

We have the greatest material wealth ever known because we are free, and our people have been encouraged
to produce it—out of themselves. It is foolish to place our
material wealth first and decide that it, rather than the freedom and energy that produced it, is our real worth.

Freedom, a willingness to work, and the desire to serve
your God through service to your fellowmen—these are the
sources of true wealth. Cling fast to these truths, and you
must inevitably increase in favor with man. "And Jesus
increased . . . in favour . . . with man."

Point 4: "And Jesus increased . . . in favour with God."

This is the most important of all man's strivings; without it, nothing is of the slightest account.

"For what shall it profit a man, if he shall gain the
whole world, and lose his own soul?" (Mark 8:36.)

Growing in favor with God is the most important because it is the veritable foundation upon which all other
worthwhile blessings rest. Concerning this fact the Savior
admonished his disciples: ". . . seek ye first the kingdom of

God, and his righteousness; and all these things shall be added unto you." (Matthew 6:33.)

Spiritual strength promotes positive thinking, positive ideals, and positive efforts. These are the qualities that promote wisdom, physical and mental well-being, and enthusiastic acceptance and response by others. "Favour with God" gives necessary incentive and perspective to life. It gives man real purpose for living and achieving.

As always, we have the example of the Master to guide us. "My meat," he said, "is to do the will of him that sent me. . . ." (John 4:34.)

And again, "Father, . . . I have glorified thee on the earth: I have finished the work which thou gavest me to do." (John 17:1, 4.)

We increase in favor with God as we do the will of God. Let us be faithful in the work he gives us, whatever it may be and whatever our station in life. Let our desires be in harmony with God's will as it is revealed to us— keeping his word in our hearts, and conquering selfish desires that would lead us astray.

If we would advance in holiness—increase in favor with God—nothing can take the place of prayer. And so I adjure you to give prayer—daily prayer, secret prayer—a foremost place in your lives. Let no day pass without it. Communion with the Almighty has been a source of strength, inspiration, and enlightenment through the world's history to men and women who have shaped the destinies of individuals and nations for good.

Will you value and take advantage of the opportunity to tap these unseen but very real spiritual powers? Will you, with Abraham Lincoln before Gettysburg and George Washington at Valley Forge, humble yourselves before Almighty God in fervent prayer?

Prayer will help you understand the apparent conflicts in life—to know that God lives, that life is eternal.

Be not ashamed to believe and proclaim that God lives; that he is the Father of our spirits; that Jesus is the Christ, the Redeemer of the world; that the resurrection is a reality; that we lived as spirits before mortal birth and will live again as immortal beings through the eternities to come. Blessed are you if you have a testimony of these things. These great spiritual truths have seen systems come and go, and so it will be in the future. These truths will, if you are wise, take precedence in your lives over all contrary theories, dogmas, or hypotheses from whatever source or by whomsoever advocated.

Therefore, go forward intelligently and yield simple and loyal obedience to all the laws of the universe and the truths of eternity. Yours is a great responsibility in this day when the need for courageous leadership is so urgent. *You* can become those leaders!

Young men and women of the free world, yours is a great challenge. You can be choice spirits in your land. Forget not that each of you has been endowed with the priceless gift of free agency. Each of you is, in very deed, the master of your fate, and Christ should be the captain of your soul. You need not be the victims of circumstance, for unto you it is given to achieve and become "perfect, even as your Father which is in heaven is perfect." (Matthew 5:48.)

Jesus lives today. He is risen. This I know.

"And Jesus increased in wisdom and stature, and in favour with God and man."

May you, by following this same path, merit the same commendation. If you follow this divine pattern established by the resurrected Christ, you cannot fail, for you will have fulfilled the measure of your creation.

Yes, Jesus Christ is divine. He lives today. He was resurrected. He is the Son of God, the Redeemer of the world. I bear this witness and pray that the young men and women of all the world may be blessed with a testimony of this all-important truth.

2

Our Lord and Master

We live in an age of doubt, faithlessness, and sin when even eternal verities are being questioned and discarded. Many of the pulpits of the land are being turned into pipelines to collectivism—preaching the social gospel and denying the basic Christian concepts and the very existence of God and the divinity of the Lord Jesus Christ.

Some time ago I attended a three-day convention known as the New England Rally for God, Family, and Country, which concluded on Independence Day, July 4.

In the evening at an informal dinner in a hotel in Boston, brief informal remarks were made by prominent participants in the conference. One of those was Tom Anderson, publisher of nine state farm papers in the South. In the course of his remarks he said, in substance:

> Ladies and gentlemen, I have been accused of leaving my church. I want you to know I did not leave my church, my church left me. My church no longer teaches that Jesus is the Christ, the Savior and Redeemer of the world, the very Son of God, as I was taught at my mother's knee and in my Sunday School class as a boy. My church no longer teaches the reality of the holy atonement, the resurrection, and the final judgment. I still believe these concepts of Christianity as taught to me in my childhood. But my church no longer teaches

these basic concepts. Instead my church is teaching the social gospel, and, like many other Christian churches, the pulpit has become a pipeline to collectivism. Again, I say, I did not leave my church, my church left me.

Thank God for faith, for testimony. Thank God for the Church of Jesus Christ. It has not left us—it will never leave us. Thank God for the eternal truths of the gospel of peace and salvation. Thank God for the anchor, the feeling of security, the inner calm that the everlasting truths of the gospel bring to every faithful child of God.

Each year as the Christmas season approaches, all true Christians direct attention to one of the greatest events of all realms and of all eternity. The Lord Omnipotent who reigneth came down to earth and mortality, becoming the Only Begotten of the Father in the flesh.

His mother, Mary, of the tribe of Judah, was undoubtedly the most marvelous and beautiful of all virgins, having been chosen for this extremely high honor. "And the angel came in unto her, and said, Hail, thou that art highly favoured, the Lord is with thee: blessed art thou among women. . . . Fear not, Mary: for thou hast found favour with God. And, behold, thou shalt conceive in thy womb, and bring forth a son, and shalt call his name JESUS." (Luke 1:28, 30-31.)

The Babe of Bethlehem became the Nazarene, the Man of Galilee, the Life and Light of the world, the Savior and Redeemer of mankind, the miracle of all time. More books have been written about him, more buildings have been erected to his honor, more men have died with his name on their lips than any other person who ever lived.

Men have tried to summarize his life. One such effort by J.A. Francis was sent to me by President Heber J. Grant in 1938 and reads as follows:

Here is a man who was born in an obscure village, child of a peasant woman. He grew up in another obscure village. He worked in a carpentry shop until he was thirty, and then for three years he was an itinerant preacher. He never wrote a book. [Not one small scrap of evidence exists that he ever wrote or dictated so much as a single personal letter.] He never held an office. He never owned a home. He never had a family. He never went to college. He never put his foot inside a big city. He never traveled two hundred miles from the place where he was born. He never did one of the things that usually accompany greatness. He had no credentials but himself. He had nothing to do with in this world except the naked power of his divine manhood.

While still a young man, the tide of popular opinion turned against him. His friends ran away. One of them denied him. Another betrayed him. He was turned over to his enemies. He went through the mockery of a trial. He was nailed upon the cross between two thieves. His executioners gambled for the only piece of property he had on earth while he was dying, and that was his coat. When he was dead he was taken down and laid in a borrowed grave through the pity of a friend.

Nineteen wide centuries have come and gone and today he is the center of the human race and the leader of the column of progress. I am far within the mark when I say that all the armies that ever marched, and all the navies that were ever built, and all the parliaments that ever sat, and all the kings that ever reigned put together, have not affected the life of man upon this earth as powerfully as has this one solitary life.

The sweetest story ever told is the story of the coming of the Christ child, through whose perfect life and by compliance with whose teachings all may find peace of mind and soul-contentment.

Yes, it is possible, even in this wicked, war-torn world, to glorify God, to have peace in the soul, and to feel a spirit of goodwill and fellowship. I have been a witness to this truth in many lands on both sides of the iron curtain. We are all brothers and sisters, members of the family of God. There is a divine spark in every soul who comes into this world.

Never has this spirit of the Christ in our Father's children impressed me as it did in a little Baptist Church in atheistic Russia in Moscow in 1959. May I let one of the twenty members of the American press who accompanied me tell the story—with apology for my name in it. This is the same man, somewhat of a humorist but a fine Christian, who affirmed that his church had left him.

His report, which was carried in several farm papers, is headlined, "A Visit to a Russian Church With Secretary Benson," and it reads as follows:

Imagine getting your greatest spiritual experience in atheistic Russia! We had just left Moscow's citadel of atheism, fantastically ugly Red Square where thousands of subservients come daily to worship the incarnation of history's foremost mummies, Vladimir "The Body" Lenin and "Good Ol' Joe" Stalin, their carcasses perfectly preserved in their glass showcase in the red marble mausoleum. They're the only well-dressed people in Moscow—all dressed up and no place to go. . . .

Sunday schools in Russia are not permitted to exist. All "education" belongs to the state—and so do the children. Six days a week for 40 years the children have been taught atheism in school. It would be inconsistent to let them be taught about God in a Sunday school!

A person can lose his job or be demoted for church attendance. Starting next year young people have to either be confirmed in church or join "youth confirmation" (Communist) groups. If they choose the church, they won't be able to get a job when they're old enough to work. Most people under 60 have sold out God for jobs, security, convenience. Or maybe they've simply concluded that co-existence, with atheism, is better than no existence.

Our Intourist guide had informed us that intelligent people don't go to church; that religion, which they refer to in the past tense, is a fairy story. With a straight face the beguiling guide had told us that churches were closed because the people no longer wanted them open; they had "learned better," she said. In spite of this unsolicited wisdom, we drove from the ornate, atheistic Kremlin to a little out-of-the-way faded stucco Baptist Church on a narrow cobblestone street. The central Baptist Church, one of the few open-for-business churches left in Moscow, was playing to its usual three-times-a-week standing room only crowd of about 1,000.

Behind the pulpit glowed a stained-glass window inscribed with *"Bog est lyubov* (God is love)." It glowed quite differently from the diffused orange-colored light which bathes the carcasses of the enshrined killers on display in Red Square.

Every face in the old sanctuary gaped incredulously as our obviously American group was led down the aisle. They grabbed for our hands as we proceeded to our pews which were gladly vacated for our unexpected visit. Their wrinkled old faces looked at us pleadingly. They reached out to touch us almost as one would reach out for the last final caress of one's most-beloved just before the casket is lowered. They were in misery and yet a light shone through the misery. They gripped our hands like frightened children.

A member of our group was unexpectedly called to the pulpit. His voice choked with emotion, he preached a sermon of love and faith, hope and truth.

"I believe very firmly in prayer," he said. "It *is* possible to reach out and tap that unseen power which gives us strength and such an anchor in time of need.

"Be not afraid. Keep this commandment: love one another. Love all mankind. Truth will endure. Time is on the side of truth." Thus spake Ezra Taft Benson, Mormon Apostle and Secretary of Agriculture.

The Secretary's wife and two beautiful daughters raptly drank in his words, with tears streaming. "God lives, I know that He lives, that Jesus is the Christ, the Redeemer of the World. We are eternal beings."

As each sentence was translated for the audience by the Russian minister the women removed their handkerchiefs from their heads and waved them like a mother bidding permanent goodbye to their only son. Their heads nodded vigorously as they moaned, *"Da, da, da!* (yes, yes, yes!)"

As their gnarled hands folded in fervent prayer, it made you think of the ancient Christians about to be thrown to the lions. Most were old women. The old can attend church. They have no jobs to lose. They can "afford" to go to church. There were a handful of teenagers, one of whom stood beside me. I wished mightily that we could break the language barrier and talk. A youth with the courage to oppose history's most godless dictatorship—to worship God!

Cynical newspaper correspondents who'd griped about a "command performance" in church with Benson stood there crying openly.

These people have what has been described by some bubbleheads as "freedom of religion." It is freedom to live out their last few years without being shot in the back of the neck; freedom to go on existing in a living hell under a forced choice between God and their own families.

These old souls live by faith alone, unlike the Communist high priests who're backed by the all-powerful state and the firing squad.

The Communist plan is that when these "last believers" die off, religion will die with them. What the atheists don't know is that God can't be stamped out either by legislated atheism or by firing squad. Then [referring to himself] this Methodist back-slider who occasionally grumbles about having to go to church, stood crying unashamedly, throat lumped, and chills running from spine to toes. It was the most heartrendering and most inspiring scene I've ever witnessed.

As we filed out, they sang, as I've never heard it sung before, "God Be With You Till We Meet Again." And all knew we never would, not on this earth.

In our group, we also knew that if we have the morality and the courage—I am convinced we have everything else it takes in super abundance—if we have the morality and the courage, the greatest force in the world, love of God and love of freedom will destroy and wipe out communism. We shall not have to co-exist with this diabolical conspiracy of hate. (Tom Anderson, *Straight Talk*, Western Islands, 1967, pp. 183-86.)

Yes, our thoughts turn to the Babe of Bethlehem, Jesus the Christ, our Savior and Redeemer. And why did he come to earth accompanied by the singing of heavenly hosts? Following his resurrection when he appeared to the Nephites on this hemisphere, as recorded in Third Nephi, he gives us the answer as he emphasizes the name for his church. These are his words:

Behold I have given unto you my gospel, and this is the gospel which I have given unto you—that I came into the world to do the will of my Father, because my Father sent me.

And my Father sent me that I might be lifted up upon the cross; and after that I had been lifted up upon the cross, that I might draw all men unto me, that as I have been lifted up by men even so should men be lifted up by the Father, to stand before me, to be judged of their works, whether they be good or whether they be evil—

And for this cause have I been lifted up; therefore, according to the power of the Father I will draw all men unto me, that they may be judged according to their works. (3 Nephi 27:13-15.)

It is my testimony that the Babe of Bethlehem, Jesus

the Christ, is the one perfect guide. Only by emulating his example and adhering to his eternal truth can men realize peace on earth and good will toward men. There is no other way. He is the way, the truth, the light.

3

Life Is Eternal

We are eternal beings. We lived as intelligent spirits before this mortal life. We are now living part of eternity. Our mortal birth was not the beginning; death, which faces all of us, is not the end.

> Our birth is but a sleep and a forgetting;
> The soul that rises with us, our life's star,
> Hath had elsewhere its setting,
> And cometh from afar;
> Not in entire forgetfulness,
> And not in utter nakedness,
> But trailing clouds of glory do we come
> From God, who is our home.
> > —William Wordsworth
> > "Intimations of Immortality"

As eternal beings, we each have in us a spark of divinity. And, as one who has traveled over much of this world, I am convinced that our Father's children are essentially good. They want to live in peace, they want to be good neighbors, they love their homes and their families, they want to improve their standards of living, they want to do what is right, they are essentially good. And I know that God loves them.

And as his humble servant, I have in my heart a love for our Father's children. I have met them in so-called high places and low. I have visited with them in their homes, in their fields, on their small farms, in their shops, on the highways of the earth, and in the air. I have had the privilege of meeting with them in large and small meetings, and worshiping with them in their churches.

Again I say, our Father's children are essentially good. I know the Lord loves them. And as his humble servant, I have love in my heart for them. May God bless you wherever you are and be close to you, as he can and will through his Spirit.

Yes, as we travel through this topsy-turvy, sinful world, filled with temptations and problems, we are humbled by the expectancy of death, the uncertainty of life, and the power and love of God. Sadness comes to all of us in the loss of loved ones. But there is gratitude also. Gratitude for the assurance we have that life is eternal. Gratitude for the great gospel plan, given freely to all of us. Gratitude for the life, teachings, and sacrifice of the Lord Jesus Christ.

Thank God for the life and ministry of the Master, Jesus the Christ, who broke the bonds of death, who is the light and life of the world, who set the pattern, who established the guidelines for all of us, and who proclaimed: "I am the resurrection, and the life: he that believeth in me, though he were dead, yet shall he live: And whosoever liveth and believeth in me shall never die. . . ." (John 11: 25-26.)

"If a man die, shall he live again?" asked Job, the prophet, anciently. (Job 14:14.) My good friend Senator Everett Dirksen, shortly before his death, responded impressively to Job's question in these words:

What mortal being, standing on the threshold of infinity, has not pondered what lies beyond the veil which separates the seen from the unseen?

What mortal being, responding to that mystical instinct that earthly dissolution is at hand, has not contemplated what lies beyond the grave?

What mortal being, upon whom has descended that strange and serene resignation that life's journey is about at an end, has not thought about that eternal destination and what might be there?

Centuries ago the man Job, so long blessed with every material blessing, only to find himself sorely afflicted by all that can befall a human being, sat with his companions and uttered the timeless, ageless question, "If a man die, shall he live again?" In the Easter Season, when all Christendom observes the Resurrection and seeks answers to many questions, there in the forefront is the question raised by Job, "If a man die, shall he live again?"

If there be a design in this universe and in this world in which we live, there must be a Designer. Who can behold the inexplicable mysteries of the universe without believing that there is a design for all mankind and also a Designer? . . .

"If a man die, shall he live again?" Surely he shall, as surely as day follows night, as surely as the stars follow their courses, as surely as the crest of every wave brings its trough. (*U.S. News & World Report*, November 8, 1965, p. 124.)

Yes, life is eternal. We live on and on after earth life, even though we ofttimes lose sight of that great basic truth.

Our affections are often too highly placed upon the paltry, perishable objects. Material treasures of earth are merely to provide us, as it were, room and board while we are here at school. It is for us to place gold, silver, houses, stocks, lands, cattle, and other earthly possessions in their proper places.

Yes, this is but a place of temporary duration. We are here to learn the first lesson toward exaltation—obedience to the Lord's gospel plan.

Yes, there is the ever-expectancy of death, but in reality there is no death—no permanent parting. The resurrection is a reality. The scriptures are replete with evidence. Almost immediately after the glorious resurrection of the Lord, Matthew records: "And the graves were opened; and many bodies of the saints which slept arose, And came out of the graves after his resurrection, and went into the holy city, and appeared unto many." (Matthew 27:52-53.)

The apostle John on the Isle of Patmos "saw the dead, small and great, stand before God." (Revelation 20:12.) And so we may quote on and on from holy writ, ancient and modern.

The spirit world is not far away. Sometimes the veil between this life and the life beyond becomes very thin. Our loved ones who have passed on are not far from us. One great spiritual leader asked, "But where is the spirit world?" and then answered his own question, "It is here." "Do spirits go beyond the boundaries of this organized earth? No, they do not. They are brought forth upon this earth, for the express purpose of inhabiting it to all eternity." ". . . when the spirits leave their bodies they are in the presence of our Father and God; they are prepared then to see, hear and understand spiritual things. . . . If the Lord would permit it, and it was His will that it should be done, you could see the spirits that have departed from this world, as plainly as you now see bodies with your natural eyes. . . ." (Brigham Young, in *Journal of Discourses,* vol. 3, pp. 367-69.)

Yes, life is eternal, so:

What though the skies seem dark today,
Tomorrow's will be blue;
When every cloud has cleared away
God's providence shines through.

—Author Unknown

What is death like? Here is a simple incident as told

by Dr. Peter Marshall, chaplain of the United States Senate:

In a certain home, a little boy, the only son, was ill with an incurable disease. Month after month the mother had tenderly nursed him, but as the weeks went by and he grew no better, the little fellow gradually began to understand the meaning of death and he, too, realized that soon he was to die.

One day his mother had been reading the story of King Arthur and the Knights of the Round Table, and as she closed the book the boy lay silent for a moment, then asked the question that had been lying on his heart. "Mother, what is it like to die? Mother, does it hurt?" Quick tears filled her eyes. She sprang to her feet and fled to the kitchen, supposedly to go get something. She prayed on the way a silent prayer that the Lord would tell her what to say, and the Lord did tell her. Immediately she knew how to explain it to him.

She said as she returned from the kitchen, "Kenneth, you will remember when you were a little boy, you would play so hard you were too tired to undress and you tumbled into your mother's bed and fell asleep. In the morning you would wake up and much to your surprise, you would find yourself in your own bed. In the night your father would pick you up in his big strong arms and carry you to your own bedroom. Kenneth, death is like that; we just wake up one morning to find ourselves in the room where we belong because the Lord Jesus loves us."

The lad's shining face looked up and told her there would be no more fear, only love and trust in his heart as he went to meet the Father in heaven. He never questioned again and several weeks later he fell asleep, just as she said. That is what death is like. (See Catherine Marshall, *A Man Called Peter*, New York: McGraw Hill, 1951, pp. 272-73.)

Yes, life is eternal. Death is not the end. As I have gratefully testified many times—

I know that Jesus is the Christ—the Savior and Redeemer of the world—the very Son of God. He was born the Babe of Bethlehem. He lived and ministered among men. He was crucified on Calvary. On the third day he rose again.

To the sorrowful, inquiring women at the tomb the angels proclaimed: "Why seek ye the living among the dead: He is not here, but is risen. . . ." (Luke 24:5-6.) There is nothing in history to equal that dramatic announcement. "He is not here, but is risen."

No other single influence has had so great an impact on this earth as the life of Jesus the Christ. We cannot conceive of our lives without his teachings. Without him we would be lost in a mirage of beliefs and worships, born in fear and darkness where the sensual and materialistic hold sway. We are far short of the goal he set for us, but we must never lose sight of it; nor must we forget that our great climb toward the light, toward perfection, would not be possible except for his teachings, his life, his death, and his resurrection.

May God hasten the day when people everywhere will accept his teachings, his example, and his divinity; yes, when they will accept as a reality his glorious resurrection, which broke the bonds of death for all of us.

Yes, we must learn and learn again that only through accepting and living the gospel of love as taught by the Master and only through doing his will can we break the bonds of ignorance and doubt that bind us. We must learn this simple, glorious truth so that we can experience the sweet joys of the spirit now and eternally. We must lose ourselves in doing his will. We must place him first in our lives. Yes, our blessings multiply as we share his love with our neighbor.

To the extent that we stray from the path marked out for us by the Man of Galilee, to that extent we are failing in our individual battles to overcome our worlds. But we are not without his help. Again and again he told his disciples, and all of us, "Let not your heart be troubled. . . ."

"If ye shall ask any thing in my name, I will do it."

"I will not leave you comfortless. . . ."

"Peace I leave with you, my peace I give unto you. . . ." (John 14:1, 14, 18, 27.)

We feel his comforting spirit in the sweet prayer of a child and the quiet abiding faith of all who have let his gospel permeate their lives. What a priceless gift it is that we can know him through our own prayers and through the sacred and solemn testimonies of those who have seen him, known him, felt his presence.

My brothers and sisters, I give you my solemn witness and testimony that I know that Jesus the Christ lives. He was in very deed raised from the dead, as we shall be. He is the resurrection and the life. He appeared unto many in the Old World after his resurrection.

And according to modern scriptures, sacred to me, he spent three glorious days, before his ascension, with his "other sheep" here in America—the New World. And he lives today.

I quote from a vision given to the Prophet Joseph Smith and his associate Sidney Rigdon, February 16, 1832:

And now, after the many testimonies which have been given of him, this is the testimony, last of all, which we give of him: That he lives!

For we saw him, even on the right hand of God; and we heard the voice bearing record that he is the Only Begotten of the Father—

That by him, and through him, and of him, the worlds are and were created, and the inhabitants thereof are begotten sons and daughters unto God. (D&C 76:22-24.)

Yes, my friends, Jesus is the Christ. He lives. He did

break the bonds of death. He is our Savior and Redeemer, the very Son of God.

And he will come again, as the Holy Bible proclaims: ". . . this same Jesus, which is taken up from you into heaven, shall so come in like manner as ye have seen him go into heaven." (Acts 1:11.)

Yes, this same Jesus has already come to earth in our day. The resurrected Christ—glorified, exalted, the God of this world under the Father—appeared to the boy Joseph Smith in 1820. This same Jesus who was the God of Abraham, Isaac, and Jacob, the God of Moses, the Creator of this earth, has come in our day. He was introduced by the Father to Joseph Smith in these words: *"This is My Beloved Son. Hear Him!"* (Joseph Smith 2:17.)

The appearance of God the Father and his Son Jesus Christ to the boy prophet is the greatest event that has occurred in this world since the resurrection of the Master. As the restored Church of Jesus Christ, we humbly and gratefully bear this witness to all men. This message is a world message. It is the truth, intended for all of our Father's children. More than three million members of the Church throughout the world bear this solemn testimony.

Today thousands of faithful missionaries throughout the nations freely carry this all-important message to the world. Jesus is the Christ, the Savior of mankind, the Redeemer of the world, the very Son of God. He is the God of this world, our advocate with the Father.

Today these missionary-messengers of truth and the three million members of The Church of Jesus Christ of Latter-day Saints—the Mormon Church—bear witness that God has again spoken from the heavens, that Jesus Christ has appeared again unto man, that the resurrection is a reality.

Today I testify to the truth of the message which they bear and add my solemn witness.

4

Joseph Smith—Man of Destiny

As a divinely called special witness of the Lord Jesus Christ, I bear testimony that God our Father in heaven lives; that Jesus is the Christ, our Savior and Redeemer; and that Joseph Smith is a prophet of God, the representative of the Lord who stands today at the head of this the last and greatest of all gospel dispensations. This I know with all my heart, and I thank God for this priceless knowledge.

It is my testimony also that that glorious event, the first vision of the boy prophet Joseph Smith, which ushered in this last dispensation, is the most important happening in this world since the resurrection of the Master.

As I have thumbed through more than a score of volumes on the Prophet in my own library, and recalled there are reported to be more than 1600 separate volumes and more than 20,000 books and pamphlets that refer to the Prophet in the library of the Church, I am prompted to ask, what except testimony and further witness can be added as we honor our greatest countryman around the world and acknowledge him as a prophet-representative of the Lord Jesus Christ without a peer?

As I have reflected on present world conditions and

reviewed the life and mission of a true and stalwart prophet of God, two impressively true and courageous statements
have come to me again and again.

The first comes from an immortal poet. James Russell
Lowell lived during the time of the Prophet Joseph; I
quote from his inspired poem of courage, "The Present
Crisis":

> Once to every man and nation comes the moment
>   to decide;
> In the strife of Truth with Falsehood, for the good
>   or evil side;
> Some great cause, God's new Messiah, offering each
>   the bloom or blight,
> Parts the goats upon the left hand and the sheep
>   upon the right,
> And the choice goes by forever 'twixt that darkness
>   and that light.
>
> * * *
>
> Careless seems that great Avenger; history's pages
>   but record
> One death-grapple in the darkness 'twixt old systems
>   and the Word;
> Truth forever on the scaffold, Wrong forever on the
>   throne,—
> Yet that scaffold sways the future, and, behind the
>   dim unknown,
> Standeth God within the shadow, keeping watch
>   above his own.
>
> * * *
>
> Then to side with Truth is noble when we share her
>   wretched crust,
> Ere her cause bring fame and profit, and 'tis
>   prosperous to be just;
> Then it is the brave man chooses, while the coward
>   stands aside,

Doubting in his abject spirit, till his Lord is crucified,
And the multitude make virtue of the faith they
    had denied.

Yes, time is on the side of truth—on the side of God's prophet.

The other item comes from the sorrowing followers in the dark days following the martyrdom of him who went "like a lamb to the slaughter" but who was "calm as a summer's morning" because he had a "conscience void of offense towards God, and towards all men."

Hear the words of his sorrowing followers:

> To seal the testimony of this book and the Book of Mormon, we announce the martyrdom of Joseph Smith the Prophet, and Hyrum Smith the Patriarch. They were shot in Carthage jail, on the 27th of June, 1844, about five o'clock p.m., by an armed mob—painted black —of from 150 to 200 persons. . . .
>
> Joseph Smith, the Prophet and Seer of the Lord, has done more, save Jesus only, for the salvation of men in this world, than any other man that ever lived in it. In the short space of twenty years, he has brought forth the Book of Mormon, which he translated by the gift and power of God, and has been the means of publishing it on two continents; has sent the fulness of the everlasting gospel, which it contained, to the four quarters of the earth; has brought forth the revelations and commandments which compose this book of Doctrine and Covenants, and many other wise documents and instructions for the benefit of the children of men; gathered many thousands of the Latter-day Saints, founded a great city, and left a fame and name that cannot be slain. He lived great, and he died great in the eyes of God and his people; and like most of the Lord's anointed in ancient times, has sealed his mission and his works with his own blood. . . . (D&C 135:1, 3.)

Thus did the Prophet Joseph Smith climax his earth life and fulfill the mortal part of his divinely appointed mission. This mortal mission, he made clear, was not to end until fully completed. Like the mission of the Savior, "a lamb slain before the foundation of the world," Joseph was truly foreordained to his great mission.

To get a vision of the magnitude of the Prophet's earthly mission we must view it in the light of eternity. He was among "the noble and great ones" whom Abraham described as follows:

> Now the Lord had shown unto me, Abraham, the intelligences that were organized before the world was; and among all these there were many of the noble and great ones;
>
> And God saw these souls that they were good, and he stood in the midst of them, and he said: These I will make my rulers; for he stood among those that were spirits, and he saw that they were good; and he said unto me: Abraham, thou art one of them; thou wast chosen before thou wast born. (Abraham 3:22-23.)

So it was with Joseph Smith. He too was there. He too sat in council with the noble and great ones. Occupying a prominent place of honor and distinction, he unquestionably helped in the planning and execution of the great work of the Lord to "bring to pass the immortality and eternal life of man," the salvation of all our Father's children. His mission had had, and was to have, impact on all who had come to earth, all who then dwelt on earth, and the millions yet unborn.

The Prophet Joseph Smith made this eternal fact clear in these words: "Every man who has a calling to minister to the inhabitants of the world was ordained to that very purpose in the grand council of heaven before this world was. I suppose that I was ordained to this very office in that grand council. It is the testimony that I want that I am God's servant, and this people His people." (*Teachings of the Prophet Joseph Smith,* p. 365.)

The calling and testing of men for assignment of responsibility in the great work of salvation is, no doubt, going on on both sides of the veil. The calling of men to sacred office is not confined to earth life only. There is organization, direction, and assignment in pre-earth life and in post-earth life also.

The greatest activity in this world or in the world to come is directly related to the work and mission of Joseph Smith—man of destiny, prophet of God. That work is the salvation and eternal life of man. For that great purpose this earth was created, prophets of God are called, heavenly messengers are sent forth, and on sacred and important occasions even God, the Father of us all, condescends to come to earth and to introduce his beloved Son.

The Prophet Joseph Smith was not only "one of the noble and great ones," but he gave and continues to give attention to important matters here on the earth even today from the realms above. For in the eyes of the Lord, the God of this world under the Father, it is all one great eternal program in which the Prophet Joseph plays an important role, all through the eternal priesthood and authority of God.

Sometimes the veil becomes very thin. Faithful men and women do sometimes get glimpses of eternity—assurance that the work here and in the realm beyond the veil is all one great program of a loving Father for the blessing of his children.

The very nearness of the world beyond was brought forcibly to the attention of my own family through the passing of a noble woman, Barbara S. Amussen, a temple officiator for more than a score of years in the Logan Temple. I know that the veil may become thin indeed.

Yes, the glorious work of salvation and exaltation goes on over there with the knowledge and, at least to some extent, the direction of the work here on this side of the veil. And in this direction the Prophet Joseph Smith, head of the greatest and last gospel dispensation, occupies a sacred place.

Let me give you one convincing item of evidence. There are others.

You will recall that President Heber J. Grant was

chosen to be an apostle October 13, 1882, at twenty-six years of age. Referring to this calling, he said that from October 1882 until February 1883, he was in a most unhappy frame of mind. He felt that he was unworthy to be an apostle and should resign. This troubled him greatly.

While on the Navajo reservation in Arizona during a visit to one of the stakes, he was riding horseback alone, pondering on this situation, when he seemed to hear a discussion going on in a council in heaven about the vacancies that existed in the quorum prior to his calling. In this council the Savior, the Prophet Joseph Smith, his father, Jedediah M. Grant, and others were present. They discussed whom they wanted chosen and decided that the way to remedy this situation was to send a special revelation to the President of the Church. "It was made known to me," said President Grant, "that the Prophet Joseph Smith and my father asked that I be called to that position. . . . It was also made clear to me that from that day on it depended upon me and me alone whether I made a success or failure of my life." (See *Gospel Standards,* pp. 195-96.) That settled forever the question that troubled him.

Yes, we operate through the Lord's organization on both sides of the veil. And in this all-important operation the Prophet plays a most important leadership responsibility.

It is but reasonable to believe that ancient prophets were permitted to see and rejoiced over the ushering in of this, our great gospel dispensation preparatory to the coming of the Lord in glory. They no doubt rejoiced in the forthcoming mission of the Prophet Joseph Smith. At least one such person saw the coming of the Prophet Joseph and caused a record to be made more than 1500 years ago, which record Joseph Smith, the Prophet, translated under the gift and power of God.

About 600 years B.C., just before the destruction of

Jerusalem, Lehi, an Israelite prophet, under the direction of the Lord, led a small colony to this western continent. Father Lehi, a direct descendant of Joseph who was sold into Egypt, brought with him sacred records, including some of the sacred writings of their famous ancestor, Joseph. Favored of the Lord, Joseph was shown what would befall some of his posterity in our day.

Lehi, quoting from the writings of Joseph, declared to his posterity:

> Yea, Joseph truly said: Thus saith the Lord unto me: A choice seer will I raise up out of the fruit of thy loins; and he shall be esteemed highly among the fruit of thy loins. And unto him will I give commandment that he shall do a work for the fruit of thy loins, his brethren, which shall be of great worth unto them, even to the bringing of them to the knowledge of the covenants which I have made with thy fathers. . . .
>
> And his name shall be called after me; and it shall be after the name of his father. And he shall be like unto me; for the thing, which the Lord shall bring forth by his hand, by the power of the Lord shall bring my people unto salvation. (2 Nephi 3:7, 15.)

As the earthly representative of the Lord Jesus Christ and his great church, many revelations were received by the Prophet. From time to time the Lord made crystal clear his support of the Prophet and admonished the Church and individuals thereof to give heed to the Prophet's counsel and support him in his holy calling.

In section 20 of the Doctrine and Covenants, given the same month in which the Church was organized, the Lord gives a revelation containing instructions regarding the duties of members and the functions of offices in the priesthood:

> The rise of the Church of Christ in these last days, being one thousand eight hundred and thirty years since the coming of our Lord and Savior Jesus Christ in the flesh, it being regularly organized and established agreeable to the laws of our country, by the will and commandments of God, in the fourth month, and on the sixth day of the month which is called April—

Which commandments were given to Joseph Smith, Jun., who was called of God, and ordained an apostle of Jesus Christ, to be the first elder of this church; . . .

And this according to the grace of our Lord and Savior Jesus Christ, to whom be all glory, both now and forever. Amen. (D&C 20:1-2, 4.)

The Lord assured the Prophet that "there is no weapon that is formed against you shall prosper; And if any man lift his voice against you he shall be confounded in mine own due time." (D&C 71:9-10.)

How often in the life of the Prophet and following his martyrdom was this promise fulfilled!

Brigham Young understood this when he declared to enemies of the Prophet who were secretly plotting the life of Joseph: "You cannot destroy the appointment of a prophet of God; but you can cut the thread that binds you to the prophet of God and sink yourselves to hell."

The Lord admonished his church that "if ye desire the glories of the kingdom, appoint ye my servant Joseph Smith, Jr., and uphold him before me by the prayer of faith." (D&C 43:12.)

Men of the world have appraised this prophet of God —Joseph Smith—as an unusual man of destiny. Many have seen him as a man of character, a man of courage, a man of deep spiritual insight.

One of the best known statements is from Josiah Quincy, mayor of Boston, whom the Prophet took on a tour of Nauvoo. A genius in sizing up men, he later published an essay on the Prophet in his book *Figures of the Past,* which included the following:

It is by no means improbable that some future textbook, for the use of generations yet unborn, will contain a question something like this: What historical American of the nineteenth century has exerted the most powerful influence upon the destinies of his countrymen? And it is by no means impossible that the answer to that interrogatory may be thus written: *Joseph Smith, the Mormon Prophet.* And the reply, absurd as it doubtless seems to most men now living, may be an obvious commonplace to their descendants. History deals in surprises and paradoxes quite as startling as this. (Page 317.)

Quincy ends his essay as follows:

Born in the lowest ranks of poverty, without book-learning, and with the homeliest of all human names, he had made himself at the age of thirty-nine a power upon the earth. Of the multitudinous family of Smith, none had so won human hearts and shaped human lives as this Joseph. His influence, whether for good or evil, is potent today, and the end is not yet. (Page 337.)

On September 4, 1843, a writer in the New York *Times* declared:

This Joe Smith must be set down as an extraordinary character, a prophet hero, as Carlyle might call him. He is one of the great men of his age, and in future history will rank with those who, in one way or another, have stamped their impress strongly upon society.

It is no small thing, in the blaze of this nineteenth century, to give to men a new revelation, found a new religion, establish new forms of worship, to build a city with new laws, institutions, and orders of architecture, to establish ecclesiastical, civil, and military jurisdiction, found colleges, send out missionaries, and make proselytes on two hemispheres. Yet, all this has been done by Joe Smith, and that against every sort of opposition, ridicule and persecution.

Stephen A. Douglas, the "little giant" as he was known in the Congress of the United States, said of the Prophet Joseph: "If I could command the following of Joseph Smith, I would resign my seat in Congress and go out to Oregon. In five years a noble state might be formed, and if they would not receive us into the union, we would have a government of our own."

From the *Weekly Bostonian* of about August 1842 comes this interesting statement:

Smith is decidedly the greatest original of the present day. He carries all before him when he undertakes an enterprise—knows no impediment—and never halts in his course till he has accomplished his object. His post, at the head of the Mormons, is a conspicuous one, and a few years, with such advancement as he has met with for the past year, will give him a numberless host of followers. We should not be surprised if he should become as omnipotent as ever the Pope was in his palmiest days. He is a genius—and a rare one—and all the armies of Satan, should they confront him in a solid phalanx, would be sure to meet with sore discomfiture, if not complete annihilation. The true philosophy of "go-a-heady"—the quintessence of concentrated moral and spiritual energy, fears no combat, and although, we cannot say it exactly courts danger, it never flies from a post of duty on its approach. We have so high an opinion of Joe Smith, that we intend to open a correspondence with him, in order to acquaint ourselves with all his secret springs of action, and thus get all the secrets of his success, public and private, worldly and ecclesiastical.

From the interesting little volume *Joseph the Prophet As He Lives in the Hearts of His People* by Daryl Chase comes this unusual statement by the poet John Greenleaf Whittier:

Once in the world's history we were to have a Yankee Prophet, and have had in Joseph Smith. For good or for evil he has left his track on the great highway of life, or to use the words of Horne "knocked out for himself a window in the wall of the nineteenth century" whence his rude, bold good-humored fact will peer out upon the generations to come.

I hope the good Lord has permitted Whittier to meet the "Yankee Prophet" in the realms above.

Much has been written and said about the Prophet. His life was an open book. He preached many sermons, wrote letters and epistles, translated the Book of Mormon (two-thirds the size of the Bible) and the Book of Abraham, and gave us scores of revelations and six volumes of journal history. Yet no one apparently has undertaken a comprehensive biography. Why? Is it too much for mere man to undertake—to write the story of him who declares "no man knows my history"?

Summaries of his noble and inspired achievements have been attempted. One sometimes quoted is from a book on the flyleaf of which appears a statement as follows:

Here is a man who was born in the stark hills of Vermont; who was reared in the backwoods of New York; who never looked inside a college or high school; who lived in six States, no one of which would own him during his lifetime; who spent months in the vile prisons of the period; who, even when he had his freedom, was hounded like a fugitive; who was covered once with a coat of tar and feathers, and left for dead; who, with his following, was driven by irate neighbors from New York to Ohio, from Ohio to Missouri, and from Missouri to Illinois; and who, at the unripe age of thirty-eight, was shot to death by a mob with painted faces.

Yet this man became mayor of the biggest town in Illinois and the state's most prominent citizen, the commander of the largest body of trained soldiers in the nation outside the Federal army, the founder of cities and of a university, and aspired to become President of the United States.

He wrote a book which has baffled the literary critics for more than a hundred years and which is today more widely read than any other volume save the Bible. On the threshold of an organizing age he established the most nearly perfect social mechanism in the modern world, and developed a religious philosophy that challenges anything of the kind in history, for completeness and cohesion. And he set up the machinery for an economic system that would take the brood of Fears out of the heart of man—the fear of want through sickness, old age, unemployment, and poverty.

In [fifty-three] nations are men and women who look upon him as a greater leader than Moses and a greater prophet than Isaiah; his disciples now number over two million; and already a granite shaft pierces the sky over the place where he was born, and another over the place where he . . . received the inspiration for his Book. (John Henry Evans, *Joseph Smith, an American Prophet*, Deseret Book, 1966.)

I testify to you that Joseph Smith was and is a prophet of God, one of the truly great prophets of all time, a man of destiny, a man of character, a man of courage, a man of deep spirituality, a God-like prophet of the Lord, a truly noble and great one of all time.

Joseph Smith the Prophet went willingly to his death. He sealed his testimony with his life—his own blood. On that fateful day in Nauvoo, Illinois, as he looked back upon his city and people whom he loved, on his way to

Carthage Jail and his martyrdom, he declared: "This is the loveliest place and the best people under the heavens; little do they know the trials that await them." (*Documentary History of the Church,* vol. 6, p. 554.)

Later the Prophet said feelingly, but calmly and courageously, "I am going like a lamb to the slaughter, but I am as calm as a summer's morning. I have a conscience void of offense toward God and toward all men. If they take my life I shall die an innocent man, and my blood shall cry from the ground for vengeance, and it shall be said of me, 'He was murdered in cold blood.'" (Ibid., p. 555.)

Following his martyrdom, his saddened and devoted followers who revered him as a prophet of God issued to the world a statement that appears in a sacred volume of scripture, the Doctrine and Covenants. (D&C 135.)

Yes, the fourteen-year-old boy stood true against the world. God knew his son when he was chosen. He knew he would be loyal and true even to death: "He had known Joseph and his loyalty and dependability in the Grand Council in Heaven before the foundations of the world were laid."

Only thirty-eight years, six months, and four days old when he was martyred, the Prophet stands alone without a peer among men of all time. As a translator of scriptures, a revealer of new truth regarding the origin and destiny of man, as a builder and as a leader and inspirer of men, he is without a mortal equal.

President J. Reuben Clark, Jr., has given this concise capsule summary of the life and labors of this young man of destiny—prophet of the living God:

He led his people through years of tragic persecutions, of burnings, plunderings, robbery, rapings, and butchery. He founded cities, erected buildings, built two temples, planned two others, and for one of them the cornerstone was laid. Men followed him to their death, because they loved him and the cause for which he stood. He led alike in prosperity and in disaster, and the Saints never stood closer to him than when fiendish persecution threatened their very existence. He performed mighty miracles. He was visited by heavenly messengers. The Father and Son came themselves to him. All of this before he was forty years old,—a record unequalled by any other mortal in the world's history. (*Church News,* December 7, 1949, p. 16.)

In view of his divinely inspired record and the ever-accumulating evidence of his prophetic powers, it is easy to understand why his rapidly increasing followers around the world join in saying: "Praise to the man who communed with Jehovah! Jesus anointed that Prophet and Seer. Blessed to open the last dispensation, Kings shall extol him, and nations revere." (*Hymns,* no. 147.)

Yes, Joseph Smith, the latter-day Prophet, was an instrument in the hands of the Lord in opening a new gospel dispensation, the last and greatest of all gospel dispensations.

He witnessed and participated in the greatest event that has transpired in this world since the resurrection of the Master. Here is a partial description, in his own words, of that great and all-important event:

After I had retired to the place where I had previously designed to go, having looked around me, and finding myself alone, I kneeled down and began to offer up the desires of my heart to God. I had scarcely done so, when immediately I was seized upon by some power which entirely overcame me, and had such an astonishing influence over me as to bind my tongue so that I could not speak. Thick darkness gathered around me, and it seemed to me for a time as if I were doomed to sudden destruction.

But, exerting all my powers to call upon God to deliver me out of the power of this enemy which had seized upon me, and at the very moment when I was ready to sink into despair and abandon myself to destruction—not to an imaginary ruin, but to the power of some actual being from the unseen world, who had such marvelous power as I had never before felt in any being—just at this moment of great alarm, I saw a pillar of light exactly over my head, above the brightness of the sun, which descended gradually until it fell upon me.

It no sooner appeared than I found myself delivered from the enemy which held me bound. When the light rested upon me I saw two Personages, whose brightness and glory defy all description, standing above me in the air. One of them spake unto me, calling me by name, and said, pointing to the other—*This is My Beloved Son. Hear Him!"* (Joseph Smith 2:15-17.)

This glorious vision of God the Father and his Son Jesus Christ, in broad daylight in the spring of 1820, is the greatest event that has transpired in this world since the resurrection of our Lord.

Joseph Smith, Jr., who witnessed it, was and is a prophet of God. Today more than 15,000 missionaries and more than three million members of the Church throughout the free world bear witness of this important fact.

The Church of Jesus Christ of Latter-day Saints, founded and directed by a prophet of God, has been before the world for nearly a century and a half. It has met mob violence, persecution, drivings, and deception by wicked men, and prejudice and misunderstandings by many people throughout the world. Yet, in spite of widespread opposition, ambassadors of truth have carried, from the very beginning, and are today carrying to the world the all-important message of the restored church as directed by Joseph Smith the Prophet.

Paraphrasing the words of Apostle Paul, this thing has not been done in a corner. (See Acts 26:26.)

The world has generally revered the ancient dead prophets and rejected the living ones. It was so with Joseph Smith. Truth is often on the scaffold, error on the throne. But time is on the side of truth, for truth is eternal. The message of Mormonism is a world message. It is the truth. The Church of Jesus Christ of Latter-day Saints is a world organization.

The message of Joseph Smith—the message of The Church of Jesus Christ of Latter-day Saints, the message of Mormonism—is the most important message in this world. And Joseph Smith the Prophet, who lives today, continues to have an important part in its direction here on earth.

The Church is a world organization—the true Church of Jesus Christ restored to the earth in its fulness—and is intended to bless all of our Father's children. These things I know, and to them I bear humble witness.

God lives, Jesus is the Christ, the Redeemer of the world, with his latter-day base of operations here in America, and Joseph Smith was and is a prophet of the living God.

This is my witness and testimony to all the world.

5

Missionary Work—A Major Responsibility

Our great objective is to help save the souls of the children of men. The Lord said to the Prophet Joseph Smith: "Remember the worth of souls is great in the sight of God." (D&C 18:10.)

This is our first interest as a church—to save and exalt the souls of the children of men. There is no richer program anywhere in the world than we have in the Church today for the building of men and women and providing the answers to the problems that face parents, families, and individuals. It is a program that is needed today as never before.

The message of Mormonism, the restored gospel of Jesus Christ, has now been before the world for over 140 years. In June 1830, Samuel Harrison Smith trudged down a country road in New York State on the first official missionary journey of the restored church. He had been set apart by his brother, the Prophet Joseph. This first missionary traveled twenty-five miles that first day without disposing of a single copy of the new and strange book that he carried on his back. Seeking lodging for the night, faint and hungry, he was turned away, after briefly explaining his mission, with the words: "You liar, get out of my house. You shan't stay one minute with your books." Continuing his journey, discouraged and with heavy heart, he slept that first night under an apple tree.

So began, in the most inauspicious way, the missionary work of this dispensation through the restored church, The Church of Jesus Christ of Latter-day Saints.

More than one hundred and forty years have come and gone since that first humble missionary set out to carry the message of salvation to a confused world. In fulfillment of the all-important God-given mandate, this great work has gone forward through the years unabated. It is a dramatic chapter in the history of a "peculiar people." But in all the annals of Christendom, there is no greater evidence of courage, willingness to sacrifice, and unbounded devotion to duty. Men, women, and children—all have joined in this heroic effort with no hope of material reward.

These ambassadors of the Lord Jesus Christ, as they firmly believe themselves to be, have trudged through mud and snow, swum rivers, and gone without the common necessities of food, shelter, and clothing in response to a call. Voluntarily, fathers and sons have left homes, families, and jobs to go to all parts of the world, enduring great physical hardship and unrelenting persecution. Families have been left behind, often in dire straits, willingly laboring the harder to provide means for their missionaries. And through it all there has been a joy and satisfaction that has caused families at home to express gratitude for special blessings received and the missionaries to refer to this period as "the happiest time of my life."

It has been conservatively estimated that between 140,000 and 150,000 full-time missionaries have served the Church since 1830, to say nothing of the thousands of local men and women who have performed valiant missionary services at home, numbering currently more than 20,000.

These faithful emissaries who have gone abroad have expended from 98 to 105 million days of missionary effort at a cost, through loss of personal income and expense for living, of more than $420 to $450 million, and this does not include any costs of transportation to and from or in the field, costs of administration at home or abroad, or expense of local missionary service.

Probably no group of people of comparable size in all the world has made such a free-will offering to the spreading of righteousness, and this from people who are not wealthy and who, in addition, are expected to contribute one-tenth of their interest annually to the work of the Lord, according to the ancient-modern law of the tithe.

Why? What is it that brings forth such sacrifice of time, means, and the comforts and sweet associations of home?

Is it not the burning conviction that God has again revealed himself to man on the earth, reestablished his church with all the gifts and blessings enjoyed in former days, and committed again to men his holy priesthood, with authority to exercise it for the blessings of his children? Yes, without doubt, it is the personal testimony of the divinity of this great latter-day work, faith in the commands that have been given in this and all past dispensations regarding the purposes of the Almighty, and our responsibility as his covenant children, the knowledge that God lives and loves his children, and the conviction that it is our mission to build and save men everywhere.

From the days of Father Adam to the days of the Prophet Joseph Smith and his successors, whenever the priesthood has been on the earth, a major responsibility has been the preaching of the saving, eternal principles of the gospel—the plan of salvation. Father Adam taught these things to his own children. (Moses 5:12.) Consider

Noah's long years of missionary effort and the preachings of all the ancient prophets. (Moses 8:16-20.) Each in his day was commanded to carry the gospel message to the children of men and call them to repentance as the only means of escaping the pending judgments. The Master made crystal clear the great mission of his ancient apostles to "go ye therefore, and teach all nations." (Matthew 28:19.)

In the early visits of the resurrected Moroni to the Prophet Joseph Smith, it was emphasized that the Prophet's name would be known for good or evil throughout the world and that the new volume of scripture and the restored gospel, which it contained, would have to be carried to the entire world "by the mouths of my disciples, whom I have chosen in these last days." (D&C 1:4.)

More than a year before the Church was organized, the Lord revealed through the Prophet that "a marvelous work is about to come forth among the children of men," and that the field was "white already to harvest." (D&C 4:1, 4.) The early converts were charged with the burden of the responsibility as follows: "Therefore, O ye that embark in the service of God, see that ye serve him with all your heart, might, mind and strength, that ye may stand blameless before God at the last day." (D&C 4:2.)

Great promises were made to these early missionaries. They were told that "the worth of souls is great in the sight of God," and that if they "should labor all your days in crying repentance unto this people and bring save it be one soul unto me, how great shall be your joy with him in the kingdom of my Father," and that if many souls were converted, their joy would be multiplied accordingly. (See D&C 18:10, 15.)

All these and many other glorious promises were made, even before the Church was formally organized on April 6, 1830.

Following the organization, men and women were baptized and worthy brethren ordained to the priesthood and set apart to cry repentance and to deliver the message of the restored gospel. Even greater promises were embodied in the revelations which followed, many of which referred in no uncertain terms to the solemn responsibility resting upon the restored church to preach the word. In the fall of that same year came the word of the Lord through the Prophet as follows: "For verily, verily, I say unto you that ye are called to lift up your voices as with the sound of a trump to declare my gospel unto a crooked and perverse generation. For behold, the field is white already to harvest; and it is the eleventh hour, and the last time that I shall call laborers into my vineyard." (D&C 33:2-3.)

The Lord made it plain to these humble ambassadors that they were "preparing the way of the Lord for his second coming." (D&C 34:6.) They were promised that their words would be prompted by the power of the Holy Ghost and would be the will of the Lord and scripture unto the people, inasmuch as they were faithful. They were told in no uncertain terms that they were being sent "out to prove the world," that they should "not be weary in mind, neither darkened," and a hair of their head should "not fall to the ground unnoticed." (D&C 84:79-80.)

Is it any wonder, then, that with their personal testimonies a new dispensation of the gospel was being opened; and coupled with these stirring promises of the Lord, they went forth in power and at great personal sacrifice, without monetary reward, even though their numbers were few and their circumstances poor? Add to this the fact that the heavenly pronouncements emphasized that this was the last time the gospel should be given to men as a witness, in preparation for Christ's second coming and the end of the world—the end of wickedness. Theirs was the responsibility of warning the world of impending judgments, as it is ours today. They knew, as do we, that the Lord has said:

> For a desolating scourge shall go forth among the inhabitants of the earth, and shall continue to be poured out from time to time, if they repent not, until the earth is empty, and the inhabitants thereof are consumed away and utterly destroyed by the brightness of my coming.
>
> Behold, I tell you these things, even as I also told the people of the destruction of Jerusalem; and my word shall be verified at this time as it hath hitherto been verified. (D&C 5:19-20.)

The time came, in late 1831, to consider the publication of revelations that the Lord had given to his church. By this time, many revelations had been received and the Church had shown considerable growth, in spite of persecution and drivings from the powers of evil. At this conference of elders, the Lord revealed through the Prophet Joseph a great revelation addressed to the people of his church and "unto all men, there is none to escape." (D&C 1:2.) No message heretofore given set forth in such clarity and power the worldwide nature of the message of the restored gospel. If there had been any question before, this left no room for doubt. Our message is a world message.

No person can read section 1 of the Doctrine and Covenants, realizing that the Church accepts it as the word of the Lord, and ask why we send missionaries into all parts of the world. The responsibility, and a major one it is, falls squarely upon the membership of the Church, for "the voice of warning," says the Lord, "shall be unto all people, by the mouths of my disciples, whom I have chosen in these last days." (D&C 1:4.) Then the Lord adds this great promise: "And they shall go forth and none shall stay them, for I the Lord have commanded them." (D&C 1:5.)

The revelation further states that all these things he has given unto his disciple-missionaries "to publish unto you, O inhabitants of the earth." (D&C 1:6.) After declaring that his voice is unto the ends of the earth, the Lord points out that he, "knowing the calamity which should come upon the inhabitants of the earth, called upon my servant, Joseph Smith, Jun., and spake unto him from heaven. . . ." (D&C 1:17.) The same as in all other dispensations—a means of escape, revealed through a prophet—is provided. Then the Lord emphasizes that he is "willing to make these things known unto all flesh," for he is "no respecter of persons." (D&C 1:34-35.)

As a closing admonition he invites all his children to "search these commandments," which have been revealed for the blessing of all mankind, because "they are true and faithful, and the prophecies and promises which are in them shall all be fulfilled." (D&C 1:37.) Though heaven and earth pass away, his word, he says, "shall not pass away, but shall all be fulfilled, whether by mine own voice or by the voice of my servants, it is the same." (D&C 1:38.) Two days after giving this great revelation, the Lord said to his church: "Send forth the elders of my church unto the nations which are afar off; unto the islands of the sea; send forth unto foreign lands; call upon all nations. . . ." (D&C 133:8.)

And so, as Latter-day Saints everywhere, with personal testimonies of these great events, we accept humbly, gratefully, this major responsibility placed upon the Church. We are happy to be engaged in a partnership with our Heavenly Father in the great work of the salvation and exaltation of his children. Willingly we give of our time and the means with which he may bless us to the establishment of his kingdom in the earth. This we know is our first duty and our great opportunity. This spirit has characterized the missionary work of the Church of Jesus Christ in all ages. It has been an outstanding mark of the ushering in of the dispensation of the fulness of times—our time. Wherever faithful Latter-day Saints are to be found, this spirit of unselfish sacrifice for the greatest cause in all the earth exists. In a statement published to the world during the last world war, the First Presidency of the Church declared: "No act of ours or of the Church must interfere with this God-given mandate." (*Conference Report,* April 1942, p. 91.)

In a word, we dedicate our all to the work of the Lord —the establishment and growth of his kingdom and the spread of righteousness. This is a major responsibility. We accept gratefully the challenge and pray ever for the Lord's sustaining power as we go forward. This great work is divine—directed by the Lord Jesus Christ through his church, The Church of Jesus Christ of Latter-day Saints. To this I bear humble and grateful testimony.

6

Missionary Memories

"Father, how old do you have to be to receive a patriarchal blessing?" asked an Aaronic Priesthood youth at the end of a Sunday School class in which two returned missionaries had made brief reports of their missions.

The rural Whitney Ward was blessed with a bishop who loved the young people and the great missionary cause. Often from the pulpit and in classes he would quote from the Bible the Lord's counsel to his ancient apostles: "Go ye into all the world, and preach the gospel to every creature." (Mark 16:15.) And then he would emphasize the great responsibility placed upon the Church in our day to "share the gospel with others" and "our duty to preach the gospel to all the world." As a true "missionary bishop," he expected every boy to be ready for a mission.

As a means of stimulating interest, the bishop had each returned missionary make a brief report of his mission in the Sunday School to the children and a more complete report in the sacrament meeting later in the day. This particular morning two missionaries had reported. Although it was sometimes difficult to understand how it could be "the happiest two years of my life," as they would conclude after recounting their hardships of opposition, we early got a desire to go on a mission.

This was the desire that prompted the question I had asked my father that Sunday morning. He told me he knew of no age requirement, but one should be old enough to understand what it means, and of course one must be worthy. I asked him if I was worthy. He informed me that he thought I was, but he was not the one to say because "that is the responsibility of the bishop. Why don't you ask the bishop if you might receive a recommend for a patriarchal blessing?" This I did. After a careful but brief interview in one corner of the chapel—because fifty or sixty years ago many chapels didn't have bishops' offices—he gave me a signed recommend.

As I proudly showed it to my father, he pointed to a tall, white-haired man and said, "Brother Dalley, our stake patriarch, is visiting here today. Why don't you present the recommend to him and ask when you might receive a blessing?" The patriarch responded kindly by putting his hand on my shoulder and saying, "If you'll come with me, we'll walk up the road to the home of my son-in-law, Brother Winward, and I'll give you the blessing right today."

Up the road, arm-in-arm with this godly man, we went to the farm home. In the parlor, a room used on special occasions, with Brother Winward as scribe, this noble patriarch placed his hands upon my head and gave a clear answer to a boy's prayer. I was promised, if faithful, of course, that I would go on a mission "to the nations of the earth, crying repentance to a wicked world." Filled with happiness and assurance that this and other promises in the blessing would be fulfilled, it seemed that I was almost walking on air during the mile walk to our farm home, where I broke the glad news to the family.

But before my promised blessing came, another rich

blessing for the entire family came as a complete surprise to all. It was during the time, many years ago, when sacrament meeting was held at 2:00 P.M. in the rural wards. We usually went to meeting in the white-top buggy, which would hold the entire family. But at this particular time there was an epidemic—chicken pox, I believe—in the ward. Parents were to attend sacrament meeting, but the children were to stay home. So Father and Mother went to meeting in the one-horse buggy.

As Father and Mother returned from sacrament meeting and we all gathered around the buggy, we saw something we had never seen before in our home. Both father and mother were crying at the same time—and they had just returned from sacrament meeting. Being the oldest, I asked what was wrong. Mother assured us everything was all right. "Then why are you crying?" we asked. "Come into the house and we'll tell you all about it."

As we gathered around the old sofa in the living room, they explained why there were tears. When sacrament meeting was over, the storekeeper opened the store just long enough for the farmers to get their mail, as the post office was in the store. There was no R.F.D. in those days, and opening the store briefly saved a special trip to the post office.

As our parents proceeded homeward, Father driving and Mother opening the mail, here was a letter from Box B in Salt Lake City. This was a call to go on a mission. No one asked if you were able, ready, or willing to go. The bishop was expected to know and the call came without warning.

Then Mother explained that they were happy and grateful that Father was considered worthy to fill a mission. Then Father explained, "We're crying a bit because we know it means two years of separation, and your mother and I have never been separated more than two nights at a time in all of our married life, and that has been when I've been in the canyon for poles, fence posts, or derrick timbers."

Father went on his mission, leaving Mother at home with seven children. The eighth was born four months after he left. In preparation, the small dry farm was sold to finance the mission. A family moved into part of our expanded farm home to rent the row cropland. We children, under Mother's day-to-day encouragement and Father's letters of blessings, took care of the dairy herd and the hay and pastureland.

You can well imagine who had the hardest end of that mission. But not once did we ever hear a murmur from Mother's lips as she would sing at her work the ballads of youth and the songs of Zion she and Father had enjoyed so much in the ward choir. In fact, my first baby tending— we call it sitting now—I remember was as a boy of seven years tending my younger brothers and sisters while Father and Mother went to choir practice on Wednesday evenings.

It was hard work, but a rich two years. Letters from Father from what seemed to us far away—Davenport, Iowa; Springfield, Illinois; Chicago, Cedar Rapids, etc.— coupled with family prayer and unity brought into that home a spirit of missionary work that never left it. Later, seven sons went on missions from that home, some of them on two or three missions.

Many years later at the bedside of that noble mother, who, as Father confided to me as the oldest child, had only a few weeks unless the Lord intervened, I heard her farewell words to her fifth son as he left for his mission. "Remember, George, no matter what happens at home, I want you to stay and finish your mission." A few weeks later a telegram from the First Presidency to President LeGrand Richards of the Southern States Mission told of her passing. And a year later a second telegram told of the passing of Father. But true to the wish of his mother and the missionary spirit of that true Latter-day Saint home, George stayed and finished his mission, and a summer later he returned to his old field of labor on a short-time mission. In the brief will, first call on the modest assets was provision for missions for the two younger sons.

My father, who as a young man had helped to support several of his twelve brothers and sisters on missions also, was spoken of by a prominent citizen, state senator, and nonmember of the Church in these words: "Gentlemen, today we buried the greatest influence for good in Cache Valley." How grateful we eleven children are for parents who always, by word and example, were faithful to the great missionary call of the Master.

7

Essentials for Missionary Success

Our message is a world message. It is not a message just intended for a handful of Latter-day Saints. When God the Father and his Son Jesus Christ come to earth, as they did in 1820 when they appeared to the young boy prophet, Joseph Smith, it is not something that concerns only a handful of people. It is a message and a revelation intended for all of our Father's children living upon the face of the earth. It was the greatest event that has ever happened in this world since the resurrection of the Master. Sometimes I think we are so close to it that we don't fully appreciate its significance and importance and the magnitude of it.

One of my favorite sections of the Doctrine and Covenants is the first section. It's not the first revelation given; it wasn't given until November 1831, but it was given at a conference of elders in the early days of the Church when they were considering whether or not the revelations given up to that time should be published to the world. At first the Lord had counseled that the revelations not be made public, but now the Church had been organized for a year and a half, and the whole consideration was what is good for the kingdom. What is best for the kingdom? What is best for our Father's work? During that conference the Lord gave a revelation to his church through the Prophet Joseph, and in the very first verses of that revelation the Lord makes it very clear that he was speaking not only to his church, but to the world, to all of our Father's children living upon the face of the earth; and he made it very clear that this work, this message, is a world message:

Hearken, O ye people of my church, saith the voice of him who dwells on high, and whose eyes are upon all men; yea, verily I say: Hearken ye people from afar; and ye that are upon the islands of the sea, listen together.

For verily, the voice of the Lord is unto all men, and there is none to escape; and there is no eye that shall not see, neither ear that shall not hear, neither heart that shall not be penetrated. (D&C 1:1-2.)

And then the Lord indicates the responsibility resting upon his disciples—you and me—to carry this message to the world, and he makes probably the most glorious promise ever made to a group of disciples when he said, in the fifth verse: "And they shall go forth and none shall stay them, for I the Lord have commanded them."

No group of workers anywhere in the world outside of the kingdom have such a promise. And so it is well that we keep in mind not only the importance of our message, but the promise that has been given that in this work we cannot fail if we do our part. This is not our work. It is the work of the Lord that we are called upon to help with, to carry this message to our Father's children. It is a message of salvation and exaltation. It is a message that will save and exalt the souls of the children of men. There is no other way, because this is the only true message and the only true church upon the face of the whole earth. Those are not my words; they are the words of the Lord Jesus Christ as found in the revelations. This gospel in its purity, now restored to the earth, is intended to reach all of our Father's children, and what a glorious thing it is to be permitted to participate in it! ". . . this is my work and my glory—to bring to pass the immortality and eternal life of man." (Moses 1:39.) That's the whole purpose of the Church, the whole purpose of the program, the whole purpose of missionary service, and we are called to help carry that out.

I am very happy to report to you, after visiting some forty nations of the world and traveling almost 100,000 miles per year, that the work of the Lord is prospering everywhere it is in operation. I think the outlook has never been more favorable than it is today. Our numbers are increasing. The devotion of our people and the faith of our people, I am confident, is increasing. And I think the devotion of our missionaries is as great as it has ever been, and the effectiveness of our work per person, per missionary, is the best it has ever been. It's not as good as it could be. It's not as good as it will be. But I think it's the best it has ever been.

And so, to our missionaries who are engaged in a wonderful work, I would like to make three or four suggestions as to how you might make your work a little more effective.

First of all, I would like to suggest that you heed the counsel of your mission president and those in authority over you, and that you accept that counsel well and willingly and readily with all your heart. Therein is safety, and by so doing you will make the maximum progress.

I would like to emphasize that it is so important that you lose yourselves in this work, that you don't worry about "what is it going to do for me." You are not out in the world with self-improvement as the major objective, but you can't help getting a maximum amount of self-improvement if you lose yourself in the work of the Lord. I don't know of any better preparation for life than two years of devoted, unselfish, dedicated service as a missionary. Now it's all right to keep that in the back of your minds, but you have been called to carry the Lord's message to the world, not to improve yourselves particularly. However, you can't carry this message to the world without doing yourself a lot of good.

The busy missionary is the happy missionary. I cannot recall a missionary who was really active and busy ever going astray. Occasionally we have missionaries who make mistakes. It usually starts when they become idle, when they stay in their lodgings when they ought to be out with the people, when they try to find excuses for not going out and tracting and knocking on doors and holding meetings with the people. Occasionally you will find a missionary who is looking for excuses for not going out—who can look out the window and see a storm coming when there isn't any, who can see rain when it isn't raining. The important thing is to get out with the people, to keep active, to be devoted. Do not sleep longer than is needful. The same Lord who gave the Word of Wisdom in the 89th section also gave that instruction in the 88th section, and it is just as binding as the counsel that you are not to use tobacco or alcoholic beverages. So cease from all lightmindedness, cease to sleep longer than is needful, and retire to your bed early. You will be more effective, you will do more work, you will be happier, and you will have better health.

There are four or five essentials for successful missionary work. Without them you cannot possibly succeed. First of all, you must have a burning testimony of the divinity of this work if you are going to succeed. Now it is almost a foregone conclusion that missionaries, when they come into the field, have that testimony. Sometimes there will be missionaries who are not quite certain. Then your first obligation is to get that testimony through prayer, through fasting, through meditation, through study, through appealing to the Lord to give you the testimony, through responding to calls when they come to you. You must have a testimony of the divinity of this work. You must know that God lives; that Jesus is the Christ, the Redeemer of the world; that Joseph Smith is a prophet of God; that the priesthood and authority of our Heavenly Father is here; and that you bear that priesthood and have the authority to represent him in the world.

Second, you will never be effective as a missionary unless you are humble in your work. The Lord has made it very clear in the 12th section of the Doctrine and Covenants when he says that no man can assist with this work unless he is humble and full of love. But humility does not mean timidity. Humility does not mean fear. Humility does not mean weakness. You can be humble and still be courageous. You can be humble and still be vigorous and strong and fearless. In the early days of the Church the elders were human also, and the Lord was not always pleased with them, as he made very clear in some of the revelations. But great teacher that he is, he would often commend them for the work they had done and then correct them. That's good psychology. My wife uses it on our children and sometimes on her husband. The Lord used it with the early elders of the Church and one time was pretty severe on some of them, and I am sure it must have caused them to have very serious reflections. Speaking to the elders, those who are the men who were called to bear his name, he said: "But with some I am not well pleased, for they will not open their mouths, but they hide the talent which I have given unto them, because of the fear of men. Wo unto such, for mine anger is kindled against them." (D&C 60:2.) That is pretty plain, isn't it? Sometimes we have among our missionaries those who are afraid because of the fear of man, and if you permit yourselves to get that spirit of fear, the adversary will back you up. He will support you. He will encourage you in it until you get to the point where you are afraid to exercise your authority and to bear testimony regarding this message. Remember the promise made in the first section: "And they shall go forth and none shall stay them, for I the Lord have commanded them." There is no place for fear. There is no place for discouragement, because you can't fail in this work if you do your part. There is no place for timidity or hesitancy. Humility, yes, but you can be humble and courageous and fearless and effective.

Third, I think that if you are going to be successful, you must develop in your heart a love for people with whom you work. They need the gospel as they need no other thing. Develop in your hearts a love for them, a desire to lift them up, and a desire to help them and to bless them by teaching them the principles of the gospel. The gospel will absolutely revolutionize their lives, change their outlook. People are hungry for something that will give them an anchor, that will satisfy the questions of their souls, that will bring peace to their hearts and a feeling of security, inner satisfaction. They are not getting it and they need it, and only the gospel can provide it.

Fourth, you must live an exemplary life. Maintain the standards of the Church fully. Adhere to the counsel and the standards that have been set up for missionary service. Be true to every requirement and every regulation. They are all given for your benefit and blessing—not to bear you down, not to limit your freedom, but to make you more effective as missionaries. The eyes of the world are upon you. As you travel among the people, you may think that nobody knows you, but there is always someone watching you. Of course our Heavenly Father always has his eyes on us, but it is surprising how many people outside the Church know who you are and what you are doing and what the requirements are for missionary service.

Let me give you an example. Many years ago, a member of our district council in the mission in Washington was traveling by plane. He had been in Canada, and on the flight back the plane developed trouble and had to land on an auxiliary landing field in Pennsylvania. It was a cold night, and the passengers were told that the plane would probably be on the ground for an hour. They got out and stretched and wandered around a little, and then they noticed over in the brush a light. They walked over toward this light and found a CCC camp, and as they opened the door they got the aroma of hot food. So they got courage and walked in, and they were invited to join the CCC boys at dinner. Now, the member of our district council found himself seated between two CCC boys, and when they brought around the hot coffee our friend, who didn't use it ordinarily, thought, "The coffee is hot and I am cold and there isn't anything else readily available to drink." So he took some and engaged in conversation with the two boys beside him. One of them said, "Where do you come from?" He said, "I come from Washington, but originally I came from Utah." "You don't happen to be a Mormon, do you?" "Yes," he replied, "I am a Mormon." The boy said, "You are not a very good one, are you." Well, he was a pretty good one, and it was an awful shock to him to hear this comment. He said, "What do you know about the Mormons?" The boy said, "Well, a couple of years ago I was in St. George, Utah, and I attended Mormon services. I know you Mormons have in your church what you call the Word of Wisdom, and that good Mormons live it." Can you imagine how the district councilor felt? It wasn't the cup of coffee—that is not going to destroy anyone—but it was the fact that he hadn't maintained that which he believed in. He hadn't kept the standards.

It never pays to let down on your standards in this church. You will be thought more of if you live the gospel, if you will be what you profess to be. You will be happier, you will have a better feeling inside, you will do more good in the world, and you will be more effective as missionaries. So live church and missionary standards wherever you go.

I wish that a record were available of the number of people who have been attracted to the Church because of the example they have seen in missionaries. I heard two wonderful women in a meeting one night bear testimony that they were first attracted to the Church by seeing a couple of Mormon elders go by their window day after day. One said that she would see them go out in the morning, come back about noon, go out shortly after lunch, and come back in the evening. She said, "Sometimes we would be working in the garden, but mostly we would be sitting in the front room and we would see them go by. They made such an impression upon us that we asked the police officer in our neighborhood who they were and what they were doing." And she said, "It was that example that first compelled us to go to one of their meetings. Now we are members of the Church."

Brother William A. Martin and his companion stood on an empty street corner in Ireland one night, trying to hold a street meeting, with only a policeman there to hear them. It was a stormy night, and they thought their effort had been in vain, but up in a second floor window were two young women who heard them sing "O My Father" and heard part of the testimony they bore, and they inquired of the police officer who those two young men were. Later one of those women became Brother Martin's wife, joined the Church, and immigrated to Utah. I heard Brother Martin tell this story when I was on my first mission in 1922 in England, when he was secretary of the mission under Elder Orson F. Whitney and later President David O. McKay.

You never know the amount of good you are doing. You are sowing seeds, you are planting a thought, you are setting an example. The Lord has said that you will not fail in this work, and so you must go forth and do your duty. Keep the commandments. Maintain the standards. Be true to your mission, to the charge that has been given you as representatives of the Lord Jesus Christ.

And then one final thought: I hope you and your companion are true to each other. I hope you feel you have the best companion in the world. I hope you draw close to each other as companions, that you uphold and sustain each other before the Saints, before our friends, before the world. I have seen many examples of this, but one of the most impressive occurred in Philadelphia some years ago. I had been in a meeting of agricultural leaders all day, and in the evening I left my hotel to mail a couple of letters. As I walked into the post office I heard the strains of a familiar Mormon hymn coming through the window from the opposite side. I dropped my letters in the box, walked over to the window, and looked out, and there were two young men in dark suits standing on the steps of the post office holding a street meeting. One of them was speaking and the other was holding in one hand two hats and in the other some copies of the Book of Mormon and some tracts. When they finished their meeting I went out and introduced myself. Then I said to the young man who was holding the hats and the copies of the Book of Mormon, "What were you doing while your companion was speaking?" His answer was most satisfying. He said, "Brother Benson, I was praying to the Lord that he would say the right thing that would touch the hearts of the people who were listening."

That's the kind of support I'm referring to. When you reach the point where you can enjoy and rejoice in the success of your companion, even when that success exceeds your own, then you've got the real missionary spirit, the real unselfish spirit of love, the spirit of the gospel. When you can rejoice in the success of your companion, then you've got a spirit that will make you effective as a missionary. Then you will really be truly, truly happy. Then you will have lost yourself in the service of this wonderful gospel, in service to our Father's children—the greatest work in all the world.

Remember what the Lord said: ". . . the worth of souls is great in the sight of God. . . . And if it so be that you should labor all your days . . . and bring, save it be one soul unto me, how great shall be your joy with him in the kingdom of my Father!" (D&C 18:10, 15.) And remember also that "any man that shall go and preach this gospel of the kingdom, and fail not to continue faithful in all things, shall not be weary in mind, neither darkened, neither in body, limb, nor joint; and a hair of his head shall not fall to the ground unnoticed." (D&C 84:80.) Now if you have become weary in this work you had better give yourself a good self-examination, because the Lord has said that no man shall be weary in this work.

There are at least twenty-seven sections of the Doctrine and Covenants that refer to missionary work. The first great responsibility placed upon this church in our day was to carry this message to the world. It is still a major responsibility. It is going on here on earth and it is going on in greater volume on the other side, and whether you do it here or over there doesn't make very much difference, just so long as you are missionaries. If you are laboring as you should, if you love this work, you will be engaged in helping to save the souls of the children of man throughout eternity until they have all heard it. And so it is the greatest work in all the world. There isn't anything like it in magnitude, in importance, in size, in promise.

And so, my brethren and sisters, I invoke God's blessings upon you. I see a great future for the work of the Lord. We have just scratched the surface of our possibilities. "The field is white, already to harvest." God bless you in your efforts. May he bring you joy and happiness—the happiness that surpasseth understanding, the happiness of which the world knows nothing, and may he crown your efforts with success, which I know he will through your faithfulness.

8

A Love for the Work

I have many happy memories associated with my brethren in the Council of the Twelve. There were eight years when I was not able to meet with them often, and how I missed being there! But I felt that I had received a call from our prophet when, on learning of the possibility of my being appointed Secretary of Agriculture in President Dwight D. Eisenhower's Cabinet, President David O. McKay said, "My mind is clear, and if the invitation comes in the right spirit, I feel you should accept."

I remember leaving with a promise of staying two years, and then at the end of two years, the insistence of President Eisenhower that I stay another two years, and then four years more.

One morning I received in my office in Washington a call from the White House. The appointment secretary on the other end of the line said, "We have a man here by the name of David O. McKay from Salt Lake City who has asked to see the President. Do you know him, and do you think we should have him see the President?" I said I was sure the President would feel honored to see David O. McKay.

After his interview with the President, President McKay came over to my office and said, "Brother Benson, I didn't even tell my counselors that I was leaving this morning. I just received the impression to get on the plane and come back here to see the President and ask if he wouldn't release you now that the 1956 campaign is over and he has been reelected. You have been here four years."

I said, "President McKay, I hope you were successful."

He said, "No, I was not. Of course they can't force you to stay, but I think we have an obligation to our country and that we should accede to his wishes. I think you should stay on."

But there were very few weeks while I was in Washington that my thoughts didn't turn to the Salt Lake Temple on Thursday, because I knew that on that day of the week the members of my quorum, whom I love most deeply, would be on their knees with the First Presidency, and then they would be gathered around the altar, dressed in the robes of the holy priesthood, and on that day I would be especially remembered.

Often wonderful things happen when you are shut out, and sometimes wonderful things happen when you are shut in. There came to my mind an experience my wife, Flora, had when she was on a mission in Hawaii.

She had been officiating part-time in the temple while on her mission, and this particular night the session had run a bit late, and she had been delayed for some reason. So when she got to the door she found that it was locked. She was in and everyone else had gone, and she was alone in the temple. The mission home in those days was situated across a stile, over a fence, and through some trees. When she found she was locked in, she tried the door and said, "Yes, I can open it from the inside." But she said a prayer that she would be protected, because in those days there was a camp in the trees just off the trail to the mission home, and there had been some incidents, so she was worried. She prayed to the Lord that she would be protected, and then she started toward the door. As she stepped outside the door, there was a circle of light all around her person and that circle of light accompanied her all the way to the mission home—over the stile, through the trees, to the door of the mission home.

I know, too, that the Lord can touch the hearts of men behind the iron curtain. I have seen it happen. I have been very close to it. I remember very well our efforts to get to Warsaw, Poland, in 1946 and my desire to get up to Selbongen in East Prussia where we had one congregation, the only congregation in Poland and the only Church-owned building in Germany at that time. There was one plane going, taking supplies to the American Embassy, but no passenger service. We had to get permission from the Russians and the Poles to get into Warsaw. Brother Fred Babbel, who was with me, had tried to make arrangements without success, and then I had tried, and we still weren't successful. But our plane was to leave in two days, and so we did some fasting and praying. At last I went to see the Russian general who was in charge of the Poles and finally, after about two hours in his office with him, he signed the document to permit us to go. Then we made arrangements to ride on the plane with the Americans who were carrying supplies to the American Embassy. I learned later that this general lost his commission because he had given permission for an American to go into Poland, and I always felt that the Spirit worked on this man, because he had previously turned us down.

In Warsaw there was only one hotel that was even partially intact, and that was the Polonia Hotel. I shared one room with seven other men, most of them members of the press. We got the Americans to loan us a jeep, and we drove up to Selbongen. It took us all day to drive there on

Sunday, through two rainstorms and with no cover on the jeep. When we drove into the little town of Selbongen we found the name had been changed to Zelback, because the Poles had changed all the names throughout the area. There was no one on the street because it was Sunday, and as we approached our little chapel, we saw a woman running away from us. She had seen this military vehicle and had thought it meant more trouble, because the people had been persecuted and their homes had been ransacked.

Well, we stopped the jeep and I jumped out. When the woman saw we were civilians, she turned around and came walking toward us. Then she recognized us—I guess from a picture, I don't know how else—and she screamed, "Oh, it's the Brethren! They have come at last!" She ran to us with tears in her eyes and then guided us to the home of the branch president. I think I never saw so many tears shed by a small group as we saw that day, as the word spread and the people came into the branch president's home. Then we held a meeting. I said, "Haven't you had your meetings today, yet?" They said, "Yes, we have had our meetings —priesthood, Sunday School, and sacrament meeting— but now that you are here we want another meeting." It was five o'clock, just starting to get dusk, and so we set the meeting for six and sent the members out to notify the Saints. At six o'clock the little chapel was filled.

During the service, as I was speaking near the time of closing, two Polish soldiers came in the front door and took a few steps into the building. I motioned for them to come forward. There were only two vacant seats, on the front row. Then, through the interpreter, I told them why I was there and on what authority and something about our work. I went ahead speaking to the people after the soldiers had taken seats at my invitation. I could tell the people were frightened of them, because as they came down the aisle the women would push away from the aisle. As we came to the end of the service and were starting to sing the closing song, they left the meeting place.

We had planned to close the meeting, but three or four people stood up immediately and asked, "Couldn't we have another meeting? This was not like a real meeting with soldiers here." One lady said, "I have a candle at home I have been saving for a special occasion [there were no lights in the building]." She said, "I will go get it if you want to read from the scriptures." And so we held another meeting for an hour and a quarter with these wonderful people.

The next morning they took me around to the side of the chapel and showed me a little mound. It was the grave of a young man. He and some other men had been lined up by the soldiers, who demanded that they give them cigarettes. In those days cigarettes were a lot more valuable than money; they were a medium of exchange in war-torn Europe at the end of the war. When they asked this brother for cigarettes, he said, "I don't have any." They thought, of course, that he was not telling them the truth, and so they repeated their demand, and, of course, he didn't have any. He was a good Latter-day Saint. And there in the presence of his young wife and his mother they shot him down. He was buried beside the little chapel where he was shot.

I thought about that experience and the manner in which we got to Poland. I thought of our first interview with General McNarney, the top general in the American forces. It was in the I. G. Farbin building in Frankfurt, which had been spared by "pin bombing," because the Americans expected it would be their headquarters when the war was over, as it was.

We had driven our little jeep up to the building, parked it, and gone in to see if we could get an appointment with the general. We had been in Europe just a few days. We wanted to get permission from him to make our own distribution of our welfare supplies to our own people through our own channels. In those days, of course, everything was being distributed through the military. We were told by the colonel at the desk that we couldn't get an appointment for three days. The general was very busy, with important delegations coming to see him. We returned to our car and had a prayer together, then went back in. In the meantime, the secretary at the desk had been changed, and, in less than fifteen minutes, we were in the presence of General McNarney.

Then I saw the Spirit operate on that man. I heard him say, "Under no conditions can you have permission to distribute your own supplies to your own people. They must come through the military." And, of course, we recognized immediately that if we had to go through the military, our Saints wouldn't get much of the supplies. And so we started telling him about the program of the Church, and when he saw we were somewhat determined, he said, "Well, you go ahead and collect your supplies, and probably by the time you get them collected the policy will be changed." I said, "General, they are already collected; they are always collected. We have ninety warehouses full of supplies. Within twenty-four hours from the time I wire our First Presidency in Salt Lake City, carloads of food, bedding, clothing, and medical supplies will be moving toward Germany." When I said this, he said, "I never heard of people with such vision." And before we left him we had written authorization to make our own distribution to our own people through our own channels, and from that moment on we had wonderful cooperation.

So I know that the Spirit can operate on nonmembers of the Church in high positions when it is in the interests of the work of the Lord. I have seen it with my own eyes.

I thank the Lord for the missionary work of the

Church, and I am thankful that even during the last world war, the First Presidency saw fit to issue an official statement in which they said, "No act of ours or of the Church must interfere with this God-given mandate" to carry the message to the world. (*Conference Report,* April 1942, p. 91.)

In the early days of the Church some of the elders, after receiving a testimony of the gospel, would ask the Prophet Joseph to inquire of the Lord as to how they could best spend their time. One of those who came was John Whitmer, who came with Peter Whitmer, Jr. This is the word of the Lord to John Whitmer through the Prophet Joseph:

> Hearken, my servant John, and listen to the words of Jesus Christ, your Lord and your Redeemer.
>
> For behold, I speak unto you with sharpness and with power, for mine arm is over all the earth.
>
> And I will tell you that which no man knoweth save me and thee alone—
>
> For many times you have desired of me to know that which would be of the most worth unto you.
>
> Behold, blessed are you for this thing, and for speaking my words which I have given you according to my commandments.
>
> And now, behold, I say unto you, that the thing which will be of the most worth unto you will be to declare repentance unto this people, that you may bring souls unto me, that you may rest with them in the kingdom of my Father. Amen. (D&C 15.)

This is the great work for which we are responsible—the greatest work in all the world. And the most profitable manner in which we can spend our time is to proclaim the word and bring souls unto him. God help us in it.

9

The Things That Endure

I would like to say a word, if I may, about our standards and our obligations as young people and leaders of youth. At a June Conference session, the general YMMIA president whispered to me, "One of our board members opened the door to a rear room in this building just before the meeting started and found one of our young speakers on his knees for a last word of prayer to his Heavenly Father for aid."

There is not anything that this nation needs more than for all of our people to be on their knees, night and morning, recognizing the need for divine guidance and divine support. As we were visiting at the home of my son in Washington, D.C., waiting until time for our plane to leave, we were talking about some of the eternal things of life, those things that never change, those things that are all-important. Our son Reed, who loves literature and has helped to make our family love and appreciate it, read, among other things, lines from a wonderful poem by William Watson, entitled "The Things That Are More Excellent."

As we wax older on this earth,
    Till many a toy that charmed us seems
Emptied of beauty, stripped of worth,
    And mean as dust and dead as dreams,—
For gauds that perished, shows that passed,
    Some recompense the Fates have sent:
Thrice lovelier shine the things that last,
    The things that are more excellent.

Tired of the Senate's barren brawl,
    An hour with silence we prefer,
Where statelier rise the woods than all
    Yon towers of talk at Westminster.
Let this man prate and that man plot,
    Or fame or place or title bent;
The votes of veering crowds are not
    The things that are more excellent.

When we talk about our standards and our ideals, our basic concepts, our principles, we are talking about those things that are more excellent. True, the Lord has given us leeway in implementing programs to move forward the great objectives that he has set. The methods may be our own, but the basic principles, the basic concepts, the eternal verities, are unchangeable, and it is my conviction that these basic principles are not on trial. You and I are on trial; the world is on trial.

I think of the story of a prominent American businessman who was visiting the Louvre, that great gallery in Paris. As he was leaving that wonderful gallery, he turned to the attendant at the door and said, with a wave of the hand, "Not a thing here, not a thing worthwhile." And the old man looked up at him and he said, "My good sir, the paintings in this gallery are no longer on trial. The spectators are."

Now, the eternal principles of the gospel are no longer on trial. The history of the race, the experience of man, the testimonies of people living and dead are evidence that these things are true and that only through adherence to those eternal concepts can men and women find happiness here and happiness and exaltation hereafter.

I am so grateful that the world is coming, at least in a measure, to recognize the value and the importance of some of these basic standards, these things that are more excellent, that form a part of our program for youth in the Church.

Many years ago when I first lived in Washington, in the early thirties, I had gone down to my office early one morning in the hope that I might get some work done before the telephone started to ring. I had just got seated at my desk when the telephone rang, and I picked it up a bit reluctantly. The man at the other end introduced himself, a total stranger, and asked me if I would have lunch with him during the day. Well, he was so sincere that I accepted finally, reluctantly, and at one o'clock I faced him across the luncheon table in a downtown hotel. He said, "I guess you wonder why I have asked you to come here."

I said, "Yes, I am a bit curious to know."

He said, "Well, two or three days ago at a businessmen's luncheon meeting in Chicago, I was talking to some of my associates, and I told them I had been asked by our corporation to go to Washington, D.C., to open an office and to employ a young man to represent our corporation there in the nation's capital. I began telling them the kind of a young man I would like to have represent our firm. First of all," he said, "I indicated to them that I wanted a young man whose integrity would never be questioned, a young man of real character. I would like a young man who did not use liquor and would not be serving liquor as a means of trying to influence people." He said, "I wanted a young man who, if married, would be devoted to his wife and family, and who if unmarried would not be chasing cheap women around. I told them that I would prefer to have a young man who did not even smoke."

Then he said, "One of them spoke up and said, 'What you want is a returned Mormon missionary.'" He told me, "I had heard about the Mormon Church a little; in fact, I remembered two young men in dark suits calling at our door one day and leaving us a copy of the Book of Mormon. But that was about the extent of my knowledge. However, as I rode to Washington on the train, I began thinking about the comment of my friend, and I said to myself, 'Well, probably, that is just exactly the kind of a young man I do want. Why not?' So," he continued, "as I registered at my hotel last night, I said to the clerk, 'Are there any Mormons in Washington?' He said, 'I don't know, I suppose there are—they seem to be everywhere.' I said, 'Do you know any?' And he said, 'No, I can't say that I do, but the manager of the hotel is right here, and he will probably know someone.'" And then my host said, "I asked the manager, and he gave me your name. Now that is why I have invited you to lunch. Can you give me the names of three or four young men whom I might interview, who meet the standards I have outlined?"

Well, of course, you know it would be an easy matter for any one of us to give to any man who makes such inquiry the names not only of three or four but of a dozen or more who meet those standards.

The dean of one of our great agricultural colleges once came to my office and said, "I have something to tell you. Your church has just organized a stake in our state, the first one in our state." I said, "Yes, I know. I read about it." He said, "I want you to know that they really pick good men for stake presidents. They have taken one of my associates, a professor in my department." He added, "I never met a finer man." And then he started to tell me about the man's standards and ideals and principles and the things that guide him.

On a visit to Purdue University, where I was attending a meeting of large stock producers from twelve Midwestern states, I was seated at a table with the president of the university. He said, "Well, I see you Mormon people have done it again." I said, "What do you mean?" And then he told me the figures that he had just been reviewing regarding the achievements of Utah in the field of education. He said, "I cannot understand this. Your state is not one of the great, wealthy states in terms of dollar income. How is it that you make such a record in the field of education?"

I said, "I am not sure that I have the answer, but probably I can give you part of the answer." Then I told him about our people and their love for education, how it has been emphasized from the very inception of our great latter-day work, and I quoted some of the revelations that the Prophet Joseph had received. I referred to the great MIA program and made reference to our great slogan, "The glory of God is intelligence." When I quoted those lines, he said, "What did you say?" I said, "The glory of God is intelligence, or in other words, light and truth." He said, "I never heard anything like that. That is wonderful."

Then he called the attention of the rest of the group at the table—there were perhaps fifteen or twenty men there—and repeated essentially the conversation we had had together.

After the luncheon we went into the Music Hall, where the meeting of some 7,000 livestock producers was to be held. We listened to a male chorus sing two numbers, one having a state setting and the other, "America, the Beautiful." After the chorus left, I was to take my part on the program. In his introduction, before 7,000 people, the university president again repeated our conversation at the luncheon table and told about the MIA and its slogan. In my talk I paid tribute to the wonderful chorus, and so afterward he said, "Would you like to go up to the room where they have been rehearsing? This building is so beautifully constructed that acoustically it is almost perfect, and you could not hear them rehearsing above, but they have been up there rehearsing all during this meeting."

So we went up and I was invited to speak briefly to them. I told them of our love for music. I quoted the Lord's words, given through the Prophet Joseph and found in the 25th section of the Doctrine and Covenants, on the important part music plays in our worship. When I had finished with my final remarks, the leader was kind enough to say, "I wish we had had the recording machine on today. I am going to make you a proposition. If, when you go back to your office, you will record essentially what you have said today and send it to us, we will record the two numbers we sang, which you liked so well, and send them to you." Well, the exchange has been made.

Why do I mention these things? I mention them because when our standards and our ideals, our concepts, our principles are understood, even by men of the world, they cannot help but appreciate them.

I have in my files tear sheets from a little national magazine of limited circulation, Listen, with a feature article under the title "The Mormons Find Fun in Abstinence." At the top of the page is a picture of our beloved President David O. McKay and a quotation from him as follows: "A spotless character founded upon the ability to say no in the presence of those who mock and jeer wins the respect and love of men and women whose opinion is most worthwhile."

There is also a quotation from Elder Richard L. Evans

regarding the Word of Wisdom, a picture of the Tabernacle Choir, a picture of our young men in action in a basketball tournament, and a comment regarding that. The editorial comment is as follows:

[From time to time *Listen* has featured various church organizations taking a strong stand in the matter of alcohol education and the personal use of intoxicants. This feature by the nationally known writer, Don K. Anthon, notes the basic philosophy and belief of the Mormon Church in this regard, along with factual evidence showing the beneficial results appearing in the every-day lives of its members.]

What at first seemed to be another routine sailing of the *Saxonia* from Montreal to Greenock, Scotland, August 13, 1955, proved instead to be one of the ship's most eventful Atlantic crossings. Plans for a concert tour of Europe led to the making of reservations on the *Saxonia* for 600 passengers, the majority of whom were members of the Church of Jesus Christ of Latter-day Saints, more commonly known as Morons, with headquarters in Salt Lake City. The passengers, including 375 members of the renowned Tabernacle Choir of the Mormon Church, and these choir members together with their families and friends, completely filled the *Saxonia.* Altogether it was a happy group, anticipating a vacation filled with new scenes and pleasant associations. And as they marched up the gangplank, they indulged in much singing and gay conversation. As the captain of the ship looked them over, he remarked to his mate, "It looks as if we are going to have a lively passage." The barkeeper beamed with delight from behind his line of glasses in anticipation of the heavy demand upon his supplies when the ship got underway.

However, it was not long after leaving port before the bartender became aware of the fact that there had not been a single call for a drink. Convinced that this was very unusual, he quieted his apprehensions by concluding, "Oh, well, they will soon be showing up. They always do." The ship was well under way, and still there was no business at the bar. The hope for eager customers dimmed, and in frustration he appealed to the captain, "I can't understand it. I haven't had a single drink. Such a thing has never happened before." The captain agreed that it was a strange situation, especially since the passengers all appeared gay and happy, and he said he would investigate to see what he could find out.

Quickly contacting one of the passengers who appeared to be a hopeful candidate for information, he asked what he considered the favorite drink of the party. The prompt reply came back. "Mormons do not drink any liquor." That seemed incredible to the captain, but he said, "Well, what do Mormons drink? Surely they must have some social drink." In reply, the honest Mormon said, "We drink milk mostly, and sometimes fruit juices." "Well," ejaculated the captain, "milk for six hundred passengers? We don't have that much on board."

The bartender who stood within hearing distance gave expression to his amazement by a doleful countenance. Between captain and bartender they agreed that the unusual situation must be met, so the ship pulled into Quebec and a king-sized supply of milk was put aboard. From that time until the end of the voyage, the barkeeper was busy serving milk straight, malts, and fruit cocktails.

Then the article goes on to tell about their arrival in Scotland, the wonderful impression the choir made, and the bartender's final comment at the end of the journey. He said, "Never in my life have I known a shipful of passengers to have so much pleasure and enjoy so much fun and at the same time be cold sober."

Of course, this is not anything new to us. But the thing that pleases me is that it seems to be appreciated a little more as time goes on—these standards, these ideals we talk about in the Church. So I am very happy that today there is more evidence in support of the truth of the Word of Wisdom than ever before, and with the passing of time, the evidence will accumulate and increase. Why? Because in the Word of Wisdom are announced the eternal, basic principles that never change, and we must always remember that time is on the side of truth and the Word of Wisdom is the truth, as are the other standards and ideals of the Church.

So our young people and our leaders of youth cannot afford in the least degree to let down in their standards. They cannot afford not to uphold wholeheartedly the ideals, the basic concepts, these eternal principles upon which our programs have been established. We have everything to gain and nothing to lose by living the standards of the Church, the standards of truth.

Sometimes our friends speak more truth than they

realize. Many distinguished visitors come to Washington, D.C. Some time ago, the King of Belgium visited, and in his address he said this: "I who am a young man come from a country old enough to have been spoken of proudly by Julius Caesar. I come to a country [meaning the United States] which for centuries God kept hidden behind the veil until its appointed hour when it took into its young arms the people of the Old World."

Well, you can imagine what I thought as I heard those words. I was determined that this wonderful, fine-appearing young monarch should read the account of the very truth that he spoke, recorded in the Book of Mormon.

At a party at the Beverly Hills Hilton Hotel in Los Angeles, I had been asked by the President of the United States to greet the president of one of our newer republics, the president of eighty-eight million people scattered on some 3,000 islands a thousand miles long, a nation that had been in existence only a few years. As we sat there at this dinner, which was sponsored in large measure by the motion picture industry and at which many movie stars were present, I could look out a beautiful bay window. Down the avenue, on the elevation, I could see the soft floodlights around our glorious Los Angeles Temple, and I had the joy of pointing it out to my guests and to friends at our table and other tables. I thought, as we sat there, "Much of what goes on tonight is simply the froth of life. The things that endure, the things that are real, the things that are important are those things represented in the temple of God."

In our experience in Washington, never once was there a single occasion when we had cause to feel any embarrassment because of our standards, our principles, our ideals, the things for which this church stands.

When my good wife entertained the First Lady and the wives of the Cabinet members in our own home, it was a different luncheon than probably they had been used to. Sister Benson said very graciously, "Now, you will find some things different in our home. There will not be any tobacco, there will not be any cocktails, there will not be any tea and coffee, but we will try to make it up to you in our own way." I wish you could have heard the comments afterward.

No, you will never have any occasion to be embarrassed among people who count, real men and women, because you live according to the standards, the teachings, and the ideals of the Church. I know whereof I speak.

I have had dinners tendered in my honor to which have been invited leaders from dozens of nations, and out of respect of me, there has not been even tea and coffee served—just fruit juices throughout the dinner. There have been other times, too, when, as host, it has been my privilege and pleasure to entertain the representatives of several other countries, and there has never been any embarrassment because there has not been liquor served or because there has been a blessing asked on the food. In fact, I have felt from my own personal experience that there has been a little feeling of appreciation and added respect, and ofttimes inquiry leading to gospel conversation, because of some of these simple things.

May I just quote from one editorial from a fine newspaper in Pennsylvania:

> We will take Ezra Taft Benson without a martini in his hand to any other public official with one. We prefer men of distinction who got that way without a cocktail calling card. We like the image of Washington we learned from the school books. We deplore the preference of some for martini-government. We think it is time officials who have the courage of their convictions against such goings-on be told they have friends and supporters back home.

There is a lot of sentiment in this country, outside the Church, in support of our ideals and standards as Latter-day Saints. Let us not fail the Church. Let us not fail ourselves by being so unwise as to feel we have to let down in our standards in order to be accepted by the world. It is not true. The world may not live by our standards, but they have respect and appreciation for those of us who have the wisdom and the courage to maintain those standards.

Some day we may be called upon as a people to exert great influence in helping to preserve the liberties and freedoms and blessings vouchsafed to us as a people in the Constitution of this land. Some of our inspired leaders have had words to say on that subject. I hope and pray that we will be ready when the time comes—in fact, I am inclined to feel sometimes it is going to be a gradual process. Maybe it is underway now. We will not be able to discharge our obligations unless we adhere strictly to the standards and ideals of the church and kingdom of God.

That we may do so with all our hearts and receive the inner satisfaction, the inner peace, and the joy that comes from keeping the commandments of God is my humble prayer.

10

The Latter-day Saints and the World

The Church of Jesus Christ of Latter-day Saints is a world organization. Our message is a world message. The Book of Mormon prophets who were permitted to see our day noted that the members of the Church of Christ would be relatively few in numbers. They also noted that they were distributed worldwide. I have been impressed with this fact, particularly while supervising our missionary work in Europe and in Asia. And even as far back as 1946, at the end of World War II, while serving an emergency mission in Europe, I was impressed with the wide distribution of our people as I traveled through the war-torn countries of the world.

Never has the Church been so well-known as it is today. Almost everywhere we are now known for what we really are, and not for what our past enemies have said about us. The interest in the Church and its message is worldwide, at least in the free world. I noted this in Japan at Expo '70, where some seven million people crowded through our relatively small pavilion, and eight-hundred thousand of them signed cards inviting missionaries to visit them.

On my last of several visits to Israel as a Cabinet member of the United States government, and later as a Church official, Sister Benson and I spent a delightful evening with Mr. and Mrs. David Ben-Gurion, at their invitation, in their home in Tel Aviv. As we were leaving that evening, Mr. Ben-Gurion said, "I want you to pray to God that he will spare me for ten more years. I'm writing a history of the Jewish people, and it will take me ten years to finish it. I would like you to send me all the information you have about Orson Hyde's visit to the Holy Land in 1841, including a copy of the prayer he gave as he dedicated the land of Palestine on the Mount of Olives. I want to incorporate it all into my history." Then as a last word as we were leaving, he said, "There are no people in this world who understand the Jews like the Mormons." To this I responded, "Mr. Ben-Gurion, there are no people in this world who understand the world like the Mormons." And he answered, "Oh, I'm not sure I'd go quite that far, but what I said is true."

Leaders of this church, called by revelation, bearers of the priesthood of God, see clearly the problems of the world and know what is needed for their solution.

We live today in a wicked world. Never in our memory have the forces of evil been arrayed in such a deadly formation. The devil is well organized and has many emissaries working for him. His satanic majesty has proclaimed his intention to destroy our young people, to weaken the home and family, and to defeat the purposes of the Lord Jesus Christ through his great church.

As Latter-day Saints, we know the adversary will not succeed. The Church stands stronger today than ever before in its history. We are not only growing in numbers, we are also increasing in faith and testimony as measured by attendance at meetings, the payment of tithes and offerings, support of the great missionary program, the building program, temple work, and other phases of our program. Today we have the fullest and the richest program for the blessing of our Father's children to be found anywhere upon the face of the earth. I know this is true.

But we live in a day of wickedness. It seems that almost everything that is good, pure, uplifting, and strengthening is being challenged as never before—yes, almost discarded by many.

From time to time I hear from my non-Mormon friends. Many of them are fine Christians, honorable men of the earth. A prominent executive in the eastern part of the United States closed his letter with these words: "God bless you—and your wonderful work. I pray that Satan will be kept out of your church, since we have failed to do so in ours."

As Christian people, as members of the true church of Jesus Christ, we face difficult days. But they are also days filled with challenge, hope, and assurance. We have clearly before us the answers to the problems facing mankind. We know what the Lord expects of us. He said that we should all "arise and shine forth" and "be a standard for the nations." (D&C 115:5.) We know the course we should follow. Do we have the faith and courage to follow that course? I hope and pray we do.

You will recall the parable of the wheat and the tares in the thirteenth chapter of Matthew. The disciples at the time seemed not to understand this parable set forth by the Savior, and they asked him for an explanation. He said to them:

He that soweth the good seed is the Son of man;

The field is the world; the good seed are the children of the kingdom; but the tares are the children of the wicked one;

The enemy that sowed them is the devil; the harvest is the end of the world; and the reapers are the angels.

As therefore the tares are gathered and burned in the fire; so shall it be in the end of this world.

The Son of man shall send forth his angels, and they shall gather out of his kingdom all things that offend, and them which do iniquity. (Matthew 13:37-41.)

In modern revelation, the Lord has said, "Behold, verily I say unto you, the angels are crying unto the Lord day and night, who are ready and waiting to be sent forth to reap down the fields." (D&C 86:5.) He also said in this same revelation that he would "let the wheat and the tares grow together until the harvest is fully ripe; then ye shall first gather out the wheat from among the tares, and after the gathering of the wheat, behold and lo, the tares are bound in bundles, and the field remaineth to be burned." (D&C 86:7.)

The Lord has also said in our day in a revelation to the Prophet Joseph, "I, the Lord, am angry with the wicked; I am holding my Spirit from the inhabitants of the earth. I have sworn in my wrath, and decreed wars upon the face of the earth, and the wicked shall slay the wicked, and fear shall come upon every man." (D&C 63:32-33.)

In section one of the Doctrine and Covenants, the introduction to the Lord's book of commandments, he made it clear that "the hour is not yet, but is nigh at hand, when peace shall be taken from the earth, and the devil shall have power over his own dominion." (D&C 1:35.)

President Joseph Fielding Smith said in 1967, "Peace *has* been taken from the earth. The devil *has* power over his own dominion. The Spirit of the Lord *has* been withdrawn. Not because the Lord desires to withdraw that Spirit, but because of the wickedness of mankind, it becomes necessary that the Spirit of the Lord be withdrawn." ("The Predicted Judgments," *BYU Speeches of the Year,* March 21, 1967, p. 6.)

Prophets of God, ancient and modern, have predicted that judgments would be poured out upon the world unless the people repented. Prophets and leaders of the Church from the days of the Prophet Joseph have spoken out clearly and courageously regarding the calamities, destructions, and plagues that would visit the earth unless the people repented of their evil ways.

President Wilford Woodruff, in an address in Brigham City, Utah, in June 1894, said:

> God has held the angels of destruction for many years lest they reap down the wheat with the tares. But I want to tell you now, those angels have left the portals of heaven, and they stand over this people and this nation now, and are hovering over the earth waiting to pour out the judgments. And from this very day they shall be poured out. Calamities and troubles are increasing in the earth and there is a meaning to these things. Remember this and reflect upon these matters. If you do your duty, and I do my duty, we shall have protection and shall pass through the afflictions in peace and safety. Read the scriptures and revelations. (*Discourses of Wilford Woodruff,* p. 230.)

Yes, peace has been taken from the earth, and "if prophecy is to be fulfilled, there awaits the world a conflict more dreadful than any the world has yet seen." ("The Predicted Judgments," p. 9.)

President Brigham Young said:

> When the testimony of the Elders ceases to be given, and the Lord says to them, "Come home; I will now preach my own sermons to the nations of the earth," all you now know can scarcely be called a preface to the sermon that will be preached with fire and sword, tempests, earthquakes, hail, rain, thunders and lightnings, and fearful destruction. (*Journal of Discourses,* vol. 8, p. 123.)

Why is the Lord angry with the wicked? Because they have rejected the gospel. They have rejected Jesus Christ as the God of this world. They have rejected the Author of salvation. As President Joseph Fielding Smith said:

> When you reject the gospel, when you reject the Author of our salvation, what have you to rely on? Nothing! Nothing but the devil's plan. What is the devil's plan? To force men; to take away from them their agency; to compel them to do the bidding of someone else, whether they like it or not. That is the feeling that has spread over

the world. Naturally, the Lord says the time was near at hand, and he said that over one hundred years ago and it is now, of course, much closer. . . .

We hear a great deal about the thought that we are fighting now for liberty—the liberty of the people, the liberty of the nations. I hope so, but if we want to insure the liberty of the people, then we must turn back again to Jesus Christ who is the God of this land. I say "we." I mean the people of the United States, the people of this continent. We cannot afford to forsake the God of this land who is Jesus Christ. If we do, we lose our strength. The Lord has promised to protect this nation, this whole continent, this whole hemisphere. He would fortify it against all other nations; He would fight our battles on one condition: That we would keep His commandments.

Now there is our danger. We must not forsake God. If we are not in this life abiding in His truth, you may be sure that He is not going to be on our side. He will leave us to ourselves. ("The Predicted Judgments," pp. 12-13.)

It should be comforting to all Latter-day Saints that the Lord has given great promises in that sacred volume, the Book of Mormon, promises that should give us comfort and assurance on the condition that we live the gospel. How I wish that every person would read the Book of Mormon, and in it the prophetic history of the Americas and the clear warnings for the future.

Read what Father Lehi said in 2 Nephi 1:6-8. Read what his son Jacob said in 2 Nephi 10:10-14. Read also 1 Nephi 22:17, when the Lord said through his prophet, "Wherefore, he will preserve the righteous by his power, even if it so be that the fulness of his wrath must come, and the righteous be preserved, even unto the destruction of their enemies by fire. Wherefore, the righteous need not fear; for thus saith the prophet, they shall be saved, even if it so be as by fire." And further, "the righteous need not fear, for they are those who shall not be confounded. . . ." (1 Nephi 22:22.) Then, in the twenty-sixth verse: "And because of the righteousness of his people, Satan has no power; wherefore, he cannot be loosed for the space of many years; for he hath no power over the hearts of the people, for they dwell in righteousness, and the Holy One of Israel reigneth." (1 Nephi 22:26.)

But we must all keep in mind the warning of the brother of Jared:

> And now, we can behold the decrees of God concerning this land, that it is a land of promise; and whatsoever nation shall possess it shall serve God, or they shall be swept off when the fulness of his wrath shall come upon them. And the fulness of his wrath cometh upon them when they are ripened in iniquity.
>
> For behold, this is a land which is choice above all other lands; wherefore he that doth possess it shall serve God or shall be swept off; for it is the everlasting decree of God.
>
> Behold, this is a choice land, and whatsoever nation shall possess it shall be free from bondage, and from captivity, and from all other nations under heaven, if they will but serve the God of the land, who is Jesus Christ. . . . (Ether 1:9-10, 12.)

My beloved brethren and sisters, these things are true. This work is true. God the Father and his beloved Son did appear to Joseph Smith. This was the greatest event that has transpired in the world since the resurrection of the Master. This is our message and our warning to the world. It is a world message from a world organization—The Church of Jesus Christ of Latter-day Saints. These warnings of the prophets, ancient and modern, shall in very deed be fulfilled. The Lord *is* "angry with the wicked." He *is* "holding his Spirit from the inhabitants of the earth." The one hope for this wicked world is to accept and live the gospel, to keep the commandments, to heed the warnings of the prophets, ancient and modern.

I bear witness that these things are true and pray that all of us will heed the inspired counsel of the priesthood of God.

11

Keeping the Sabbath Day Holy

Few, if any, subjects in the great, eternal gospel plan of the Lord have been spoken of more frequently than that of the Sabbath. Ancient prophets of God have proclaimed it, Presidents of the Church and other General Authorities have repeatedly emphasized it, lay Christians and men of good will throughout Christendom have spoken approvingly of its place and value in the lives of men, women, and children of all races and climes.

In the Church, it has been the subject of much preaching and writing. A call to the Church Historian's office for a few items on the Sabbath brought to my office 132 specific references and the generous comment, "If you need more, please let us know." I assure you, I didn't.

The period allotted for this discussion could be filled and more—and quite profitably—by simply quoting from my beloved brethren, past and present. I am grateful for their counsel and admonition on the important subject of the Sabbath. And I am also thankful that I find myself in full harmony, insofar as I can tell, with what they have said and written. I am also pleased that the record is clear and full. No Latter-day Saint need stumble or be in doubt as to his duty in reference to this divine law.

I believe in honoring the Sabbath day. I love a sacred Sabbath. I am grateful that as a boy I had a constant example and sound parental counsel as to the importance of keeping the Sabbath day a holy day. I am also grateful that my beloved wife and children and grandchildren have been true to the direction of the priesthood of God in regard to the Sabbath day. My memories of the Sabbath from infancy have been joyful, uplifting, and spiritually profitable, for which I am deeply grateful.

Men from time immemorial have recognized the need for blessed rest—time for physical and spiritual refreshment. The human body and the spirit of man require it for happy, purposeful living.

Over sixty years ago an item from the *Daily News* appeared in the *Liahona, the Elders' Journal* under the caption "The Day of Rest."

> One of the facts upon which all men are agreed, whatever may be their view of life, is the need of a frequently recurring season of spiritual and physical refreshment. The life which was an unending vista of dusty days in the city would be a life from which we should all turn in despair. The hum of the wheels would drive the world mad. The soul would perish under the strain of material things and the body would perish with it. There is, therefore, no question of can't in the desire to keep our Sunday: it is a supreme necessity, and never more supreme than in these days, when the pace of life is always being quickened and men are becoming more and more like the parts of a giant machine whose operations they do not understand and whose roar dulls the mind. (January 1, 1910, vol. 7, p. 445.)

Well over fifty years ago, Joseph L. Townsend penned these lovely lines about the Sabbath for the *Improvement Era.*

> O, blessed day of peace and rest,
> Thou art the day I love the best!
> Through precious hours thy gifts are sown
> With blessings from the Savior's throne.

With songs of joy attune my lyre,
And feed my soul's celestial fire;
Let love with love its pleasures meet,
And happiness be mine complete.

I know the joy of rest and peace
That from my toil brings sweet release;
And when the evening hours have passed
Yet shall thy precepts ever last.

And so repeated days replace
Thy happy hours of love and grace;
And Heaven, each departed year,
In vision thou hast made more clear!
—July 1920, p. 833

Henry Ward Beecher said: "A world without a Sabbath would be like a man without a smile, like a summer without flowers, and like a homestead without a garden. It is the joyous day of the whole week."

Samuel Taylor Coleridge: "I feel as if God had, by giving the Sabbath, given fifty-two springs in every year."

Ralph Waldo Emerson: "The Sunday is the core of our civilization, dedicated to thought and reverence. It invites to the noblest solitude and to the noblest society."

Henry Wadsworth Longfellow: "Sunday is the golden clasp that binds together the volume of the week."

Yes, Sunday is wonderful, but how much more wonderful it might be if honored as a sacred Sabbath. Man has tried on several occasions to change God's law of the Sabbath. Each attempt has resulted in failure.

After the War of 1870, England and France decided to observe the Sabbath only every twenty-one days in order that they might have time to build up the war-torn countries. After a period of trial, however, a careful check showed that they had accomplished less total work than when they rested every seventh day as the Lord prescribed.

In the hope that it may be of some little help, I have chosen to discuss the subject of the Sabbath briefly under the following seven important subtopics:

1. Scriptural basis anciently
2. Scriptural basis in modern latter days
3. Purpose of the Sabbath
4. What fits that purpose
5. What does not fit that purpose
6. Helps toward a sacred Sabbath
7. Consequences of disobedience and obedience

1. The Church accepts the Sabbath as a law unto man from the beginning. Said Elder James E. Talmage:

> The Sabbath was prefigured if not definitely specified in the record of the creation, wherein we read, following the account of the six days or periods of creative effort: "And God blessed the seventh day, and sanctified it: because that in it he had rested from all his work which God created and made." (Gen. 2:3.)
>
> In the early stages of Exodus the Israelites were commanded to lay in a double portion of manna on the sixth day, for the seventh was consecrated as a day of holy rest; and this was signalized by the Lord's withholding manna on the Sabbath day. (See Exod. 16:23-30.) There is no proof that Sabbath observance by Israel at this early date was an innovation; and it may be reasonably regarded as a recognition of an established order by re-enactment in the new dispensation. Later, when the Decalog was codified and promulgated on Sinai, the Sabbath law was made particularly explicit, and the Lord's rest was cited as its foundation (in these well-known words):
>
> "Remember the Sabbath day, to keep it holy. Six days shalt thou labour, and do all thy work: But the seventh day is the sabbath of the Lord thy God: in it thou shalt not do any work, thou, nor thy son, nor thy daughter, thy manservant, nor thy maidservant, nor thy cattle, nor thy stranger that is within thy gates: For in six days the Lord made heaven and earth, the sea, and all that in them is, and rested the seventh day: wherefore the Lord blessed the sabbath day, and hallowed it." (Exod. 20:8-11.) ("Remember the Sabbath Day, a Law Unto Man from the Beginning," *Improvement Era*, December 1917, p. 114.)

Holy prophets of God throughout Israelite history

admonished and rebuked the people regarding this divine law of the Sabbath. The affliction of the nation was due to Sabbath violation, according to Nehemiah. (Nehemiah 13:15-22.) To Isaiah (Isaiah 58:13-14) and Ezekiel (Ezekiel 20:12-24) and the Book of Mormon branch in America (Jarom 5; Mosiah 18:23), Sabbath observance was an imperative requirement.

Apostate Israel, long before the birth of Christ, had departed from the purpose and spirit of Sabbath observance.

This condition was strongly denounced by our Lord in reply to the many criticisms heaped upon him because of the healings and other good works wrought by him on the Sabbath. *"The sabbath was made for man, and not man for the sabbath,"* said he, and then continued with the profound affirmation: *"The Son of man is Lord also of the sabbath."* (Mark 2:27-28.)

Christ came not to destroy the Law of Moses but to fulfill it; and through him the law was superseded by the gospel. The Savior rose from the tomb on the first day of the week; and that particular Sunday, as also the next, was rendered forever memorable by the bodily visitation of the resurrected Lord to the assembled apostles and others. To the believers in the crucified and risen Savior Sunday became the *Lord's Day* (Rev. 1:10), and in time took the place of Saturday as the weekly Sabbath in the Christian churches. (Talmage, *op. cit.,* p. 115.)

2. As Latter-day Saints, we accept Sunday as the Christian Sabbath and proclaim its sanctity. And, as Elder James E. Talmage has so well summarized:

We admit without argument that under the Mosaic Law the seventh day of the week, Saturday, was designated and observed as the holy day, and that the change from Saturday to Sunday was a feature of the apostolic administration following the personal ministry of Jesus Christ. Greater to us than the question of this day or that in the week, is the actuality of the weekly Sabbath, to be observed as a day of special and particular devotion to the service of the Lord. (Ibid., p. 114.)

By direct revelation authority, the Church teaches

that Sunday is the acceptable day for Sabbath observance as the Lord's day.

> In this, a new dispensation, and verily the last—the Dispensation of the Fullness of Times—the law of the Sabbath has been reaffirmed unto the Church. It is to be noted that the revelation, part of which follows, was given to the Church on a *Sunday* (August 7, 1831).
>
> "And that thou mayest more fully keep thyself unspotted from the world, thou shalt go to the house of prayer and offer up thy sacraments upon my holy day. For verily this is a day appointed unto you to rest from your labors, and to pay thy devotions unto the Most High. Nevertheless thy vows shall be offered up in righteousness on all days and at all times. But remember *that on this the Lord's day*, thou shalt offer thine oblations and thy sacraments unto the Most High, confessing thy sins unto thy brethren, and before the Lord. And on this day thou shalt do none other thing, only let thy food be prepared with singleness of heart that thy fasting may be perfect, or, in other words, that thy joy may be full." (D&C 59:9-13.) (Ibid., pp. 115-16.)

President Joseph Fielding Smith, commenting on the Lord's day, said: "The Lord's day was, of course, Sunday, and on this day the Latter-day Saints have been commanded to observe the weekly Sabbath. So far as the Latter-day Saints are concerned, the Lord has spoken. This settles the question." (*Answers to Gospel Questions,* Deseret Book, 1958, vol. 2, p. 59.)

"We believe that a weekly day of rest is no less truly a necessity for the physical well-being of man than for his spiritual growth but, primarily and essentially, we regard the Sabbath as divinely established, and its observance a commandment of him who was and is and ever shall be, *Lord of the Sabbath."* (Talmage, *op. cit.,* p. 116.)

On Sunday, April 11, 1830, five days after the Church was organized in the Whitmer home, the Prophet called together his followers and held the first sacramental service in the Church in this dispensation. The first Sunday on the plains, April 18, 1847, moving westward from Winter Quarters, Howard Egan wrote: "Today, being a day set apart by the Almighty God for His people to rest, we do not intend to travel." The day following the arrival of the Mormon pioneers in the Salt Lake Valley, Sunday was strictly observed, and at two o'clock, the worshipers met in their first sacramental service in their new home.

3. What is the purpose of the Sabbath? The Lord gives the answer in Doctrine and Covenants, section 59: "And that thou mayest more fully keep thyself unspotted from the world, . . . this is a day appointed unto you to rest from your labors, and to pay thy devotions unto the Most High." (D&C 59:9-10.) And as we offer our religious offerings and sacraments with thanksgiving, and confess our sins, the Lord has promised that our joy will be full and—

the fulness of the earth is yours, the beasts of the field and the fowls of the air, and that which climbeth upon the trees and walketh upon the earth;

Yea, and the herb, and the good things which come of the earth, whether for food or for raiment, or for houses, or for barns, or for orchards, or for gardens, or for vineyards;

Yea, all things which come of the earth, in the season thereof, are made for the benefit and use of man, both to please the eye and to gladden the heart;

Yea, for food and for raiment, for taste and for smell, to strengthen the body and to enliven the soul.

And it pleaseth God that he hath given all these things unto man; for unto this end were they made to be used, with judgment, not to excess, neither by extortion.

And in nothing doth man offend God, or against none is his wrath kindled, save those who confess not his hand in all things, and obey not his commandments. (D&C 59:16-21.)

These, then, are the promises if we keep a sacred sabbath "in righteousness," with glad hearts, "and a contrite spirit." (D&C 59:8.)

The purpose of the Sabbath is for spiritual uplift, for a renewal of our covenants, for worship, for rest, for prayer. It is for the purpose of feeding the spirit, that we may keep ourselves unspotted from the world by obeying God's command.

"The Lord's plan is perfect," said Elder Orson F. Whitney.

> . . . his commandments have in view the salvation of the body as well as the spirit, for it is the soul that will be redeemed from the grave and glorified. God has commanded us to care for the spirit, as well as for the body, and give it food in due season, and He set aside the Sabbath day that man might rest from his temporal labors and go to the house of the Lord and be fed with that holy influence which nourishes the spirit of man. That is why we meet together on the Sabbath day. Our spirits need their food, the same as do our bodies and if we neglect them, they will starve and dwindle and die upon the same principle that the body will die when deprived of its proper nourishment. (*Liahona, the Elders Journal,* February 5, 1910, vol. 7, p. 530.)

As President Joseph Fielding Smith has pointed out, "The Lord has never given a commandment to the members of the Church, or to the world, except it has been given for the everlasting welfare and blessing for all who obey it." (*Answers to Gospel Questions,* Deseret Book, 1957, vol. 1, p. 101.)

4. What fits the purpose of the Sabbath? Here are a few suggestions:

a. Activities that contribute to greater spirituality.

b. Essential Church meetings in the house of prayer.

c. Acquisition of spiritual knowledge—reading the scriptures, Church history and biographies, and the inspired words of the Brethren.

d. Resting physically, getting acquainted with family, relating scriptural stories to children, bearing testimony, building family unity.

e. Visiting the sick and aged shut-ins.

f. Singing the songs of Zion and listening to inspiring music.

g. Paying devotions to the Most High—prayer, personal and family; fasting, administrations, father's blessings.

h. Preparing food with singleness of heart—simple meals prepared largely on Saturday.

Remember, Sunday is the Lord's day—a day to do his work.

The May 1902 issue of the *Improvement Era* carried an excellent article by Colonel R. M. Bryce Thomas entitled "How Shall We Find the Sabbath of Profit?" which closed with these words:

> Thus, by an honest and conscientious observance of the Sabbath day, the spiritual life is strengthened and built up, and the blessings and favors of God our Father are vouchsafed to us. But let us remember that we are not entitled to devote the Sabbath to any secular purpose, and that if we do so, we do it at our peril.

5. Numerous are the activities that do not fit the spirit or purpose of the Sabbath. Here are a few:

> a. Overworking and staying up late Saturday, resulting in exhaustion on Sunday.
>
> b. Filling the Sabbath so full of extra meetings that there is no time for prayer, meditation, family fellowship, and counseling.
>
> c. Doing gardening and odd jobs around the house.
>
> d. Taking trips to canyons and resorts; visits to friends, amusements, joy riding, loafing, etc.
>
> e. Children playing vigorously and seeing picture shows.
>
> f. Sports, golf, fishing, and hunting "wild animals," which God made for the use of man only "in times of famine and excess of hunger." (D&C 89:15.) "Let the boys have their exercise. Let them have amusements at the proper time, but let them be taught better things on the Sabbath day," said President Joseph F. Smith. ("What Shall We Do on the Sabbath Day?" *Improvement Era*, August 1916, p. 864.)
>
> g. Reading Sunday papers—the largest edition of the week. Why? Because it is diverting and time-consuming on a day we need to build the spirit.
>
> h. Shopping or supporting with our patronage Sunday business —grocery stores, supermarkets, restaurants, gas stations, etc. (First Presidency's statement, June 19, 1959; Nehemiah 10:31.)

President Joseph Fielding Smith made it a practice not to turn on radio or TV on Sunday except for Church-sponsored programs.

This is from a statement of the First Presidency on the Sabbath, dated June 19, 1959:

> The Sabbath is not just another day on which we merely rest from work, free to spend it as our light-mindedness may suggest. It is

a holy day, the Lord's Day, to be spent as a day of worship and reverence. All matters extraneous thereto should be shunned. . . . Latter-day Saints, with a testimony of the Gospel and a knowledge of the spiritual blessings that come from keeping the Sabbath, will never permit themselves to make it a shopping day, an activity that has no place in a proper observance of the Holy Day of the Lord, on which we are commanded to pour out our souls in gratitude for the many blessings of health, strength, physical comfort, and spiritual joy which come from the Lord's bounteous hand. (*Church News,* July 11, 1959, p. 3.)

6. Here are a few helps toward a sacred Sabbath:

a. Houseclean, straighten up, refuel car, and prepare clothing and food in advance, on Saturday.

b. Provide for recreation and amusements during the week and provide for a half holiday during the week. "We stand for a sacred sabbath and a weekly half holiday" is a good slogan for families especially. (Heber J. Grant, in *Latter-day Prophets Speak,* p. 363.)

c. Students should study their school subjects during the week and keep a sacred Sabbath—it pays.

d. Get a good rest on Saturday night.

Businesses that close on Sunday can succeed. There are many examples. Here is one example from the owner of a restaurant in Salt Lake City, excerpted from his letter of January 13, 1971:

You will note a number of reasons why I have closed my place of business on Sunday. . . .

1. The foremost reason, it was a commandment of the Lord which we wanted to obey.

2. I did not feel like I wanted to ask thirty or forty fine people to break the Sabbath every week. . . .

3. We had young children we wanted to teach the importance of keeping the Sabbath day holy. . . .

4. The year we closed our business on Sunday we made more money than any previous year.

5. It is my testimony that the Lord has blessed us over the years and that we are far better off financially and spiritually than we ever would have been had we remained open on Sunday.

6. I am so sure the Lord has blessed us that I would not dare open our place of business on Sunday. It is my firm conviction, if I

were to open my place on Sunday and stop paying an honest tithing, I would be broke in one year.

I have a firm conviction that the greatest guarantee for success in business for a Latter-day Saint is to honor the Sabbath day as the Lord has commanded. I would be glad to bear this testimony to anyone any time. (W. A. Sorensen.)

7. What are the consequences of disobedience? President George Albert Smith said, ". . . much of the sorrow and distress that is afflicting and will continue to afflict mankind is traceable to the fact that they have ignored His [God's] admonition to keep the sabbath day holy." (*Conference Report,* October 1935, p. 120.) Our spiritual natures, needing spiritual food, shrink and die without it. Physical deterioration also results. "Let us, therefore, in the midst of our worldly callings and associations," says President Joseph F. Smith, "not forget that paramount duty which we owe to ourselves and to our God." (*Juvenile Instructor,* vol. 47, March 1912, p. 145.)

What are the consequences of obedience to this divine law? Spiritually it will help to "keep ourselves unspotted from the world." Temporally, "the fulness of the earth" will be ours—all this through cheerfully keeping this divine law.

Yes, it is verily true that:

A Sabbath well spent, brings a day of content,
And strength for the trials of tomorrow,
But a Sabbath profaned, whatever be gained,
Is a sure forerunner of sorrow.

12

The Power of Prayer

Rearing eleven vigorous children to honorable manhood and womanhood on a small farm is no easy accomplishment. Yet, as my father and mother devoted themselves to this task, they never seemed to have any fear of the future. The reason was their faith—their confidence that they could always go to the Lord and he would see them through.

"Remember that whatever you do or wherever you are, you are never alone," was my father's familiar counsel. "Our Heavenly Father is always near. You can reach out and receive his aid through prayer."

All through my life the counsel to depend on prayer has been prized above any other advice I have ever received. It has become an integral part of me, an anchor, a constant source of strength.

Prayer came to my aid during a terrifying experience of my early life. I was a missionary in England for the Church. My companion, William Harris, and I were standing back to back, facing a hostile crowd that was swelled by a rowdy element from the pubs, men who were always eager for excitement and not averse to violence. What had started out to be a customary missionary street meeting soon took on the proportions of an angry, unmanageable mob. Many false, malicious rumors had been spread about our church activities.

The crowd started swaying. Someone from the rear called out, "What's the excitement?" Several voices shouted, "It's them bloody Mormons!" This touched off a clamorous demonstration: "Let's get 'em under our feet!" "Throw 'em in the river!"

The mob surged forward and tried to force us to the ground so they might trample us.

In my anxiety, I silently prayed for the Lord's guidance and protection. When it seemed that I could hold out no longer, a husky young stranger pushed through to my side and said, in a strong, clear voice, "I believe every word you said tonight. I am your friend."

As he spoke, a little circle cleared around me. This, to me, was a direct answer to my fervent prayer. The next thing I knew, a sturdy English bobby was convoying us safely through the crowd and back to our lodgings.

Resorting to prayer in such a time of crisis was not born of desperation. It was merely the outgrowth of the cherished custom of family prayer with which I had been surrounded since earliest childhood. How well I remember that while the family was small we frequently knelt together in the kitchen. As we grew in numbers and size we moved into the dining room, which had been added. As children we all took our turns in offering simple, heartfelt prayers. How grateful I am that we have continued that practice in my own home, and that my devoted wife and children look upon it as a never-failing source of strength and contentment.

With the ending of World War II in Europe, I was sent to London to direct relief activities for our Latter-day Saint membership in fourteen nations of Europe and the

Near East. Since our staff was specifically and efficiently organized to furnish and distribute supplies, we were anxious to handle the work ourselves. But in Germany and Austria, where the need was most acute, permission was not forthcoming. The military authorities were determined to avoid even the appearance of making special concessions.

I sought an audience with the general in charge. It was flatly refused. Having seen the desperate plight of many of these people, I resolved to seek divine guidance through fasting and prayer.

Before long a spirit of assurance replaced my troubled anxiety. "The Lord," I thought, "is sharing his strength with me." An impelling force urged me to seek another audience with the general.

I approached the general's adjutant with a surge of confidence. Minutes later I was granted an audience. The general heard me through and graciously acceded to our request.

Several scattered groups of people in Poland were in critical condition. Yet, after six weeks of negotiation, our visas were not forthcoming. Again I retired to my room for prayer and meditation. And again I received assurance that the Lord would go before us and prepare the way. As I entered my companion's room, I said simply, "Pack your bags. We're leaving for Poland."

The events that followed would seem incredible to many. That Unseen Power removed every barrier. The very same official who had refused us permission now sent us on our way in less than ten minutes.

In Warsaw we explained our mission to a fellow American. "Mr. Benson," he remarked, "if you think you can do all that traveling in one week, you're crazy. I've been here over a month now and haven't been able to get so much as a jeep to take me beyond the city limits."

We saw him again a week later, while waiting for the plane that would fly us out of Poland. When we recounted the successful completion of our mission, he exclaimed incredulously, "I don't believe it!"

It is soul-satisfying to know that God is mindful of us and ready to respond when we place our trust in him and do that which is right. There is no place for fear among men and women who place their trust in the Almighty, who do not hesitate to humble themselves in seeking divine guidance through prayer. Though persecutions arise, though reverses come, in prayer we can find reassurance, for God will speak peace to the soul. That peace, that spirit of serenity, is a great blessing.

If I could wish for anyone a priceless gift, it would not be wealth, profound wisdom, or the honors of men. I would rather pass on the key to inner strength and security that my father gave to me when he advised, "Receive His aid through prayer."

13

How to Improve Prayers, Public and Private

I know not by what method rare,
But this I know, God answers prayer.
I know that He has given His word
That tells me prayer is always heard,
And will be answered, soon or late,
And so I pray and calmly wait.
I know not if the blessing sought
Will come just in the way I thought,
But leave my prayers with Him alone,
Whose ways are wiser than my own,
Assured that He will grant my quest
Or send some answer far more blessed.
                    —Author Unknown

There is no unanswered prayer. What is prayer?

Prayer is the soul's sincere desire,
Uttered or unexpressed;
The motion of a hidden fire,
That trembles in the breast.
                    —*Hymns,* no. 220

Prayer is man's means of communicating with his Heavenly Father, the Almighty, Creator of heaven and earth. Only the deceived and the fool refuse to pray. An urgent need today is for more prayer—secret, individual prayer, family prayer, prayer in organizations, associations, and meetings generally, in schools, and in government bodies. People of all nations need more prayer. We need to be on our knees. While in the act of prayer, the greatest single event since the resurrection of Christ occurred—the appearance of God the Father and his Beloved Son to Joseph Smith.

A few years ago in the lobby of the old Savoy Hilton Hotel, which stood where the new General Motors Building now stands at 59th Street and Fifth Avenue in New York City, there was an impressive picture and prayer: The picture was of Uncle Sam on his knees in prayer. The caption read, "America on Its Knees." Then followed these words:

. . . not beaten there by the hammer and sickle, but freely, intelligently, responsibly, confidently, powerfully. America now knows it can destroy Communism and win the battle for peace. We need fear nothing or no one . . . except God.

And then this prayer:

Now darkness gathers around us, and we are confused in all our counsels. Losing faith in Thee, we lose faith in ourselves.

Inspire us with wisdom, all of us of every color, race and creed, to use our wealth, our strength to help our brother, instead of destroying him.

Help us to do Thy will as it is done in heaven and be worthy of Thy promise of peace on earth.

Fill us with new faith, new strength and new courage, that we may win the Battle for Peace.

Be swift to save us, dear God, before the darkness falls.

I have carried a miniature of this poster in my wallet for many years and have had occasion to discuss its message with the author, Conrad Hilton of worldwide hotel fame, and others.

America as a nation has been built on prayer. It has a spiritual foundation, a prophetic history. When the God-fearing Pilgrims arrived in the Western Hemisphere, Governor William Bradford recorded these words: "Being thus arrived in good harbor and brought safe to land, they fell upon their knees and blessed the God of Heaven."

America's Declaration of Independence opened and closed with a firm recognition of God: Men are "endowed by their Creator with certain unalienable rights . . . with a firm reliance on Divine Providence we mutually pledge to each other our lives, our fortunes and our sacred honor."

Abraham Lincoln soberly declared: "God rules this world. It is the duty of nations as well as men to owe their dependence upon the over-ruling power of God, to confess their sins and transgressions in humble sorrow . . . and to recognize the sublime truth that those nations only are blessed whose God is the Lord."

Thank God for the Church and its emphasis on the all-important matter of prayer, from the cradle to the grave. What an influence in our childhood came from the frequently sung reminder:

> Ere you left your room this morning,
> Did you think to pray?
> In the name of Christ, our Savior,
> Did you sue for loving favor
> As a shield today?

> When your heart was filled with anger,
> Did you think to pray?
> Did you plead for grace, my brother,
> That you might forgive another
> Who had crossed your way?

When sore trials came upon you,
Did you think to pray?
When your soul was full of sorrow,
Balm of Gilead did you borrow
At the gates of day?

(Chorus)
O how praying rests the weary!
Prayer will change the night to day;
So when life gets dark and dreary,
Don't forget to pray.
                                        —*Hymns,* no. 31

Family prayer night and morning and special prayers
in between are a unifying, strengthening anchor in Latter-
day Saint homes. Just before mealtime in the morning and
the evening is usually the best time for getting all of the
family together for family prayers. This practice, so very
important, was once widely practiced. The journals of the
early pioneers, not only in the West but in the Midwest
and East also, reveal the widespread practice of daily devotion in the home. The scriptures were read and a hymn
was often sung.

The practice of daily family devotion has almost left
much of the world, and in our busy lives of getting and
spending, Latter-day Saints also are often neglectful of this
important matter.

We need daily devotion in the home. We need to return to the practice of family prayer, secret prayer, the
old-fashioned practice of devotion in the home, daily, night
and morning, the singing of hymns, the reading of the
scriptures. How much more happiness there would be, how
many fewer divorces, how much less delinquency there
would be if these simple practices were followed as was
the custom in the pioneer home.

The holy scriptures are replete with convincing admonitions regarding the importance of prayer, impressive examples of prayer; the power of prayer. Even prophets of God have been chastised for failing to call on the Lord. Consider the hours-long interview of the brother of Jared with the Lord and the serious warning given as recorded in Ether 2:14-15:

> And it came to pass at the end of four years that the Lord came again unto the brother of Jared, and stood in a cloud and talked with him. And for the space of three hours did the Lord talk with the brother of Jared, and chastened him because he remembered not to call upon the name of the Lord.
>
> And the brother of Jared repented of the evil which he had done, and did call upon the name of the Lord for his brethren who were with him. And the Lord said unto him: I will forgive thee and thy brethren of their sins; but thou shalt not sin any more, for ye shall remember that my Spirit will not always strive with man; wherefore, if ye will sin until ye are fully ripe ye shall be cut off from the presence of the Lord. And these are my thoughts upon the land which I shall give you for your inheritance; for it shall be a land choice above all other lands.

Through Joseph Smith the warning came: "And in nothing doth man offend God, or against none is his wrath kindled, save those who confess not his hand in all things, and obey not his commandments." (D&C 59:21.)

Isaiah counseled, "Seek ye the Lord while he may be found, call upon him while he is near." (Isaiah 55:6.)

During his early ministry Jesus said, ". . . men ought always to pray, and not to faint." (Luke 18:1.) In this dispensation he said, ". . . pray always lest that wicked one have power over you, and remove you out of your place." (D&C 93:49.) And again, "Watch and pray that ye enter not into temptation." (Matthew 26:41.)

To the early inhabitants of the Western Hemisphere the Lord, through his prophets, gave much counsel. Often quoted is the timely practical counsel of Alma's companion Amulek:

Therefore may God grant unto you, my brethren, that ye may begin to exercise your faith unto repentance, that ye begin to call upon his holy name, that he would have mercy upon you;

Yea, cry unto him for mercy; for he is mighty to save;

Yea, humble yourselves, and continue in prayer unto him;

Cry unto him when ye are in your fields, yea, over all your flocks;

Cry unto him in your houses, yea, over all your household, both morning, mid-day, and evening:

Yea, cry unto him against the power of your enemies;

Yea, cry unto him against the devil, who is an enemy to all righteousness.

Cry unto him over the crops of your fields, that ye may prosper in them.

Cry over the flocks of your fields, that they may increase.

But this is not all; ye must pour out your souls in your closets, and your secret places, and in your wilderness;

Yea, and when you do not cry unto the Lord, let your hearts be full, drawn out in prayer unto him continually for your welfare, and also for the welfare of those who are around you. (Alma 34:17-27.)

And also this passage from Nephi:

But behold, I say unto you that ye must pray always, and not faint; that ye must not perform any thing unto the Lord save in the first place ye shall pray unto the Father in the name of Christ, that he will consecrate thy performance unto thee, that thy performance may be for the welfare of thy soul. (2 Nephi 32:9.)

Most inspiring of all is the example and counsel of the risen Lord as he ministered among the Nephite people:

So they brought their little children and sat them down upon the ground round about him, and Jesus stood in the midst; and the multitude gave way till they had all been brought unto him.

And it came to pass that when they had all been brought, and Jesus stood in the midst, he commanded the multitude that they should kneel down upon the ground.

And it came to pass that when they had knelt upon the ground, Jesus groaned within himself, and saith, Father, I am troubled because of the wickedness of the people of the house of Israel.

And when he had said these words, he himself also knelt upon the earth; and behold he prayed unto the Father, and the things which he prayed cannot be written, and the multitude did bear record who heard him.

And after this manner do they bear record: The eye hath never seen, neither hath the ear heard, before, so great and marvelous things as we saw and heard Jesus speak unto the Father. . . . (3 Nephi 17:12-16.)

And then the resurrected Christ gave this inspiring counsel:

Verily, verily, I say unto you, ye must watch and pray always, lest ye be tempted by the devil, and ye are led away captive by him.

And as I have prayed among you even so shall ye pray in my church, among my people who do repent and are baptized in my name. Behold I am the light; I have set an example for you.

And it came to pass that when Jesus had spoken these words unto his disciples, he turned again unto the multitude and said unto them;

Behold, verily, verily, I say unto you, ye must watch and pray always lest ye enter into temptation; for Satan desireth to have you that he may sift you as wheat.

Therefore ye must always pray unto the Father in my name;

And whatsoever ye shall ask the Father in my name, which is right, believing that ye shall receive, behold it shall be given unto you.

Pray in your families unto the Father, always in my name, that your wives and your children may be blessed.

And behold, ye shall meet together oft: and ye shall not forbid any man from coming unto you when ye shall meet together, but suffer them that they may come unto you, and forbid them not. (3 Nephi 18:15-22.)

Prayer can be combined with other gospel principles to accomplish marvelous things. Combined with fasting, it can cast out devils. (See Matthew 17:21.) Combined with faith, the brother of Jared saw Christ. (See Ether 3.)

Turning now to the more practical details of the subject under consideration, we note quotations from two modern revelations. To Martin Harris the Lord said: "And again, I command thee that thou shalt pray vocally as well as in thy heart; yea, before the world as well as in secret, in public as well as in private." (D&C 19:28.)

And the Lord told Joseph Knight, Jr.: ". . . you must take up your cross, in the which you must pray vocally before the world as well as in secret, and in your family, and among your friends, and in all places." (D&C 23:6.)

Now, as a practical matter, I present in topical outline form only, with scriptural references, items that may help to improve our prayers, public and private. These items are presented in three parts:

I. How to Improve Our Communications with Our Heavenly Father

    A. We should pray frequently.

        1. We should be alone with our Heavenly Father at least two or three times each day: ". . . morning, mid-day, and evening" (Alma 34:21); at night and in the morning (Alma 37:37). (Someone has said that when you wake up in the morning, the first thing to hit the floor should be your knees.)

        2. In addition, we are told to pray always. (Luke 21:34-36; 2 Nephi 32:9; D&C 61:39; 88:126; 93:49.) This not only shows we should pray frequently but also continually have a prayer in our heart. (Alma 34:27.)

        3. Even when the Lord's time was most in demand, he was not too busy to pray. (Luke 5:15-16.)

    B. We should find an appropriate place where we can meditate and pray.

        1. ". . . in your closets, your secret places, and in your wilderness." (Alma 34:26.)

        2. It should be free from distraction, i.e., in "secret." (Matthew 6:6; 3 Nephi 13:5-6.)

C. We should prepare ourselves for prayer. If we don't feel like praying, then we should pray until we do feel like praying.

1. Be humble. (D&C 12:8; 112:10; 52:14; Alma 34:19; James 4:3-10.) Be not like the Pharisee who was condemned—not because he failed to live the outward commandments, but because he lacked humility in prayer. (Luke 18:10-14.)

2. Our prayers will be vain if we "turn away the needy, and the naked, and visit not the sick and afflicted, and impart of [our] substance. . . ." (Alma 34:28.)

3. We must forgive anyone against whom we have bad feelings. (Mark 11:25.)

4. We should live to have the Spirit of the Lord, which will teach us to pray. (2 Nephi 32:8.)

5. We should cultivate such a strong testimony that when we pray, we follow the example of Joseph Smith and have faith with "nothing wavering." (James 1:5-6; Moroni 10:4-5.)

D. We should develop a feeling that we are talking directly with our Father in heaven.

1. ". . . he that cometh to God must believe that he is, and that he is a rewarder of them that diligently seek him." (Hebrews 11:6.)

2. "You cannot imagine an effective prayer without visualizing and feeling a personal God." (David O. McKay, *Treasures of Life,* Deseret Book, 1963, p. 308.)

E. Our prayers should be meaningful and pertinent.

1. Do not use the same phrases at each prayer. Each of us would become disturbed if a friend

said the same few words to us each day, treated the conversation as a chore, and could hardly wait to finish in order to turn on the TV and forget us.

2. We should pray about our work, against the power of our enemies and the devil, for our welfare and the welfare of those around us. (Alma 34:20; 22:25, 27.)

3. We should counsel with the Lord pertaining to all our activities. (Alma 37:36-37.) Some of us are afraid to ask the Lord about certain matters for fear he will give us an answer we don't want to hear.

4. We should be polite and grateful enough to give thanks for all we have. (Psalm 107:17-21; Philemon 4:6; D&C 78:19; 59:21.) As the Son directs, we should count our many blessings and give thanks for our calls in the Church. Ingratitude is one of our great sins.

5. We should make known our needs (Philemon 4:6; Alma 7:23), so long as it is not because of pride or for selfish reasons. (James 4:3). Sometimes we have not, because we ask not. (James 4:2.) Think of all the revelations that came to the Prophet Joseph Smith because he was willing to ask the Lord about certain matters and needs.

6. We should ask for strength to overcome. (Alma 31:31-33.)

7. We should pray for the inspiration and well-being of the President of the Church, the General Authorities, our stake president, our bishop, our quorum president, our home teach-

ers, etc. Our exaltation depends to an extent upon the inspiration of our leaders.

8. We should pray for mercy. (Alma 34:18.)

9. Many other suggestions could be made; but with the spirit of prayer, we will know what to pray. (Romans 8:26.)

F. After making a request through prayer, we have a responsibility to assist in its being granted.

1. We should listen. Maybe while we are on our knees, the Lord wants to counsel us. In addition to asking and thanking the Lord for things, we might well stay on our knees long enough to report for duty and ask him if he has any marching orders for us.

2. "Sincere praying implies that when we ask for any virtue or blessing, we should work for the blessing and cultivate the virtue." (David O. McKay, *True to the Faith,* Bookcraft, 1966, p. 208.)

II. How to Become More Effective in Praying in Behalf of a Group

A. For whom do we speak?

1. As the prayer is in behalf of a group, the prayer should, in general, express the thinking, the needs, and the desires of the group—not so much those of the individual.

2. Prior to praying, some thought should be given to the nature of the group and its needs and desires.

3. Prayer should be loud enough for the entire congregation to hear.

4. All in the audience should audibly say "amen" after the prayer. This shows we agree with the prayer and are a part of it.

B. The language of prayer.

1. Our language should be meek, yet it should edify. (D&C 52:16.)

2. Since the prayer is in behalf of a group, it should be phrased in terms of "our," "we," etc., instead of "my," "I," etc.

3. As with any prayer, it should be addressed to our Heavenly Father. The Lord set the proper example in saying, "Our Father which art in heaven." (Luke 11:2.) There is no need for flowery descriptions. We are just reverently calling him by name before we begin talking to him.

4. "Thy," "thou," and "thine" should be used so proper reverence can be shown.

5. We should always end by asking in the name of Jesus Christ, but not "Thy name," etc. (John 16:24-26.)

C. Of whom should we think when we pray?

1. Too frequently we may think of how we sound to the audience rather than concentrating on communicating with our Father in heaven. It then becomes merely another talk to the audience. It lacks sincerity. It may not even be considered by our Father in heaven. (James 4:3.) We do not feel the spirit of prayer. As said by Shakespeare's Hamlet, "My words fly up; my thoughts remain below. Words without thought never to heaven go."

2. Sometimes the so-called "good prayers" are called upon to the exclusion of the humble but less articulate members. But the Lord expects all to qualify to pray in meetings. (D&C 19:28.)

3. We must consciously tune ourselves spiritually to our Heavenly Father so we actually feel we are talking to him.

D. Our public prayers need not be everlasting to be immortal.

   1. We are advised not to multiply many words (3 Nephi 19:24) and to avoid vain repetitions (Matthew 6:7).

   2. An invocation should set the spiritual tone of the meeting, and the benediction should leave the people on a high spiritual plane, because they have been present when one has talked with God. It is the feeling rather than the length which determines a good public prayer.

E. We should assist others in preparing for public prayer.

   1. We should teach them to pray privately. Offering frequent vocal prayers gives experience in forming phrases and adds to confidence.

   2. We should provide experience in small groups where they will be more comfortable—family prayer, group meetings, quorum meetings, home teachers prior to visits, etc.

   3. We should teach that an effective public prayer depends more on the feeling of the individual than the words he uses. Therefore, developing a spirit of prayer through a proper life can best qualify a person to give a meaningful public

prayer. Without this, the prayer becomes hollow and does not inspire.

III. How People Will Be Blessed by Praying More Meaningfully

    A. Meaningful private and public prayers provide necessary prerequisites so we can lead our people back to our Heavenly Father.

        1. Inspiration comes from prayer. (D&C 63:64.)

        2. Inspiration is essential to properly lead. (D&C 50:13-14.)

        3. We must have the spirit of inspiration whether we are teaching (D&C 50:13-14) or administering the affairs of the kingdom (D&C 46:2).

        4. If we do our part in preparation and work and have the Spirit of the Lord, we can be led, though we do not know beforehand what needs to be done. (1 Nephi 4:6; Alma 17:3.)

        5. Therefore, we should always pray, especially prior to commencing the work of the Lord. (2 Nephi 32:9.)

    B. Challenge each person present:

        1. To be alone with God at least twice a day and have more meaningful communication;

        2. To be prepared to offer more effective public prayers; and

        3. To teach, inspire, and motivate others to do the same.

Never before in this gospel dispensation has there been a greater need for prayer, and never in history has there been a greater threat to our God-given right to pray when, how, or where we wish. How timely and appropriate for the true Church of Christ to emphasize this basic right and all-important need!

William Penn stated: "Those people who will not be governed by God, must be ruled by Tyrants." Government without God is tyranny.

A prophet of God, Brigham Young, said, "Prayer keeps a man from sin, and sin keeps a man from prayer."

Called upon unexpectedly to offer a prayer in the pre-inauguration Cabinet meeting of the Eisenhower Administration, I was later blessed to have a major part in establishing a policy of prayer in weekly Cabinet meetings. For both terms (eight years) of the Eisenhower presidency, Cabinet meetings were opened with prayer. Rich blessings resulted. Ofttimes a humble suggestion will cause meetings to be opened with prayer—even non-church meetings, such as service clubs, school meetings, professional, business, agricultural, and scientific groups. In the U.S. Department of Agriculture from 1953 to 1961, all staff meetings began with prayer, with the staff members leading in rotation. Priceless blessings resulted.

As I left the Administration Building of the USDA to fill a particularly difficult visit in areas critical of some policies I was advocating, entailing press conferences, public meetings, radio, TV, etc., I was handed a sealed envelope by Assistant Secretary Earl Butz, a non-Mormon, who is now U.S. Secretary of Agriculture. Safely on the plane, I opened the envelope and read:

Ezra: As you enter into a very difficult weekend, we want you to know that a lot of us are hoping and praying for you.

Remember always that many of your friends feel that a great source of your personal strength is that you walk beside God, whereas most of the rest of us only report to Him.

Keep in full step with your Senior Partner, and you surely will emerge the victor from this test.

We're counting on you.

/s/ Earl Butz

In the little book *Long and Short Range Arrows,* a compilation of short talks given by Dr. George H. Brimhall when he was president emeritus of Brigham Young University, is a talk that touched my heart as a student. It is entitled: "Keep Up Your Correspondence with Your Heavenly Father."

That we may do so effectively—publicly and privately—in spirit and in truth, is my humble prayer.

14

How to Delegate Wisely

The term *delegation* is widely used and generally understood. But the delegation we speak of is so different—so much more important—so far reaching. It is Church delegation through and by the authority of the holy priesthood of God. And as the Church grows in total membership and regional distribution, wise delegation becomes more and more important—in fact, imperative for continued success. The character of our Church membership distribution is changing and will continue to change. This emphasizes the increasing need for leadership training and the wise delegation of responsibility.

We are engaged in the greatest work in all the world—yes, the greatest in the whole universe: the saving and exaltation of our Father's children, our brothers and sisters. We are the custodians of the truth, the saving principles which, where applied, will build, save, and exalt men.

The Lord has given us the broad organization outline, the purposes, and the objectives. But he leaves to us much of the working out of the methods. And this is where correlation and leadership training come in and why various segments of the program, such as wise delegation of responsibility, are under study. And as time passes we will come to appreciate and realize more fully the place and magnitude of this training and of the correlation program.

The Apostle Paul said:

And he gave some, apostles; and some, prophets; and some, evangelists; and some, pastors and teachers;

For the perfecting of the saints, for the work of the ministry, for the edifying of the body of Christ:

Till we all come in the unity of the faith, and of the knowledge of the Son of God, unto a perfect man, unto the measure of the stature of the fulness of Christ. (Ephesians 4:11-13.)

This is our task—our responsibility. It is to be done through and under the direction of the priesthood. No men anywhere have a greater love for our Father's children than those who hold and honor the priesthood. We are all in it together—yes, on both sides of the veil, because I feel sure there is organization and wise delegation of authority over there, and most important decisions also.

This is the Lord's organization through which we operate. We are dealing with voluntary workers—our Father's children whom he loves, regardless of their mistakes and weaknesses. There must be no force, coercion, or intimidation in our delegation. To be effective, we must seek and obtain the Spirit if we are to delegate wisely. Without the Spirit we flounder, unsure of our decisions and counsel. Wise delegation requires the same Spirit required to preach the gospel, of which the Lord said this:

Wherefore, I the Lord ask you this question—unto what were ye ordained?

To preach my gospel by the Spirit, even the Comforter which was sent forth to teach the truth. . . .

Therefore, why is it that ye cannot understand and know, that he that receiveth the word by the Spirit of truth receiveth it as it is preached by the Spirit of truth?

Wherefore, he that preacheth and he that receiveth, understand one another, and both are edified and rejoice together. . . .

That which is of God is light; and he that receiveth light, and continueth in God, receiveth more light; and that light groweth brighter until the perfect day. (D&C 50:13-14, 21-22, 24.)

Wise delegation requires prayerful preparation, as does effective teaching or preaching. The Lord makes this clear in these words from the Doctrine and Covenants: "And the Spirit shall be given unto you by the prayer of faith; and if ye receive not the Spirit ye shall not teach." (D&C 42:14.) And we might add, ye shall not delegate without the Spirit.

In this same spirit—serving him with all our "heart, might, mind and strength" (D&C 4:2)—we may seek help from the good and wise men of the earth. There has been much done in this field of managing the services of men, delegation of responsibility, outside Church organization that may be helpful—tried and tested procedures, approaches, and principles. Many of these when used in company with the Spirit can be helpful. Here are a few examples:

1. Good management means delegating authority.
2. Delegating part of the workload helps you and your organization.
3. Effective management is the art of multiplying yourself through others.
4. The jobs to delegate are the ones you do best.
5. The number of subordinates who can report directly to one supervisor is limited, because of time, distance, human limitations, and type of work.
6. Authority and responsibility may be delegated. Accountability may not be delegated.
7. The most eligible candidate for a bigger job is the man who has already trained his own replacement.
8. Why delegation goes wrong:
   Failing to delegate enough,
   Delegating by formula,
   Failing to keep communication lines open,
   Failing to define the assignment,

Failing to make the assignment stick,
Failing to delegate enough authority to do the job,
Being too narrow in your delegation,
Failing to allow for mistakes.

These are but a few guidelines from American business and industry. More and more, experience proves that the spirit of the Golden Rule—the spirit of the gospel—pays off in wise delegating, in the Church and outside. Fear is a powerful motivating force. It is in constant use under dictatorship. It usually gets quick action. The trouble is that fear is also upsetting and distracting and reduces efficiency of performance.

In the Church especially, asking produces better results than ordering—better feeling, too. Remember to tell why. Follow up to see how things are going. Show appreciation when people carry out instructions well. Express confidence when it can be done honestly. When an order gets fouled up, it is well to check back and find out where you slipped up—and don't be afraid to admit that you did. Remember, our people are voluntary, free-will workers. They also love the Lord and his work. Love them. Appreciate them. When you're tempted to reprimand a fellow worker, don't. Try an interesting challenge and a pat on the back instead. Our Father's children throughout the world are essentially good. He loves them. We should also.

Why do some people fail to delegate? There are a number of reasons. Here are a few of the main ones:

1.   They feel the subordinate won't be able to handle the assignment.
2.   They fear competition from subordinates.
3.   They are afraid of losing credit or recognition.
4.   They are afraid their weaknesses will be exposed.
5.   They feel they will not have the time to turn over the work and provide the necessary training. Sometimes they are just too lazy. It takes time to delegate wisely. But in the long run it saves time, builds people, and increases output.

At the time of delegation there is usually excellent opportunity to get close to people, to build them up and give them needed counsel and direction.

My son Mark, who has had some responsibility as sales manager for the direction of 4,000 salesmen doing direct selling, sent me this list of six main principles for delegating responsibility:

1.   Select the jobs to be delegated and get them organized for the person to be assigned.
2.   Pick the proper person for the job.
3.   Prepare and motivate the delegate for his assignment.
4.   Assign the work and make sure it is fully understood.
5.   Encourage independence.
6.   Maintain supervisory control—never relinquish the reins.

Theodore Roosevelt said, "The best executive is the one who has sense enough to pick good men to do what he wants done, and self-restraint enough to keep from meddling with them while they do it."

But more important than all worldly knowledge, helpful though it be, is the example and direction found in holy writ—in the great plan of a loving Father for us, his children. What beautiful and impressive examples speak out to us! Here are just a few—there are many.

The very foundations of the world were laid by delegated authority. Many times Jesus reminded people that his mission on earth was one through delegated authority. The restoration of his church had its very beginning with delegated authority.

In speaking to the Jews in the synagogue, Jesus told them that he had been delegated by his Father: "For I came down from heaven, not to do mine own will, but the will of him that sent me." (John 6:38.)

In the opening lines of his gospel book, the apostle John noted that, at the very beginning of the foundations of the earth, Jesus acted as a divine Son delegated by the

Father: "In the beginning was the Word, and the Word was with God, and the Word was God. The same was in the beginning with God. All things were made by him; and without him was not anything made that was made." (John 1:1-3.) Christ's impressive delegation to his apostles is set forth in John, chapters 14, 15, and 16.

Think of the impressive example of the conversion of Saul, persecutor of the saints, who became the great missionary apostle to whom the Lord directed Ananias, his humble servant.

Christ also revealed that judgment had been committed to him by the Father: "For the Father judgeth no man, but hath committed all judgment unto the Son: That all men should honour the Son, even as they honour the Father. He that honoureth not the Son honoureth not the Father which hath sent him." (John 5:22-23.)

On four momentous occasions the Father introduced Jesus as one who was delegated and as "my beloved Son":

1. When Jesus was baptized of John the Baptist in Jordan, a voice from heaven spoke out: "This is my beloved Son, in whom I am well pleased." (Matthew 3:17.)

2. At the transfiguration, a voice proclaimed to Peter, James, and John: "This is my beloved Son, in whom I am well pleased; hear ye him." (Matthew 17:5.)

3. When Jesus first appeared to the Nephites, a voice was heard saying: "Behold my Beloved Son, in whom I am well pleased, in whom I have glorified my name—hear ye him." (3 Nephi 11:7.)

4. Almost the same words were spoken when two heavenly personages appeared to the boy Joseph Smith in that first vision which began the restoration of the Church: *"This is My Beloved Son. Hear Him!"* (Joseph Smith 2:17.)

In each instance, through the introduction the Father indicated that Jesus had been delegated. The Father said no more. He merely introduced. The Son had been delegated to not only preside over the world but also to redeem it.

Three years after the first vision under the direction of the Beloved Son, Moroni came to Joseph Smith. Later other important messengers came with essential keys. Then came Peter, James, and John, ancient apostles, and under them John the Baptist, to restore the Aaronic Priesthood, all delegated appropriately for their important work.

Jesus, who was delegated by the Father to come to the earth, gives us the master example of good administration through proper delegating. His leadership was perfect. Rugged, able men whom he called to be his apostles gave up prosperous business careers to follow him. Many of his delegated missionaries traveled without purse or scrip. Men suffered great hardships in carrying out his instructions. Some of them died cruel deaths in his service. But his delegated disciples went forth into the world bold as lions through his charge. They accomplished things they had never dreamed of. No leader ever motivated men and women as did he.

There are at least eight lessons in wise and effective delegating that Jesus has given those who are called to positions of leadership in his service today. Let us now consider them.

First, the organization Jesus established (the Church) was structured in a framework of delegated authority.

This was true of the church when he was on the earth: it is true in his restored church today. The Church of Jesus Christ builds leaders through involving people delegated through authority. When he was on earth, he called twelve apostles to assist him in administering the church. He also called the seventy. He delegated others. There were to be no spectators in his church. All were to be involved in helping build the kingdom. And as they built the kingdom, they built themselves.

Jesus aimed to exalt the individual. In that momentous meeting with Moses on the Mount, the Lord declared: "For behold, this is my work and my glory—to bring to pass the immortality and eternal life of man." (Moses 1:39.)

Jesus aimed to make of every man a king, to build him in leadership into eternity. On that memorable night after the last supper, he said to the eleven (after Judas had slunk out into the night to go about his dark mission), "Verily, verily, I say unto you, He that believeth in me, the works that I do shall he do also; and greater works than these shall he do; because I go unto my Father." (John 14:12.) Through delegating, Jesus desired to lift, rather than suppress, the individual. And all through the Church today, men and women are growing in stature through positions delegated to them.

Second, in delegating, Jesus did not make the assignment sound easy but he made it sound exciting and challenging.

Peter was a prosperous fisherman. When Jesus called him to his service, he did not ask him to give up his business and become a preacher or missionary. Jesus made the call much more interesting. Mark's account describes the call this way: "Now as he walked by the sea of Galilee, he saw Simon and Andrew his brother casting a net into the sea: for they were fishers. And Jesus said unto them, Come ye after me, and I will make you to become fishers of men. And straightway they forsook their nets, and followed him." (Mark 1:16-18.)

Similarly, in delegating the seventy to go forth as missionaries, Jesus made the assignment sound interesting: "Therefore said he unto them, The harvest truly is great, but the labourers are few; pray ye therefore the Lord of the harvest, that he would send forth labourers into his harvest." (Luke 10:2.)

Yet Jesus did not make his assignment sound easy. At the outset he was realistic. He added: "Go your ways:

behold, I send you forth as lambs among wolves. Carry neither purse, nor scrip, nor shoes: and salute no man by the way." (Luke 10:3-4.)

Third, in delegating responsibility, Jesus let those called know fully their duties.

He helped prepare them for their assignments. Elder James E. Talmage, in *Jesus the Christ* (p. 228), comments: "For a season following their ordination the apostles remained with Jesus, being specially trained and instructed by Him for the work then before them; afterward they were specifically charged and sent forth to preach and to administer in the authority of their priesthood. . . ."

In the great revelation on priesthood, Doctrine and Covenants, section 107, the Lord gives us an inspiring direction, our responsibility to learn our duty. Hear his words:

"Wherefore, now let every man learn his duty, and to act in the office in which he is appointed, in all diligence. He that is slothful shall not be counted worthy to stand, and he that learns not his duty and shows himself not approved shall not be counted worthy to stand. Even so. Amen." (D&C 107:99-100.)

Fourth, Jesus gave those delegated his confidence as had his Father given him.

It is significant that on at least three occasions in speaking of Jesus, the Father said: "This is my beloved Son, in whom I am well pleased." Jesus likewise sent his delegated servants forth with the feeling of confidence. For example, to the seventy he said: "He that heareth you heareth me. . . ." (Luke 10:16.)

A wise administrator in the Church today will not try to do the job himself, giving the impression that no one else is quite qualified. And as he delegates, he will give an assurance that he who has been delegated has his full backing.

Jethro taught Moses a great lesson in not trying to do everything himself. Jethro gave wise counsel to an otherwise great leader regarding the wise delegation of authority— the spreading of responsibility through building men and easing the load on Moses. You can read this great account in chapter 18 of Exodus, verses 14 to 27.

Fifth, to those he called, Jesus gave his loyalty, and he expected their loyalty in return.

Jesus told the eleven of the oneness of him with the Father. He said: "Believe me that I am in the Father and the Father in me. . . ." (John 14:11.) Jesus asked for their loyalty to him as their leader: "If ye love me, keep my commandents." (John 14:15.) Then he reaffirmed his loyalty to them: "I will not leave you comfortless: I will come to you." (John 14:18.) He added: "Peace I leave with you, my peace I give unto you. . . . Let not your heart be troubled, neither let it be afraid." (John 14:27.)

A good leader expects loyalty from those whom he delegates. He in turn gives his loyalty. He backs up those to whom he has given a job. The loyalty extends to matters beyond the call of duty. He is loyal when honors come to those with whom he serves. He takes pride in their successes. He does not overrule unless he first confers with him whose decision he overrules. He does not embarrass an associate before others. He is frank and open with him.

Sixth, Jesus expected much from those to whom he delegated responsibility.

At the time of his ascension, Jesus charged his eleven: "Go ye into all the world, and preach the gospel to every creature." (Mark 16:15.)

In the Church today a leader generally gets in performance what he truly expects. He needs to think tall when he delegates. He should assure those to whom he gives assignments that in the service of the Lord they have even greater powers than in ordinary responsibilities. There can be no failure in the work of the Lord when men do their best. We are but instruments; this is the Lord's work. This is his church, his gospel plan. These are his children we are working with. He will not permit us to fail if we do our part. He will magnify us even beyond our own talents and abilities when necessary. This I know. I'm sure many of you have experienced it as I have. It is one of the sweetest experiences that can come to a human being.

In the last solemn interview with the eleven before his ascension, Jesus said: "But ye shall receive power, after that the Holy Ghost is come upon you: and ye shall be witnesses unto me both in Jerusalem, and in all Judaea, and in Samaria, and unto the uttermost part of the earth." (Acts 1:8.)

President John Taylor said: "If a thing is well done, no one will ask how long it took to do it, but who did it." There is no room for shoddy performance in the Church. An able leader will expect quality, and he will let those whom he assigns know that he expects quality.

Seventh, Jesus seemed to invite feedback from those to whom he gave assignments.

This is shown in Mark's account: "And the apostles gathered themselves together unto Jesus, and told him all things, both what they had done, and what they had taught. And he said unto them, Come ye yourselves apart into a desert place and rest awhile. . . ." (Mark 6:30-31.) Jesus not only received feedback; he was also considerate. While he expected much, he was no "slave driver." He invited the apostles, after a strenuous period, to come "into a desert place, and rest awhile. . . ."

No wise leader believes that all good ideas originate with himself. He invites suggestions from those he leads. He lets them feel that they are an important part of decision making. He lets them feel that they are carrying out *their* policies, not just *his.*

The home teaching program of the Church offers a most excellent system for feedback. Home teachers will invite feedback from their families; priesthood leaders, from the home teachers; the bishop, from the priesthood leaders; and the stake president, from the bishops. In this way the leader will not only receive many helpful ideas; he will also keep his finger on the pulse of those whom he leads.

Eighth, Jesus taught that he who leads should follow the progress of those to whom responsibility has been delegated, giving praise and reproof in a spirit of love.

In his parable of the talent, the Master said: "Well done, good and faithful servant; thou hast been faithful over a few things, I will make thee ruler over many things: enter thou into the joy of the Lord." (Matthew 25:23.)

When responsibility has been given, the leader does not forget the person assigned nor his assignment. He follows with interest but does not "look over the shoulder." He gives specific praise when it is deserved. He gives helpful encouragement when needed. When he feels that the job is not being done and a change is needed, he acts with courage and firmness but with kindness. When the tenure of an office has been completed, he gives recognition and thanks.

Even harder to bear than criticism, oftentimes, is *no* word from our leader on the work to which we have been assigned. Little comments or notes, which are sincere and specific, are great boosters along the way.

I close by returning to the all-important matter of delegating by the Spirit, for there is no satisfactory substitute for the Spirit. In this regard I know of no more impressive scripture than the inspiring words of the Lord to the Prophet Joseph in Liberty Jail, recorded in section 121 of the Doctrine and Covenants, verses 34 to 44. Read them today. Sublime in spirit, ever timely for instruction, and ever profound in deep meaning for the priesthood of God are these words, which every leader in the Church should follow.

May we ever heed this counsel and all other scriptural direction as we strive earnestly and prayerfully to delegate wisely.

15

Suggestions on Making Decisions

Our decisions have made us what we are. Our eternal destiny will be determined by the decisions we yet will make.

Wise decisions are the stepping stones of progress. They are the building blocks of life. Decisions are the ingredients of success. For individuals and institutions, they mark the way of progress. The mind of an individual or the collective mind of the council, committee, or board of directors decides what the present state and the future direction of the individual or institution will be.

Wise decisions will show the way to progress.

We live in a wicked world. Never in our memory has the adversary been so well organized and never had he had so many emissaries working for him. As a people we face difficult days—days of pressing decisions, for young and old.

In The Church of Jesus Christ of Latter-day Saints we face momentous decisions. Our people—heads of families, parents, children—must make important decisions. Help is needed and help is available.

As a church we hold the saving truths and ordinances which will bring salvation and exaltation to members of the human race. It is therefore most important that church leaders make the right decisions and guide those under them in the paths of truth and righteousness toward the accomplishment of our goals, but also our families, wards, stakes, missions, the Church, and the world.

If we are to make proper, Christ-like decisions, we must first of all live so we can reach out and tap that unseen power without which no man can do his best in decision making.

One of the greatest decisions of this age was when the boy Joseph Smith decided that he would follow the admonition in James: "If any of you lack wisdom, let him ask of God, that giveth to all men liberally, and upbraideth not; and it shall be given him. But let him ask in faith, nothing wavering. For he that wavereth is like a wave of the sea driven with the wind and tossed." (James 1:5-6.)

The very salvation of millions of men and women in the dispensation of the fulness of times depends upon that decision! We must keep in mind that individuals do matter and that decisions they make may greatly affect the lives of others.

In addition to heavenly sources, it is important also that we realize that individual effort and resourcefulness are necessary not only in solving the day-to-day problems of the Church, but also in bringing growth and development to those required to make decisions.

There are some guiding principles that will assist church leaders in making decisions both in their own personal lives and in their important responsibility of leading others to their eventual goal of exaltation in the kingdom of God.

The biggest business of any life is making decisions. While one of the greatest gifts of God to man is free agency or the right of choice, he has also given man responsibility for these choices. We may choose between good and evil. We put our own lives in the direction of success or failure. We may not only choose our ultimate goals, but we may also determine and decide for ourselves, in many cases, the means by which we will arrive at those goals, and by our industry or lack of it determine the speed by which they may be reached. This takes individual effort and energy and will not be without opposition or conflict.

Making decisions is probably the most important thing people ever do. Nothing happens until someone makes a decision. Even the world itself circled into being as the result of God's decisions. God said, ". . . In the beginning I created the heaven, and the earth," "Let there be light; and there was light," "Let there be a firmament in the midst of the water, and it was so. . . ." (Moses 2:1, 3, 6.)

Fortunately the ability and judgment necessary to make decisions can be acquired. Certain methods and practices can bring to us all greater skill in everyday, every-week, every-month opportunities to make decisions.

There are some basic principles recommended and used by specialists in the field. It is generally recognized that there are five fundamental steps in decision making:

1. Defining the problem, its scope and significance:
   a. What kind of problem is it?
   b. What is its critical factor?
   c. When do we have to solve it?
   d. Why solve it?
   e. What will it take to solve it?
   f. What is the value or gain in solving it?
2. Collecting facts and analyzing and using them.

3. Developing and weighing possible solutions to arrive at conclusions.

4. Carrying a decision into action with plans and controls.

5. Follow-up on the results of the decisions and action.

Decisions should be based on correct principles and facts. A thorough knowledge of the principles and facts surrounding any particular problem usually leads to an easy and correct decision. A thorough knowledge of the facts surrounding a welfare problem, for example, will, when considered in connection with fundamental welfare principles, bring the bishop to the right answer in that particular case. One of the most basic elements of decision making, therefore, is to have possession of the facts and to understand and be familiar with the basic and underlying principles.

For another example, a bishop may feel that his ward should be doing better in temple work. How does he make a decision on this problem? He would first want to determine the facts by asking and finding the answers to several questions. How many temple recommends do my ward members hold? How is this number divided between the high priests, seventies, elders, and sisters? How many endowments have been performed this year compared with last? this month compared with last? How does my ward record compare with other wards in the stake? Even if it compares favorably, is it good enough? How important is this work anyway? (See Malachi 4:5-6.) Why would the whole earth be smitten with a curse had not Elijah come with the keys of sealing which he held?

After discussing the problem and its solution with his counselors and the high priests group leader and perhaps the entire ward executive committee, the bishop would then decide on a course of action. He would write down the various steps to implement the course of action decided upon, activate the program by making assignments and delegation of responsibility, and then remember to follow up.

On a personal basis, a decision to turn down a proffered cigarette or a drink of liquor will be easy to make if one has the facts, understands the underlying principles and concepts of the Word of Wisdom, and has already determined in his mind that he will uphold and sustain this divinely revealed principle.

Again, if one understands the principle, he will already know the right decision when he is faced with a problem involving morality. All he will need under the pressure of the moment will be the fortitude to make the decision he already knows is the right one.

One of the best ways for leaders to understand correct principles is to have a thorough knowledge and understanding of the scriptures and the appropriate handbook. Most situations have already arisen before, perhaps many times, and policy and procedure have already been determined to handle the problem. It is always wise, therefore, to refer to and be familiar with existing written instructions and church policy on questions as they arise.

Decisions should be timely. Sometimes a lack of decision on a point is actually a decision in the opposite direction. We need to make up our minds. Elijah said to ancient Israel: "How long halt ye between two opinions? if the Lord be God, follow him: but if Baal, then follow him. And the people answered him not a word." (I Kings 18:21.)

Joshua advocated this principle when he gathered all the elders and judges of the tribes of Israel to Shechem and told them, in effect, to make up their minds today. He said: "And if it seem evil unto you to serve the Lord, choose you this day whom ye will serve;

whether the gods which your fathers served that were on the other side of the flood, or the gods of the Amorites, in whose land ye dwell; but as for me and my house, we will serve the Lord." (Joshua 24:15.)

Some people intend to make a decision and then never get around to it. They intend to paint the barn, to fix the fence, to haul away that old machinery or remove that old shed, but the time of decision just never arrives.

Some of us face a similar situation in our personal lives. We intend to pay a full tithing, to begin keeping the Word of Wisdom, to make our initial home teaching visits early in the month. However, without actual decision followed by implementation, the weeks and months go by and nothing is accomplished. We could drift into eternity on these kinds of good intentions. Thus lack of decision becomes our decision *not* to do those good things for which we had the best of intentions. The Lord apparently sensed this weakness in his children, for he said: "Wherefore, if ye believe me, ye will labor while it is called today." (D&C 64:25.)

Get the facts—then decide promptly. As an excuse for postponing decisions, do not rely on the old clichés some people use, such as "I want to sleep on it." We don't make decisions in our sleep. However, don't jump to conclusions or make snap judgments. Get the facts, be sure of the basic principles, and weigh the consequences. Then decide!

The prophet Joel recognized the principle of timeliness as priesthood leaders should today, for now, as then, wickedness is almost everywhere. Sound decisions are needed. Joel said: "Put ye in the sickle, for the harvest is ripe: come, get you down; for the press is full, . . . for their wickedness is great. Multitudes,

multitudes in the valley of decision: for the day of the Lord is near in the valley of decision." (Joel 3:13-14.)

The decisions of which Joel spoke are the decisions that lead to eternal exaltation. May we help in showing the way.

Wise decisions are usually arrived at following work, struggle, and prayerful effort. The Lord's response to Oliver Cowdery's ineffective effort makes this clear: "But, behold, I say unto you, that you must study it out in your mind; then you must ask me if it be right, and if it is right I will cause that your bosom shall burn within you; therefore, you shall feel that it is right." (D&C 9:8.)

Let us begin, therefore, by saying that earnestly seeking our Father in heaven, having faith that he will answer our prayers, is a comforting base on which to begin. Joseph Smith also said the Lord will not take water from a dry well, so we must do our part. Sometimes attempting to find a correct decision takes great amounts of energy, study, and long-suffering.

Here are some effective suggestions our leaders can use to assist them in correctly deciding what actions should be taken.

1. Is the problem clearly understood? All too often our leaders haven't defined what is to be decided. The problem must be expressed clearly on paper.

2. Is the stated problem the real one? Is our leader treating the symptoms or the causes? For example, a stake president was concerned with home teaching in his stake and wanted to make some decisions in order to improve it. The records established that fewer families were being visited each month. The stake president was upset with the home teachers without realizing that he wasn't properly communicating on a continuing basis with the bishops and quorum leaders about home teach-

ing and its importance. The real problem wasn't low home teaching activity; the difficulty was inadequate communication between the stake president and his subordinates. Once the stake president realized the difficulty and corrected it, the home teaching improved greatly in his stake.

3. Does the problem "feel" right? We in the Church are open to inspiration and should seek it, and our Father in heaven will let us know if the problem we are concerned about is one demanding a decision. Inspiration is an important aspect of decision making.

4. Diagnose the problem. The problem must be analyzed and divided into its parts. Common sense dictates that the items to be decided should be written down and each facet be listed. Assess the whole situation, looking to the experience of the past and present as much as possible. Keep an open mind.

5. Evaluate the available alternatives. Justice Benjamin Nathan Cardozo of the Supreme Court said, "There is in each of us a stream of tendency that gives coherence and direction to thought and action." The selected facts must be carefully evaluated and listed in their order of importance as we best see them. How the Saints are affected must be of primary concern.

6. Pray and fast for inspiration. "Counsel with the Lord in all thy doings, and he will direct thee for good. . . ." (Alma 37:37.) After an adequate evaluation of the situation, prayer and fasting must then be brought in as the final step before the decision. Listen for an answer. Too often we pray without listening.

7. Make the decision. "Decision making is a lonely business," said my good friend Clarence B. Randall, former head of Inland Steel Company, "and the greater the degree of responsibility, the more intense the loneliness." After following the six steps previously men-

tioned, however, most decisions our priesthood brethren make will be for the best.

8. Determine how to accomplish the decision. Action must follow the decision. The procedures of accomplishment must be listed and assignments made.

9. Follow up and reevaluate. One good brother said, "If a decision has come from inspiration, then why evaluate?" Circumstances change and with change comes time to review and, at least some of the time, to begin the decision-making process all over again. In any event, a follow-up to see if the job is being done must be part of the procedure.

Our fellow workers will make better decisions in their callings if they will follow these nine steps. But remember, while the Lord will give us help in making decisions, he expects us to do our homework.

What are the tests that might well be applied to a proposed course of action—a pending decision? Here are six:

1. Could it retard or injure spiritual or moral progress?

2. Could it create unhappy or unpeaceful memories?

3. Is it contrary to the revealed will or commandments of God? "I, the Lord, am bound when ye do what I say; but when ye do not what I say, ye have no promise." (D&C 82:10.)

4. Could it harm any individual, family, or group?

5. Would the decision make a better person or a better associate as it pertains to God's laws? For example, by living the Word of Wisdom, we are promised that we "shall find wisdom and great treasures of knowledge, even hidden treasures." (D&C 89:19.)

6. Could a blessing be derived from this particular action? "There is a law, irrevocably decreed in heaven

before the foundation of this world, upon which all blessings are predicated—And when we obtain any blessing from God, it is by obedience to that law upon which it is predicated." (D&C 130:20-21.)

May I, in conclusion, offer the following ten points for the consideration of leaders as helps in making wise decisions:

1. Ask for guidance from the Lord in making decisions.

2. Do you get a burning in your bosom after you have made the decision?

3. Is it in keeping with the words of the prophets— that is, the Presidents of the Church, particularly the living President?

4. Some decisions are simply a matter of making good judgment, and simply coming to a decision. For instance, in the Doctrine and Covenants, the Lord tells the brethren he is not concerned whether they go by land or by sea, as long as they get going. (See D&C 61:22.)

5. There are a few cases where a decision cannot be made immediately, because the Lord wants to bring other factors to the attention of the decision maker. In that case, a man must learn to wait on the Lord or, as the Lord would say, "Be still, and know that I am God." (Psalm 46:10.)

6. In decisions of crucial importance, fasting combined with prayer can bring great spiritual insight.

7. While it is usually advisable to try to see the long-range view of the decision you make, sometimes the Lord will inspire you to make only temporary decisions that will lead to an end that only he knows about. A man should never hesitate to make such decisions. Wilford Woodruff had to make a number of those decisions that required him to say "I know not save the Lord com-

manded it." Nephi returned to Jerusalem without knowing exactly what his plan of action was going to be.

8. President Harold B. Lee tells, in his book *Decisions for Successful Living* (page 45), about talking with a church leader who sometimes, in trying to come to a decision on a given matter, would say to himself, "What would Jesus do in this situation?" This would mean, of course, that a man would have to know Jesus well enough through study and righteous living that he might ask that question intelligently.

9. A man should always be sure that he consults the Spirit in his decision making. In other words, he should keep the door ajar in case the Spirit wants to dictate a course other than the one he might have naturally followed. Brigham Young at one time said that he wanted to do a certain thing, but that the Spirit dictated otherwise.

10. It's always good to know what other Church leaders have done in making decisions on similar matters. That's why, in part at least, the Prophet Joseph had records kept of various meetings. Therefore a man should study the records, the prophets, and Church history.

We are engaged in a work in which we cannot fail —be it decision making or other—if we do our part. The Lord will not permit us to fail. This is his work. These are his children we are called to labor with, and he loves them. This is his program through which we work, his authority, and he will magnify us—yes, when necessary, even beyond our natural abilities. This I know, and I thank God for this priceless knowledge and blessing.

16

Listen to a Prophet's Voice

While Saul was on the road to Damascus, he was stopped by a heavenly vision and the voice of the Lord Jesus Christ. And Saul responded with these momentous words: "Lord, what wilt thou have me to do?" (Acts 9:6.) To this the Lord responded by sending Saul to see one of his authorized servants to receive direction and a blessing.

A man can ask no more important question in his life than that which Paul asked: "Lord, what wilt thou have me to do?" A man can take no greater action than to pursue a course that will bring to him the answer to that question and then to carry out that answer. What would the Lord Jesus Christ have us do? He has answered that question by saying, "Be ye therefore perfect, even as your Father which is in heaven is perfect" (Matthew 5:46), and, "Therefore, what manner of men ought ye to be? Verily, I say unto you, even as I am" (3 Nephi 27:27).

Christ, then, has set us the example of what we should be like and what we should do. While many men have admirable qualities, there is only one man who ever walked the earth who was without sin, whose father of his physical body was God the Father, and who had the power to resurrect his own body. This Jesus is our exemplar and has commanded us to follow in his steps.

God the Father has given Jesus Christ a name above all others, so that eventually every knee will bow and every tongue confess that Jesus is the Christ. He is the way, the truth, and the light, and no one can come back into the presence of our Father in heaven except through him. Christ is God the Son and possesses every virtue in its perfection. Therefore, the only measure of true greatness is how close a man can become like Jesus. That man is greatest who is most like Christ, and those who love him most will be most like him.

How, then, does a man imitate God, follow his steps, and walk as he walked, which we are commanded to do? We must study the life of Christ, learn his commandments, and do them. God has promised that to follow this course will lead a man to an abundant life, a fulness of joy, and the peace and rest for which those who are heavy-burdened long. To learn of Christ necessitates the study of the scriptures and the testimonies of those who know him. We come to know him through prayer and the inspiration and revelation that God has promised to those who keep his commandments.

And how do you learn the commandments? You learn the commandments through the words of the Lord in the scriptures, through the revelations received by his authorized servants, through the Light of Christ, like a conscience that comes to every man, and through personal revelation.

It is significant that when Paul asked the question, "Lord, what wilt thou have me to do?", Christ directed Paul to one of the Lord's authorized servants. So it was with Cornelius, who after prayer was so instructed; whenever God has had his prophets upon the earth, men could go to them to learn of Christ and his commandments.

The inspired words of these prophets, when written down, have become scripture, and whenever God has his representatives on the earth, there is always new revelation and new scripture. Only when men become so corrupt that the prophets are taken out of their midst do scriptures cease. And God has stated that only through his authorized representatives could men receive the ordinances essential for salvation and the commandments necessary for the perfection of his children.

Speaking to his prophets, the Lord said: "He that receiveth you receiveth me. . . ." (Matthew 10:40.) Always the words of the living prophet have taken precedence, for it has been God's message to the people at that particular time. Had any man accepted the ancient scripture in the days of Noah but refused to follow the revelation that Noah received and failed to board the ark, he would have been drowned. Always the words of the living prophets are of the most vital concern to the people; and always, if a man would know of Christ and learn his commandments so that he can obey them, he must seek to find his authorized representatives.

For centuries, because of the wickedness of men, prophets of God no longer walked the earth, so scripture ended with the last words in the New Testament. Confusion and contention reigned in so-called Christendom, for all they had was the ancient scripture, but they were without the prophets of God to explain it to them and to receive new revelation, new scripture, and to be authorized to direct the work of the ministry.

Then in 1820, the greatest single event since the resurrection of the Christ occurred. God the Father and his Son, Jesus Christ, personally visited a young boy by the name of Joseph Smith, who had been praying to know which church to join. God, our Father, spoke to the lad and said, *"This is My Beloved Son, Hear Him!"* (Joseph Smith 2:17.)

God the Son told Joseph Smith not to join any of the churches. Joseph was to learn that the Lord's true church was not on the earth; that living prophets of God, who were the foundation of the church, had not walked the earth for centuries; and that with their deaths, the rock of revelation on which the church was built had ceased; and so there was no new scripture.

Eventually, to Joseph Smith appeared the men who were the last authorized servants to direct the church of Jesus Christ—Peter, James, and John. These glorified beings ordained Joseph Smith with the same authority they had received from Jesus, so that once again there was a prophet of God on the earth who could say, ". . . thus saith the Lord." (D&C 44:1.) Joseph Smith ordained others with the authority that he received, and so the Church of Jesus Christ was restored in these latter days—The Church of Jesus Christ of Latter-day Saints, commonly known as the Mormon Church.

In due time, another heavenly messenger came to Joseph Smith to tell him that God was about to give to the earth a scriptural account of the early inhabitants of America, as the Bible is a scriptural account that covers the other side of the world. This American scripture that was translated by Joseph Smith, through the inspiration of heaven, is called the Book of Mormon. It tells, among other things, of Christ's personal appearance to God's children here in America after his resurrection in Jerusalem and of his instructions to them. The mission of the Book of Mormon is to be a companion volume with the Bible, to serve as a second witness that Jesus is the Christ, to show that God loves one nation as another, and to reduce contention by making clear many of the doctrines that have confused Christendom.

Joseph Smith received many revelations from Jesus Christ, as have the prophets who have succeeded him, which means that new scripture has been given. The Lord's mouthpiece and prophet on the face of the earth today received his authority through a line of prophets going back to Joseph Smith, who was ordained by Peter, James, and John, who were ordained by Christ, who was and is the head of the Church, the Creator of this earth, and the God before whom all men must stand accountable.

Now this marvelous message—that God has spoken to prophets in our day and reestablished his church—is for all the world. When Nathanael questioned Philip, telling him that he had found Jesus, Philip responded by saying, "Come and see." (John 1:46.)

So do we respond, "Come and see." Men can deceive you, but God will not. If you sincerely desire to know of the truthfulness of this message, then make it a matter of fervent prayer, study it out, test it out, and God will let you know.

Would you like to know if Joseph Smith was a prophet of God and if the Book of Mormon is scripture sent from God? Then put it to the test. Read the Book of Mormon, and near its close you will find a promise that is given to everyone who reads that volume; and this is the promise: if you will ask God, the Eternal Father, in the name of Jesus Christ, if this book is true, and if you will ask with a sincere heart, with real intent, having faith in Christ, then our Heavenly Father will manifest the truth of it unto you by the power of the Holy Ghost. (See Moroni 10:4.)

This is the challenge and the test. I testify to you that I have read the Book of Mormon and that I have put it to the test; that God has revealed unto me the truthfulness of this added volume of scripture and revealed unto me that Joseph Smith is a prophet of God; and that Spencer W. Kimball is his prophet and representative and stands today as the earthly President of The Church of Jesus Christ of Latter-day Saints, the one man on the earth who holds the keys of God's kingdom, as did Peter anciently.

Let me ask, do we need a true prophet of the Lord on the earth today? Did the people in Noah's day need a prophet to warn them spiritually and temporally? Had a man refused to follow Noah, would he have been saved from the flood? Yet the Bible tells us that in the last days in which we live, the wickedness of the people will become comparable to the wickedness of the people in Noah's day when God cleansed the earth by flood. Do you think we need a prophet today to warn us and prepare us for the cleansing that God promised will come, this time by fire?

Men's hearts are failing them, spiritually and temporally. Is it of interest for you to know that God has revealed many things for your blessing? He has revealed to a modern prophet a law of health which, if obeyed, promises a man that he can run and not be weary, and walk and not faint. (See D&C 89.)

Do you think men would despair so much or commit suicide if they knew through latter-day revelation about their preexistent state, where they came from, why they are here, where they are going, and the great possibilities that lie in store for them?

With the satanic attempts to break apart the family and create disunion and strife in the home, would you be impressed with a program that was inaugurated by a modern prophet of the Lord some fifty years ago and is called the home evening program? This one-night-a-week program brings together all the members of the family for some spiritual and character guidance, a discussion of family goals and plans, a display of family talent, and games and refreshments.

The Church distributes to its members each year a manual with suggestions for this home evening program. Those members who diligently hold these home evenings are given a promised blessing by a prophet of God of what will result. Listen to this promised blessing: "Love at home and obedience to parents will increase, faith will be developed in the hearts of the youth of Israel, and they will gain power to combat the evil influences and temptations which beset them." (*Family Home Evening Manual*, 1965, p. v.)

Would you like that blessing for your home?

Would you be interested to know that by latter-day revelation the Lord has said that marriage is ordained of God, and that a couple married in one of our temples by those who hold the authority to bind on earth and it will be bound in heaven, can be married not till death do you part, but for time and all eternity? Would you like the assurance that comes to that couple that if they and their children are faithful, they shall continue together as a family unit in the next life?

Are you concerned about the increasing subversion in this blessed country, and other countries of the free world, and the spread of wickedness by a giant conspiracy? Would you be interested in reading the Book of Mormon, which records the downfall of two great ancient American civilizations as a result of internal secret conspiracies and contains a warning to us today that when we see these conditions in our midst, the Lord commands us to awake to our awful situation? With the increasing amount of aid and trade that we are providing the enemy of freedom, you might be interested to know what the Book of Mormon says will happen to a nation that upholds this conspiracy. Would you like to know of the warnings of the prophets about our increasing descent down the soul-destroying road of socialism and what they have told us to do about it?

Jesus knew of the calamities that would befall the world, which is one of the reasons why he gave revelations to Joseph Smith and other prophets. Would you like to know of a program that we have had for many years of instructing our members to have on hand at least a year's supply of food, clothing, and, where possible, fuel, and of getting out of financial bondage? And did you know that God is giving his church direction to make it independent of the world?

These and many, many more revelations of great blessings and help for today, with programs of preparation for tomorrow and eternity, are available now through The Church of Jesus Christ of Latter-day Saints.

What manner of men are we to be? Verily, even as Jesus Christ. To be like him, we must study his life, learn his commandments, and do them. That is the pathway to joy and abundant and eternal life.

Prophets of God have known him; they have told us of him and of his commandments. They have been sent of God and through revelation have instructed us in the way we should go. There is no more crucial question that a man should be constantly asking than that which Paul asked: "Lord, what wilt thou have me to do?" There is no more essential answer than that which he received: to go to those who are authorized by the Lord to give directions.

Come, listen to a prophet's voice,
And hear the word of God.
And in the way of truth rejoice,
And sing for joy aloud.
We've found the way the prophets went
Who lived in days of yore;
Another prophet now is sent
This knowledge to restore.
—*Hymns,* no. 46

I leave you my witness that I know that God lives—he is not dead; that God loves his children; that we are all brothers and sisters, children of the same Father in the spirit; that he blesses us and wants to further bless us, and to that end he has established his church and sent his prophets. I know this as I know that I live, and I bear this testimony humbly and gratefully.

FAMILY

"Americans, from the very inception of our nation, have been lovers of home. It has been our primary educational institution and the center of economic, social, and cultural interest. Our homes have been the bulwark of the nation and the most fundamental institution of society. . . .

"Marriage, the home, and family are sacred institutions. They are not man-made, but have been established by a kind Providence for the blessing of his children. . . . There can be no satisfactory substitute for the home. Its foundation is as ancient as the world. Its mission has been God-ordained."

—ADDRESS DELIVERED MARCH 18, 1956

17

The Family—A Sacred Institution

Our most basic institution is the home, because, after all, it is still our greatest and most primary educational institution. It is, in very deed, the center of our economic, social, and cultural interest. The home is the bulwark of the nation and our most fundamental and basic institution.

Marriage, the home, and family are sacred institutions. They are not man-made. Thank God for that. They are divine. The first marriage performed was the marriage of two immortal beings. Following the consummation of that marriage, the Lord gave important scriptures and instruction to us regarding the home and the family.

The Lord made it clear that it is not good for man to be alone. Woman was created as a helpmeet for man, and the two united in the sacred bonds of eternal marriage become one flesh.

"What therefore God hath joined together," said he, "let not man put asunder." (Mark 10:9.) And later, he said, "Thou shalt love thy wife with all thy heart, and shalt cleave unto her and none else." (D&C 42:22.) How we need that counsel today in America! What heartaches could be avoided if men would only heed that counsel wholeheartedly. How much less unfaithfulness and infidelity there would be if we could live by that admonition.

Then, as though to strengthen further the marriage bond in the home, the Lord gave instructions to children through his prophets. The apostle Paul, echoing the admonition of Moses on Sinai, said:

"Children, obey your parents in the Lord: for this is right.

"Honour thy father and mother; (which is the first commandment with promise;)

"That it may be well with thee, and thou mayest live long on the earth." (Ephesians 6:1-3.)

And in modern revelation, the Lord has made it very clear that parents have great and serious responsibilities. Listen to these words as the Lord speaks to the parents of the Church: "And they shall also teach their children to pray, and to walk uprightly before the Lord." (D&C 68:28.)

"And again, inasmuch as parents . . . teach them not to understand the doctrine of repentance, faith in Christ the Son of the living God, and of baptism and the gift of the Holy Ghost by the laying on of the hands, when eight years old, the sin be upon the parents." (D&C 68:25.)

That is a serious responsibility, and I believe that the early history of this church clearly indicates that our grandparents, the pioneers—in fact, the Pilgrims who came and settled the great American continent—honored these obligations and were blessed in their homes for so doing.

I realize that many changes have come about in the past century. Our industrialization, specialization, concentration of populations in great cities, the reduction in the number of people living on farms, changes in agriculture—all these have had their effects. Great emphasis upon material things and the seeking after money, after pleasure and personal gratification, and the insidious inroads of liquor, tobacco, and gambling—all these have had a pulling-away influence on this most sacred institution, the American home.

It is difficult to realize that some fifty years ago there was only one divorce in sixteen marriages in America. Now it is reported in some cities that there are actually more divorces each year than marriages. Our best authorities indicate that most of the delinquency in America is the result of broken, bad, and neglected homes. As J. Edgar Hoover, the late head of the Federal Bureau of Investigation and one of the best authorities, indicated, referring to delinquents, "The actions of the majority of them were, and are, directly related to the conduct of their parents." Yes, crime begins at home.

Now, as Latter-day Saints, what can we do? What can be done? I am sure that we all agree no nation ever rises above its homes. This church will never rise above its homes. We are no better as a people than are our firesides, our homes. The school, the church, and even the nation, I feel confident, stand helpless before weakened and degraded homes. The good home is the rock foundation, the cornerstone of civilization. It must be preserved. It must be strengthened.

There has never been and there never will be a satisfactory substitute for the home established by the God of heaven. If this nation is to endure, then the home must be safeguarded, strengthened, and restored to its rightful importance.

May I suggest five simple things that I believe we might well give attention to, as some of the needs of our homes today.

First of all, I am convinced—and this is no reflection on our devoted mothers, who spend day after day, week after week, obediently serving their families—but I feel sure that one of our greatest needs is more time of parents in the home. Youth of the Church and of the nation need more than physical comforts. We will need to leave them more than lands and stocks. They need more than a modern automobile and a lovely modern building to live in. There is no satisfactory substitute for mother, and no one can take care of her children as she can. No so-called social obligations, social enticements, or outside interests should impel any mother to neglect the sacred charge that is hers of caring for her own flesh and blood. Her first loyalty in the eyes of God is to her church and her family. I feel confident that while civic and social activities may return much good, she will serve her community and her nation best if she first devotes herself to the needs of her own children.

Second, we need daily devotion in the home. We need to return to the practice of family prayer, secret prayer, the old-fashioned practice of devotion in the home, daily, night and morning; the singing of hymns; the reading of scriptures. How much more happiness there would be, how many fewer divorces there would be, if these simple practices were followed as was the custom in the pioneer home, as well as in the early days of this country, according to the diaries of our early founders.

Third, I think one of the great needs is more parental instruction in life's problems. I know there is a tendency for parents to shrink from this responsibility, the instructing of their own children in the problems of sex, the relationship with other young people, the problems of dating, and all of the many temptations that confront a growing boy and girl. These instructions should not be left to the school or to a class in sociology. The safest place, the best place, to give this vital counsel, these sacred instructions in matters of moral purity, should be in the home on a basis of confidence between parent and child. As parents, we should instruct our children. The sacred books of the ancient Persians say: "If you would be holy, instruct your children, because all the good acts they perform will be imputed unto you."

Fourth, I believe there is a great need for family recreation and cultural activities together. We should do things together as a family. It may mean a reduction in participation in women's clubs, in men's clubs, but if families could only seek their recreation and cultural activities more as a family unit, I am sure that untold benefits and blessings would accrue. A little boy was asked, after he said he was going to a summer camp, "What is a summer camp?" And he answered, "Those places where little boys go for mother's vacation." Let us take more of our vacations together as families. Can we have a weekly evening at home, as has been admonished and counseled for years by the First Presidency of the Church? Having more wholesome activities is a great need of the families of America.

And fifth, we need a closer parent-child relationship. This is closely related to the other four needs. One of the greatest needs of our young people is a closer, more frequent companionship with father and mother. There is no satisfactory substitute. I was thrilled some time ago, as I picked up a paper in the East and read an account of a letter that a rich industrialist had sent to his son, his sixteen-year-old boy, as a Christmas present. This man could have given his son anything that money could buy—an automobile, a yacht, I guess, if he wished. But when the boy came down from his room on Christmas morning and went over to the mantel where he usually found his present, there was a plain envelope with his name on it, and he opened it and read:

To my dear son:
    I give to you one hour each weekday and two hours of my Sun-

days to be yours as you want, without interference of any kind whatsoever.

Lovingly,
Dad

As I read that, I thought, what a wise father, and what a fortunate son! Yes, that is what they need.

God bless us that we may give personal attention now to these vital matters:

1. More time of parents in the home.
2. Daily family devotion in the home.
3. Parental instruction in life's problems.
4. Family recreation and cultural activities together.
5. A closer parent-child relationship.

May we be faithful to this great obligation of parenthood, this sacred obligation, that we may build our homes solidly upon eternal principles, that we may have no regrets. May we never be recreant to the great trust that has been imposed in us. May we always keep in mind that these spirits that have entered our homes are choice spirits. Many of them have been born under the covenant. As we look into their faces and contemplate their needs, we might well consider that some of them were probably choicer spirits up there than we were. It is a grave responsibility. May we not shirk it.

18

Family Joys

Dr. Henry C. Link has said that "nothing does so much to put order in a man's life as do sound principles. They are worth more to him than a library full of books, or a den decorated with diplomas, or a lifetime of round table discussions. They are standards which clarify and simplify his thinking. They are points of reference which help him to avoid complexity and confusion. They rescue him from the necessity of prolonged and useless debate. They give him a base for decision and action."

It is in the home and family that the bases for wise decisions and fruitful actions are established. There is no other place of such challenge and such opportunity. Thank God for the heritage of a good home and family and the challenge and opportunity to build such.

Our homes are divinely ordained. Americans, from the very inception of our nation, have been lovers of home. It has been true of nations generally. What fond memories and emotions have surged up in our hearts at the mere mention of home, family, parents, children, brothers, and sisters! Some of the sweetest, most soul-satisfying impressions and experiences of life are associated with home and family ties.

How precious are the memories of daily devotion in the home, the simple but powerful practice of family prayer, secret prayer, and the old-fashioned practice of the singing of hymns and the reading of the scriptures.

My heart fills with gratitude as I recall the joys of our rich family life when all six children were at home. May I mention just a few that have enriched our lives and continue to do so.

Prayer has been and is the ever-present anchor for strength and a source of direction in our family activities. I remember kneeling at the bedside of our young children, helping them with prayers in their younger years, and later seeing the older brothers and sisters helping the younger ones.

We had family prayer night and morning, with children given the opportunity to lead, and had special prayers to meet particular problems. Mention was made in family prayer, for instance, of children with assignments such as a $2\frac{1}{2}$-minute talk in Sunday School or a new teaching assignment in the MIA. We asked for help when one of the children faced a difficult examination in high school. Special mention was made of members of the family away at girls' camp, Scout camp, school, or working. This special mention of particular concerns in our family prayers gave confidence, assurance, and strength to members of the family facing difficult problems and assignments.

The inspired home evening and family council program, which carries such promise and which dates back more than forty years, has provided many happy hours and great joy together. It has built faith, strengthened testimonies, and created a family solidarity and unity that will endure throughout all eternity.

When the children were young, we enjoyed personal, intimate visits with them at their own bedsides or curled up before the fire. Later it was a joy to have them travel with me on Church and business trips throughout the state of Idaho and later throughout the nation. Sometimes these trips were a reward for achievement. Our oldest son, Reed, was taken on a trip from Washington, D.C., to the west coast when he became the first Eagle Scout in the stake. His achievement was followed a year later by that of his brother Mark. It was on a day during this trip with Reed that I was called to a position of leadership in the councils of the Church. The intimate conversation and experience of that day will remain a precious memory always.

I remember taking a trip to fulfill a speaking engagement at a great convention in Omaha. In reporting the event, the Omaha *World Herald* showed Bonnie, our third daughter, who later became a ward Relief Society president at eighteen years of age, in a picture on the front page and reported her father's speech on the back page. This trip was reported in some detail at the weekly home evening of the family.

Another family joy was to have guests in our home. At such times we always tried to arrange to have the children at the table also, to participate in the delightful conversation of the evening. The impression made on a judge and national farm leader as our daughter Barbara, age nine, led in family prayer at our dinner table was reported later by this beloved leader at a meeting of farm, labor, and business leaders in Florida.

It seemed that the family happiness increased as the children advanced in years. It was a joy to see daughters Beverly and Beth teaching in Sunday School, as they each in turn prepared for marriage. Their classes of girls came to the home where our daughters displayed and talked about their trousseaus, their temple clothes, and their plans for marriage. What a joy to hear the young girls pledge that they would follow the examples of their teachers and all be married in the temple.

One source of family joy was the correspondence that came from the children when they were away. We would gather around the kitchen table and enjoy together letters from sons and brothers at Scout camp or on missions, letters from our son Reed while he was a chaplain in the Air Force, or news from older sisters away at college. Joy came to the home when recordings were received at Christmastime or on birthdays, recordings filled with faith-promoting experiences, expressions of love, testimony, and gratitude for the gospel. These we shall never forget.

There were difficult and challenging days also, like the one when I returned from a distant trip to find my faithful and ever courageous wife directing our sons with boxing gloves on their hands, sparring with each other. One son had challenged the high school bully, who had been teasing and trying to make fun of younger classmates. The coach had set a time for the fight. Preparations were on—training, diet, and prayer were all a part of making ready. Our prayers were answered. The outcome brought increased respect and strong friendship, even with the bully.

Even when I was a busy Cabinet member serving as Secretary of Agriculture, we kept close together through picnics in the park, travel into the country, and exploration in jeeps and on horses into the hills of Virginia.

The invitation to appear on *Person to Person,* the popular Edward R. Murrow show on CBS, to present a typical Mormon home evening was a serious challenge. The eyes of the nation would be focused on this popular show. Not only the family but, to a great extent, the Church would be on trial before the people. There was some reluctance on the part of the wise mother. She did not want her daughters publicized; but with the persuasion of her sons that this would be an opportunity to do missionary work, she readily agreed. There followed prayer and fasting, but no rehearsing. It was to be an informal Mormon home evening. Questions were to be answered, as the children decided, with "a Church answer." The Lord heard our prayers, and afterwards letters came in by the hundreds. Later, in a national magazine article, Mr. Murrow expressed his pleasure and surprise when he received more fan mail on the Mormon home evening with Secretary Benson's family than on any other program of his years-long *Person to Person* series.

As I traveled on trade trips to many nations of the world as Secretary of Agriculture, family joys were still an important part of our lives. Whenever all the space was not taken by members of the press and my staff, President Eisenhower urged me to take members of my family along with me so that "the people of the world might see an American family in action." Although space on the government plane was provided, meals, hotels, and other expenses were borne by the family.

Yes, these were busy trips, but always family joys were realized. Members of the family traveling with me would be assigned various jobs, such as keeping a diary, making memoranda, keeping a record of letters of thanks to be written later, checking carefully the ever-present questions of protocol, and always, teaching the gospel by word and example.

And now, with all six children happily married in the temple of God and with families of their own, the joys continue and are multiplied. Weekly contacts are made by telephone or letter. Birthday cards are sent to each one. Family reunions are held with 100 percent attendance, and we join together in prayer and fasting as the signal goes out of illness or serious problems facing any member of the family.

And the joys continue, such as the report from our son Mark that his family had achieved its missionary goal of bringing into the Church one neighborhood family each year for five years—parents and six children cooperating, using the home evening, to bring some thirty new converts into the Church.

So much more could be said. Thank God for the joys of family life. I have often said there can be no genuine happiness separate and apart from a good home. The sweetest influences and associations of life are there. Life cannot be fully successful, no matter what goals we attain in the material world, no matter what honors of men come to us in our lives, if we fail as fathers, mothers, and children.

God bless us as Latter-day Saints that our family life may be such that we will have no serious regrets. May we heed the counsel given us and follow the inspired programs of the Church.

It is my conviction that even in this richly endowed world, there can be no enduring prosperity and happiness in nonreligious homes. The integrity of the home must be maintained. The spiritual foundation of our homes must be strengthened. Happiness here and hereafter is tied up with our successful discharge of this great responsibility. Thank God for family joys.

19

Putting Father at the Head of the Family

Recently I received in the mail a note from a missionary to whom I am somewhat close, and he was talking about how to reach people with the gospel. "The golden questions are fine," he said, "but I think we have some approaches that are better."

Then he continued: "You can approach people with many types of conversations. They don't have to be 'golden contacts.' First, ask them, 'What is the most important thing in the world to you?' They will almost always answer, 'My family.' If they say something else, you say, 'And what else?' and they will say, 'My family.'

"Then ask them, 'What do you want most for you and your family in this life and the life hereafter?' They will answer, 'To be happy,' or some similar answer. Third, ask, 'Can you imagine being happy without your family?' They answer, 'No.' You respond, 'You can have your family and have complete happiness throughout eternity. Would you like to know more about the plan whereby this is made possible for you?' "

I think this appeal of home and family for our prospective elders and our inactive elders is one of the great appeals we have today, because the thrust of the adversary seems to be at the home and family and at our young people. Parents are concerned—even inactive fathers are concerned—and our concern, of course, is to get these brethren into activity, get them to the point where they can take their families to the temple of God and have them sealed for time and all eternity.

I received a telephone call from a bishop in Ogden during the time of the construction of the Ogden Temple. He said, "Brother Benson, do you think you could spend one night for our good ward?"

"Well," I said, "Bishop, I would like to, if I can. There are only about five thousand wards in the Church, but I am sure yours is one of the best."

"Oh," he said, "there's no question about that."

I said, "What do you wish me to do?"

He replied, "We have five wonderful men who have been taken from the ranks of the prospective elders and inactive elders. We've been working with them now for about a year, or a little more. They have all been given the Melchizedek Priesthood, ordained elders, and they are now ready to go to the temple of the Lord. We'd like you to meet us in a sealing room in the Salt Lake Temple and perform the sealings of wives to husbands and children to families. You name the night."

I have often thought it is very hard to say no when they say, "You name the night." So I named the night, and I spent one of the happiest evenings of my life in the sealing room in the Salt Lake Temple. All these families had children. One pair of parents had nine children under eighteen years of age. I think I shall never forget that wonderful mother. She sat in the far corner of the sealing room, so filled with emotion she could hardly control herself. She wiped away the tears and they kept coming back. Finally, when the work was all done and they were leaving the room, she came up to me and began to apologize. She said, "Brother Benson, you'll just have to forgive me for the way I have acted tonight, but I've waited nineteen years for this moment, and all during that nineteen years I've prayed to God night and morning that the time would come when my husband would be considered worthy to receive the Melchizedek Priesthood and could bring me and the children here to the house of God, and tonight my prayers have been answered." I don't suppose it is possible for us to realize what that meant to that wonderful woman, wonderful mother and wife.

I often think, as I visit the stakes, that there are probably many such mothers and wives who are praying nightly and every morning that the time will come when their husbands will be considered worthy. So there is really a lot at stake in dealing with these inactive fathers, these prospective elders, men who should stand as the patriarchs of their families.

We are engaged in the greatest work in all the world, and that is the building of men and women of character, men and women of strength and courage, and men and women of deep spirituality—Godlike men and women; and I have a feeling that in this work we cannot fail. These men are sons of our Heavenly Father. He loves them as we love our own sons, yes, even with a deeper love, and I am thrilled when I see the progress that is being made.

I think one of the greatest thrills I have received at a stake conference was in Tokyo, where Brother Gordon B. Hinckley and I had organized a stake. I had the privilege of going back two years later to visit that stake, and in the general session on Sunday morning, they called the names of forty-one men to stand. They had been approved to receive the Melchizedek Priesthood and be ordained to the office of elder. Thirty-one of the forty-one were from the ranks of the prospective elders. I thought, "What a blessing." I said to the stake president, "Brother Tanaka, more important than anything I say or anything you'll do here today is this item of business transacted in the morning session—forty-one men who can now take their families to the house of the Lord."

This has a great appeal, I think, to our inactive brethren, particularly because fathers today are worried and concerned about their families. They are having difficulty at home. They hear a lot about the generation gap, which is another tool of the adversary to try to drive parents and children apart. They need all the help they can get, and I think now, more than any other time in the past, we have an opportunity to draw close to them and to help them to get their lives in order so they can go to the temple of the Lord, take their families with them, and be strengthened in their priesthood duties.

The Lord has given us the broad outline of organization. He has set forth the objectives and the purposes, but he leaves to us pretty much the working out of the methods.

Here are some of the basic principles to guide us in this program:

1. *The home and family is the eternal unit and the basis of the righteous life.*

I wish we could have more family reunions. It seems to me they used to be more common than they are today. It's a great opportunity to warm up inactive members of the Church, inactive heads of families, to get them into a reunion. It is also a good thing to get them to funerals when you can. A funeral is a great time to reach people because of the surroundings and the spirit generally.

I was at a reunion some two or three years ago, and after the reunion, someone sent me a definition of family, headed "What Is a Family?" This is what it said: A family is the greatest security and the dearest possession. A family is living together and praying together; understanding one another; sharing tears, toothpaste, and small change; swapping sweaters, chores, jokes; borrowing records, talents, wisdom; keeping snapshots, letters, homemade gifts and memories; giving first aid, parties, and lots of advice; and taking part in everything and in every member of the family. A family is living together and loving one another, and being loyal to each other.

2. *The father is the presiding authority in the home. He is the patriarch or head of the family.*

3. *The mother is the helpmate, the counselor.*

4. *You cannot talk about father without talking about the role of the mother—they are one, sealed for time and all eternity.*

I make it a practice, whenever I perform a marriage, to suggest to the young couple that they return to the temple as soon as they can and go through the temple again as husband and wife. It isn't possible for them to understand fully the meaning of the holy endowment or the sealings with one trip through the temple, but as they repeat their visits to the temple, the beauty, the significance, and the importance of it all will be emphasized upon them. I have later had letters from some of these young couples expressing appreciation because that item was emphasized particularly. As they repeat their visits to the temple, their love for each other tends to increase and their marriage tends to be strengthened.

5. *The quorum is organized to teach, inspire, and strengthen the father in his responsibility, and it must let him learn his duty.* That suggests involvement—involving him in the programs of the Church, giving him something to do, assuring him that he is needed and wanted in the Church.

6. *If the father fails in his responsibility, the priesthood representative must work with him to strengthen and help him to do his duty.* This involves, of course, a lot of person-to-person work and informal contacts.

7. The father has the responsibility for the physical, mental, social, and spiritual growth and development of himself, his wife, and each of his children.

A young man came to my office a short time ago for a blessing. He had problems—not moral problems, but he was neurotic; he was confused; he was concerned and worried. And so we talked for a few minutes and I said to him, "Have you ever asked your father for a blessing?" "Oh," he said, "I don't know that Dad would do a thing like that. He is not very active." I said, "But he's your father." "Yes." "Does he hold the priesthood?" "Yes, he is an inactive elder." I said, "Do you love him?" And he said, "Yes, I love him. He is a good man, he's good to the family, good to the children." I said, "Do you ever have family prayer?" He said, "It has been a long time since we had family prayer." I said, "All right, would you be willing to go home and watch for an opportunity, and ask your father if he will give you a blessing? And if it doesn't work out, you come back, and I will be glad to help you."

So he left, and in about three days he came back. "Brother Benson, this has been the sweetest thing that's happened in our home," he said. "Mother and the children sat there, my younger brothers and sisters, with my mother wiping the tears from her eyes. She expressed her gratitude later. Father gave me a lovely blessing." He added, "I could tell it came from his heart."

There are a lot of fathers who would enjoy giving their own children blessings, if they had a little encouragement. As patriarchs of their families, that is one of their obligations and duties, responsibilities, and, of course, opportunities.

8. A father cannot be released from his responsibility. Bishops are called and serve for a while and then are released, but a father is never released. He may release himself through sin, but his is an eternal calling.

9. A father has the responsibility to lead his family by—

—loving God and looking to him for daily counsel and direction. That means family prayer as well as personal prayer. I often wish there were some way to measure accurately the value of family prayer. What it would mean to little Mary, who is giving her first talk in Sunday School or perhaps her first little talk in Primary, to have the family go onto their knees that morning and make special mention of her that she will do her best and not be too frightened. What it would mean to a special teenage son who is facing a stiff examination in high school, to have him specially mentioned in family prayer. Family prayer can greatly increase the unity and solidarity in the family.

—loving his wife and being one with her. One of the greatest things a man can do for his children is to love his wife and let them know he loves her.

—desiring to have children and loving them.

—letting virtue garnish his thoughts unceasingly. This is one of the great needs today, particularly. We have so much sin, so many men attracted by a pretty face and untrue to their companions.

—being an example of all he wants to teach.

—teaching and training his children in the word of the Lord, in light and truth.

—teaching them repentance, faith in Christ, baptism, the gift of the Holy Ghost, enduring to the end, praying vocally and in secret.

—governing, commanding, correcting, nurturing, and blessing them in meekness, tenderness, and love, and upon the principles of righteousness.

—provoking not so that the family or the child is discouraged.

—creating an environment in the home conducive to order, prayer, worshiping, learning, fasting, growth, happiness, and the Spirit of the Lord.

—dedicating his home to the Lord.

10. The father must hunger and thirst and yearn to bless his family, go to the Lord, ponder the words of God, and live by the Spirit to know the mind and will of the Lord and what he must do to lead his family.

11. The Church exists to assist the father to get his family back into the presence of our Father in heaven.

12. The father will solve his problems in the Lord's way.

As heads of families, we have four major responsibilities. Certainly the first is the home and the family. I have in my office two great statements in one frame. One is by President Harold B. Lee: "The most important of the Lord's work that you will ever do will be the work that you do within the walls of your own home." The other is that great statement by President David O. McKay: "No other success can compensate for failure in the home." I wish that every father in Israel could have those emphasized to him.

The second responsibility is a man's Church responsibility: exercising his priesthood in righteousness, responding to calls, paying tithing and fast offerings; supporting the missionary program, the welfare program, the building program, the entire program of the Church.

Third, a father has responsibility to his job, to his occupation, to his employment, so that he can support those dependent upon him, for the scriptures indicate that he who will not provide for his own is worse than an infidel.

And fourth, he has a citizenship responsibility and a special responsibility to the Lord's government for free men. We must realize that the gospel can prosper only in an atmosphere of freedom.

The family is under attack today, I think, as never before, at least in my memory, and it is very real. Yet the family is the rock foundation, the cornerstone of civilization. The Church will never be stronger than its families, and this nation will never rise above its homes and its families.

Home teachers, quorum leaders, all of us, including stake missionaries, need to get the father to recognize his great responsibility to perform his duty as a father and as a patriarch to his own children.

I give you one experience in closing. At a stake presidency's meeting in Boise, Idaho, years ago, we were trying to select a president for the weakest and smallest elders quorum in the stake. Our clerk had brought a list of all the elders of that quorum, and on the list was the name of a man whom I had known for some years. He came from a strong Latter-day Saint family, but he wasn't doing much in the Church. If the bishop made a call to do some work on the chapel, he'd usually respond, and if the elders wanted to play softball, you would sometimes find him out playing with them. He did have leadership ability; he was president of one of the service clubs and was doing a fine job.

I said to the stake president, "Would you authorize me to go out and meet this man and challenge him to square his life with the standards of the Church and take the leadership of his quorum? I know there is some hazard in it, but he has the ability."

The stake president said, "You go ahead, and the Lord bless you."

After Sunday School I went to this man's home. I'll never forget the look on his face as he opened the door and saw a member of his stake presidency standing there. He hesitantly invited me in; his wife was preparing dinner, and I could smell the aroma of coffee coming from the kitchen. I asked him to have his wife join us, and when we were seated, I told him why I had come. "I'm not going to ask you for your answer today," I told him. "All I want you to do is to promise me that you will think about it, pray about, think about it in terms of what it will mean to your family, and then I'll be back to see you next week. If you decide not to accept, we'll go on loving you," I added.

The next Sunday, as soon as he opened the door I saw there had been a change. He was glad to see me, and he quickly invited me in and called to his wife to join us. He said, "Brother Benson, we have done as you said. We've thought about it and we've prayed about it, and we've decided to accept the call. If you brethren have that much confidence in me, I'm willing to square my life with the standards of the Church, a thing I should have done long ago." He also said, "I haven't had any coffee since you were here last week, and I'm not going to have any more."

He was set apart as elders quorum president, and attendance in his quorum began going up—and it kept going up. He went out, put his arm around the inactive elders, and brought them in. A few months later I moved from the stake.

Years passed, and one day on Temple Square in Salt Lake City, a man came up to me, extended his hand, and said, "Brother Benson, you don't remember me, do you?"

"Yes, I do," I said, "but I don't remember your name."

He said, "Do you remember coming to the home of a delinquent elder in Boise seven years ago?" And then, of course, it all came back to me. Then he said, "Brother Benson, I'll never live long enough to thank you for coming to my home that Sunday afternoon. I am now a bishop. I used to think I was happy, but I didn't know what real happiness was."

So, when we bring the fathers back into activity, we bring them happiness in this life, to say nothing about the eternal blessings that are opened up to them. My heart goes out to these men, heads of families, who are inactive, prospective elders. I don't believe we have a greater challenge in the Church today than to activate these men and bring them to the point where they can take their families to the house of the Lord and have opened to them the richest blessings known to men and women in this world, and closely related to the blessings in the world to come.

20

A Challenge to Youth

I'm very anxious that the young people of the Church measure up in every way to that which the Lord expects of them. They are a choice group. They are a peculiar group also. Peter, in writing to the Saints anciently, said, ". . . ye are a chosen generation, a royal priesthood, an holy nation, a peculiar people." (1 Peter 2:9.) And our young people today are peculiar in many ways. Certainly they are peculiar in their standards if they are living the gospel.

Many predictions have been made by the enemies of the Church regarding this work. I remember as a boy it was not uncommon to read predictions by some who professed to have made a study of Mormonism. They predicted that Mormonism would not endure beyond the third and fourth generation. I remember reading books written by critics of that time to this effect, and as a young boy before I got a burning testimony, I used to wonder about it. There has never been any real doubt—just a little wonder during my early years. How wrong they have been! I'm now the fourth generation; I have sons and daughters who are the fifth generation, and grandchildren who are the sixth generation, and I'm sure their faith is just as strong as their parents' was at their age—possibly stronger. No, Mormonism is not going to peter out.

Even in recent years there have been sociologists and others who have made similar predictions or who have at least raised questions regarding the faith of the youth of the Church. I remember one such case that came to my attention through the kindness of President David O. McKay. It was during World War II. There came into the office of Brother McKay in Salt Lake City a very distinguished educator from the East. The two men visited together for some time, and during the course of the conversation this distinguished educator said to President McKay, in substance, "I presume that the young people of the Church today are not like their fathers and grandfathers were. No doubt they're more realistic—they don't accept the miraculous as their fathers did—you know, the story of the early pioneers, of visions, and things of that sort."

Well, of course, this was a great shock to President McKay. He had just been opening some of his mail, so he drew from the stack of letters one letter which he handed to his guest, saying, "I think this will probably answer your question." The letter was from a Mormon boy stationed with the U.S. Navy in Farragut, Idaho. He started out by saying this was the first time he had been far from home on his own. He told how he missed his home and how he had come to appreciate more fully his parents and their teachings regarding the standards of the Church. Then he went on enumerating his blessings. As he concluded his letter, he bore a fervent testimony concerning the mission of the Prophet Joseph Smith and thanked the Lord through his letter for that testimony, for that faith.

The distinguished visitor handed the letter back to President McKay and asked, "Is this somewhat typical?" President McKay answered, "Every mail delivery brings many such letters from our boys in the service. Of course, they don't all have that faith, but the great majority of them do." Then the distinguished visitor exclaimed, "I would to God that every young man in America had such an anchor!"

If we are living the gospel, we do have such an anchor. What does the Lord expect of young men and women in his church? Someone has said, I think a bit facetiously, that the younger generation isn't so bad—it's just that they have more critics than models. That may be true in the world. We do hear a lot about juvenile delinquency.

But certainly in the church and kingdom of God the young people have plenty of models. I don't mean by that that our parents are all perfect. There are parents who are not living the gospel, few proportionately, but certainly we do come in contact, all of us, with many, many models —men and women who are living the gospel, who have translated into their lives the beauty and the fruits of Mormonism. We have no valid excuse.

Of course, it's easier where every member of the Church has come from a good Latter-day Saint home. There are some, however, who haven't been so fortunate. Some have probably come from homes where there has been a lack of spirituality, a lack of devotion, a lack of unity, a lack of the real spirit of the gospel of Jesus Christ. But the Lord has a way of compensating those of his children who are not privileged to enjoy some of these valuable blessings. Sometimes he makes up to them in his own way those things of which they seem to have been deprived. We do have many models, many examples, confirming the value of living the good life, of adhering to the standards of the Church.

So I ask, What does the Lord expect of our young men and women?

First, I believe they are expected to be happy. "Men are, that they might have joy." The purpose of life, of course, is manyfold, and through it all I'm sure the Lord expects our young people to live a full life—a joyous life, not a frivolous life. Certainly he expects them to be happy. He expects their living to be purposeful. He expects them to know where they are going and to get on their way, but to be happy in so doing—to live a full, wholesome, joyful life.

In order to do that, a young person must have a testimony of the gospel. You can't live the full life without the anchor that comes from a testimony. Oh, it's glorious to have a testimony of the truth! I have seen so much evidence of the strength of testimony under the most adverse economic and social conditions that I've reached this conclusion in my own mind: a man and woman can endure anything and keep their spirits sweet and wholesome provided they have a testimony of the divinity of this work. One must seek for it, pray for it, live for it. Assuredly it will come, because the God of heaven wants every one of his children to know that he lives, that Jesus is the Christ, and that Joseph Smith is a prophet. Each person may know that as he lives for it.

Furthermore, I believe that he expects of every young man, if he is going to be fully happy, that he enjoy the blessings of the priesthood. I can't conceive of a young man in this church being fully happy without the Melchizedek Priesthood. I don't believe that the Lord blesses his children with full happiness, if they're members of the Church, unless they receive the priesthood, a priceless possession. So much of the joy of this life and of eternity is tied up in priesthood.

If we are going to be fully happy, we need to be married in the temple of God. Marriage can never mean the same outside the temple as it does inside. It is God's way. We can afford to sacrifice almost anything for that blessing, in order to complete our plans and realize our dreams of being married *right*—in the house of the Lord. Ofttimes feeble excuses are given. Temples may be far away. Yet it's no farther, in point of time, from New York to Salt Lake City today than it was from Salt Lake to St. George when President Heber J. Grant was married. President Grant made it in a wagon. Young people should devote at least as much planning to marriage as they do to their vacation plans. Marriage in the temple is absolutely essential if we would be truly happy.

For the ultimate in happiness, we need to experience the glorious blessings of honorable parenthood—at least we need to be worthy of it. I realize that some of the choicest spirits of our Heavenly Father go through mortality without that glorious privilege, but in the Lord's own due time they'll realize that blessing, if not in this life, then in the life to come.

No girl or boy can afford to lower his or her standards just to get married to someone. The Lord expects all of us who have accepted membership in his church and kingdom to live worthy of experiencing the glorious and honorable blessings of marriage in his holy house and of honorable parenthood.

Further, the Lord also wants us to be successful. Oh, I know he doesn't worry too much about material things. All material things are but a means to an end. The end is spiritual, yet if we'll read the revelations, we will discover that many of them have to do with material things.

I'm sure the Lord wants each young man and woman of his church to excel in his or her chosen field, whatever it may be, whether it be in business, in the professions, teaching, medicine, dentistry, government, or agriculture. I'm sure it is pleasing to the Lord to see his sons and daughters who have taken upon themselves the covenants of membership in his church—and particularly young men who bear the priesthood—to be more than just average. He wants them to succeed, to be outstanding. He'll open the way before them if they will just live worthy of it.

By that I don't mean that all a person has to do is go to church in order to succeed in his chosen field, but I do mean that if we put forth an effort equal to our associates outside the Church, and live the gospel at the same time, the Lord will bless us with *added* success. If we keep the Sabbath day holy and devote ourselves to spiritual things, in the long run I'm convinced the Lord will add his blessings. He will bless us with hidden treasures of knowledge, as the Word of Wisdom so clearly indicates. He will give us the power to tap that Unseen Source of knowledge and strength that is beyond the knowledge of the men of the world. He will make us pillars of strength and power among our associates.

The world is seeking for the services of young men and women who are trained according to Mormon standards, who have the technical training, plus that training in character, in spirituality, and in faith, that gives them confidence, assurance, a feeling of security, and makes them a safe risk for the employer.

I think the Lord wants us to be good citizens of this country. I believe he wants us to keep our economic and social thinking straight and not be influenced by policies and programs that strike at the very foundation of all that we hold dear in this country.

We have a measuring rod that no other group has. We have the revelations of the Almighty to indicate to us whether a thing is right or wrong. The Lord has spoken. He has placed a responsibility upon us to see that our form of government is preserved and that good men and honest men are elected for public office. His counsel is found in the 98th and 101st sections of the Doctrine and Covenants. We're not left to move in the dark.

No Latter-day Saint—no true Latter-day Saint—will

be a communist or a socialist or a proponent of the welfare state. If we are true Latter-day Saints, we will be real Americans, devoted to our American way of life and willing always to uphold the Constitution of this land. We will oppose any program or any policy or any legislation that would weaken that Constitution or that way of life.

The God of heaven expects his children to stand on their own feet and not depend on any over-paternalistic government. I care not what political leaders say! I know what the God of heaven has said, and he expects us to ask for nothing of the government that we can provide ourselves, because you can't help people permanently by doing for them what they should do and could do for themselves.

I think it was one of the members of the First Presidency who said: "An uncorrupted citizenry builds a great state. No state ever built an uncorrupted citizenry." We've got to adhere to those old-fashioned virtues of our parents and grandparents if we are going to be true Americans in the eyes of God. Through revelation he has approved of the Constitution of this land. The founders of this nation were inspired. They were raised up for this very purpose. So if we're going to measure up in the eyes of our Heavenly Father, we must be good citizens of this great land and measure every policy, every proposal by those eternal principles which the God of heaven has been kind enough to reveal to us.

I think also that our Heavenly Father expects the youth of our church to become exalted in the celestial kingdom. We're not striving for the lower kingdoms. We're not candidates for the telestial or terrestrial kingdom. The young people of this church are candidates for the celestial kingdom and the highest degree of glory in that kingdom. That requires a great deal that has to do with our day-to-day standards. This means not just being married in the temple; not just being a good citizen; not just being happy, as measured by the world. It means living every standard of the Church fully.

To our young people it means keeping themselves clean in body and in mind. It means that they go to the marriage altar pure and clean. It means that they will reserve for the marriage relationship those sweet and intimate associations which the God of heaven intended should be a part of marriage, and not be indulged in outside the marriage covenant. The curse of this age is unchastity—next to murder in the category of crimes.

No, we cannot let down our standards. We cannot indulge in promiscuous relations outside the marriage covenant without suffering ill effects from it. Any time we break a law of God, we pay the penalty in heartache, in sadness, in remorse, in lack of self-respect.

Now, I would not have anyone believe that there is no hope if there are some who have made such a grievous mistake, because repentance and forgiveness are also a part of the gospel. Thank God for that! But it must be real repentance. Such repentance is a deep, heartfelt sorrow for sin that produces a reformation of life. It is not just a confession of guilt. Sometimes we regard all too lightly the principle of repentance, thinking that it only means confession, that it only means feeling sorry for ourselves. But it is more than that. It is a deep, burning, and heartfelt sorrow for sin that will drive us to our knees in humility and tears —a deep, heartfelt sorrow for sin that produces a reformation of life. That is the right test: a reformation of life. Only then may the God of heaven in his mercy and his goodness see fit to forgive us. He—not the priesthood on the earth— is the judge. Priesthood holders can only carry out certain requirements. They can require certain things set forth in the revelations, but forgiveness comes from above.

Sin and evil are so rampant in the world today—especially the loose relationships between young men and women—that it is well for us to see them in their proper perspective. We can't build a happy home, we can't build a happy married life on the foundation of immorality. It can't be done. So I would beseech our young people to reserve for the marriage relationship those sweet and lovely and intimate associations. Not only that, but when those associations come, let them be primarily for the purpose of procreation, for the having of a family, because it is not pleasing in the sight of God to enjoy the pleasures of those associations and refuse to accept the responsibility of parenthood. I care not what the world says; these are the standards of the kingdom of God.

The undue postponement of parenthood is bound to bring disappointment and is not pleasing in the sight of God. Yes, of course, one can always find excuses. The young husband is going through school. His wife needs to work for a few years. I know how difficult it is. I remember our first year of married life on seventy dollars a month for both of us. I thank the Lord for my noble companion and her fervent determination to put first things first.

Generally speaking, unless it's an unusual emergency, the place for the wife is in the home as the homemaker, as the planner, and she will save dollars upon dollars. She'll make her husband stand on his own feet as the provider. As a married couple they'll be drawn closer together through the years if she fulfills her responsibilities of motherhood and homemaker than if she attempts to share the responsibility of economic provider.

Now I don't say this critically. Each person must make his own decisions, of course. I am, however, giving the best counsel I know on the subject. Don't postpone unduly the blessings of honorable parenthood following proper marriage.

It thrills me to witness young couples where the husband is struggling through medical school or dental school or some other school and they have the courage and strength and the faith to know that in some way the God of heaven will assist them if they do their duty and have their families.

When the God of heaven said it was our responsibility to multiply and replenish the earth, that marriage was primarily for that purpose, he didn't insert any provisos.

So, I would ask our young people to think seriously about these things, pray about them, fast about them. The Lord will give them the answers, because he wants them to succeed. He wants them to be happy. He wants them to have the blessings of a righteous posterity. Sometimes marriage may be postponed to the point where, for physical and other reasons, parenthood is denied. Oh, what a loss when the time comes! Children are jewels. Blessed is the man or the woman who has a family of children. The deepest joys and blessings in life are associated with family, parenthood, sacrifice. It's worth practically any sacrifice to have those sweet spirits come into the home and to have them come early, that the parents might enjoy them for a longer period; that they might enjoy their parents for a longer period; and that the children might enjoy their grandparents for a longer period.

May I again assure our youth that the Lord wants them to be happy. He wants them to be successful. He wants them to be good citizens. But above all, he wants them to live so that they will be exalted in the celestial kingdom of God. The door is open. The plan is here. The authority and the power are here. It's up to us. If we live according to that plan, we'll be happy, we'll be successful, we'll love this country and be good citizens of it, and we will be exalted in the celestial kingdom.

21

Receive All Things with Thankfulness

Each year as we approach the Thanksgiving season, our thoughts turn to our blessings. In the Doctrine and Covenants we read: "And he who receiveth all things with thankfulness shall be made glorious; and the things of this earth shall be added unto him, even an hundred fold, yea, more." (D&C 78:19.) "Thou shalt thank the Lord thy God in all things. Thou shalt offer a sacrifice unto the Lord thy God in righteousness, even that of a broken heart and a contrite spirit." (D&C 59:7-8.)

The Prophet Joseph said at one time that one of the greatest sins of which the Latter-day Saints would be guilty is the sin of ingratitude. I presume most of us have not thought of that as a great sin. There is a great tendency for us in our prayers and in our pleadings with the Lord to ask for additional blessings. But sometimes I feel we need to devote more of our prayers to expressions of gratitude and thanksgiving for blessings already received. We enjoy so much. Of course we need the daily blessings of the Lord, but if we sin in the matter of prayer, I think it is in the lack of our expressions of thanksgiving, for blessings that we receive daily.

This was driven home to me as a young man when I heard my grandfather, who had been bishop of a little country ward in Whitney, Franklin County, Idaho, for some twenty-odd years. In those days it was not uncommon to have stake conferences run for three days, and it was not uncommon for the visiting General Authority to take advantage of the opportunity to visit in the homes, not only of the stake presidency but also of some of the bishops.

President Joseph F. Smith was visiting the old Oneida Stake, and, due to this custom, he had arranged to honor my grandfather and to take a meal at his home. Grandfather said that they were seated in the big combination living-dining room of their farm home. The table was laden with good things to eat, and the family was gathered around. (There were thirteen children in that wonderful family, and I assume some of them were there that day.) Just before they were ready to start the meal, President Smith turned to my grandfather, stretched forth his long arms, and said, "Bishop Benson, all this and the gospel, too." What did he mean, "All this and the gospel too"? The food represented the good things of life, the material blessings. This family represented home, family, loved ones. Thus, here was all that the world has—and the gospel too.

We are so inclined to take our blessings for granted. Most of us haven't known anything else. I haven't. I was born into the Church under the covenant. I received the priesthood as a boy twelve years of age. It came so easy to me. I don't know if I fully appreciated it. We live in this wonderful land where we have enjoyed freedom and a standard of living unequaled anywhere in the world. Most of us have never lived out in the world and seen the suffering and the shortages of things we consider necessary for civilized living. Sometimes I wish that every American could in some way be required to live abroad for three or four years as other people live in order that we might come back to these shores with a deeper appreciation for all that we have. We are a very blessed people.

At the end of the last war, I was seated in my office in Salt Lake City when I received a telephone call from a man in New York, a multimillionaire and one of our great industrialists. He had a son in a camp just outside Salt Lake City who had been expecting to be shipped overseas, and then the war had ended and so the servicemen were crowded into that camp. This boy was discouraged and his father was worried about him, so he called and said, "Would you please call him on the telephone and see if you can cheer him up a bit." I said, "Of course, I would be happy to." And so I called him and said, "Wouldn't you like to come into the office for a little visit?" He said, "I surely would."

He was a bit delayed coming in and I was just ready to leave for home when he arrived. I said, "Wouldn't you like to go out to the house with me and take pot luck with the family? My wife doesn't know you are coming, but you will be welcome." He said, "I can't imagine anything I'd rather do tonight than that." So he went with me and we had our dinner and we had our prayer. Then we gathered around the piano afterward and enjoyed ourselves in some singing. After we visited for a while, I drove him down to the bus. In a few days, I got a letter from his father. And you know, you would have thought I had saved the boy's life! In the letter, the father quoted a letter from his son in which the son had said, "Father, I didn't know there were any people in this world who lived like that."

Yes, we take it all for granted. Here was a man worth millions of dollars, who could buy his son anything that dollars could buy and never miss the dollars, and yet this simple thing of prayer and devotion in the home had passed him by. We need to be more grateful. I think there is no true character without gratitude. It is one of the marks of a real strong character to have a feeling of thanksgiving and gratitude for blessings. We need more of that spirit in our homes, in our daily association, in the Church, everywhere. It doesn't cost anything, and it is so easy to cultivate. It is so easy also to be dissatisfied and to be envious of other people.

I learned a lesson once while I was visiting in Pocatello, Idaho, on a Sunday. I was thinking about my family, who were 350 miles away, in northern Idaho, and I thought, "I'll run down to Whitney and see if I can attend the sacrament services and renew acquaintances with some of the wonderful people there." So I drove down and arrived just as the meeting was about to start. The bishop was going into the church and invited me in with him. He liked to be on the stand ten minutes before the meeting started so he could see who came in. And as we sat there, I watched the people come in—family groups, father, mother, children—and I knew practically all of them. I thought again of my family 350 miles away and was wishing I was with them.

After the meeting started, the counselor who was conducting called on me to say a few words, and in the introduction he said, "Brothers and sisters, wouldn't it be wonderful if we all had a job like Brother Benson's. He's traveling this great state of Idaho all the time. He is always on a trip." I thought, "Yes, how true to life. Distant pastures usually do look greener." I hope we can be happy where we are and be grateful for our blessings now, here; accept the challenge that is ours and make the most of it; and not be envious of others. God help us to be grateful.

Someone has said that an ungrateful man is like a hog under a tree eating apples and never looking up to see where they come from. Do we look up to see where our blessings are coming from?

I well remember a young couple who started farming a few years ago. Though they had only modest means, they made a down payment on forty acres of raw land. They were going to raise fruit—peaches particularly. They had leveled the land, brought out the laterals, planted the trees, and then they waited and watched for the time to come when they would have a harvest. That particular spring the orchard was a sea of blossoms, and it looked as though they were going to have a bounteous harvest. Then one night without warning there came a frost, which practically wiped out the entire crop overnight. Well, young John didn't go to church the next Sunday, nor the next Sunday, nor the next. Finally his bishop went out to see what was wrong. He found John out in the field and said, "John, we haven't seen you at church for several weeks. What is the matter? Anything wrong?" John said, "No, Bishop, I'm not coming anymore. Do you think I can worship a God who would permit this to happen to me?" And then he explained to the bishop what had happened.

At first the bishop felt sorrowful too, and he expressed it to John. Then, as he looked down at the ground for a moment, he said, "John, I'm sure the Lord knows that you can't produce the best of peaches with frost, but I'm sure also he knows that you can't produce the best man without frost. John, the Lord is interested in producing men, not peaches." Well, John went to church the next Sunday, and another year of harvest came. He later became a bishop in the Church.

We do have our reverses in life. "Whom the Lord loveth, he chasteneth." It is in the depths that men and women learn the lessons that help to build strong men and women—not at the pinnacles of success, but in the hour of a man's greatest success is his greatest danger. It takes reverses sometimes to make us appreciate our blessings and to develop strong, courageous characters. When reverses come, we need the Church and the gospel all the more. I am satisfied that it is possible for any person who has a testimony of the divinity of this work to meet any possible reverse and still keep his spirit sweet and his faith strong.

I saw members of the Church in Europe right after World War II, after the worst war, as far as we know, in the history of modern nations. I saw persons who were the only remaining members of once happy and prosperous families with their homes destroyed, every other family member killed in the war. I saw them and I heard them stand on their feet and bear testimony to the divinity of this work and thank God for their blessings—the blessings of the eternal nature of the marriage covenant, the conviction that the family continues beyond the veil, that there is life after death, that there will be a happy reunion for those who live worthily.

Yes, we can meet any reverse that can possibly come with the help of the Lord and the blessings of the gospel. And every reverse can be turned to our benefit and blessing. It will make us stronger, more courageous, more Godlike.

Many people have had reverses in this latter day. I often think of the Prophet Joseph, to me the greatest prophet who has ever lived upon the face of the earth, save Jesus only, whom he represented and served. I think of his trials and tribulations. I thought of them as I stood in Liberty Jail, where he had been, surrounded by vile men, not for a period of days or weeks, but for months. And finally when it seemed as though he could stand it no longer, he cried out in these words:

O God, where art thou? And where is the pavilion that covereth thy hiding place?

How long shall thy hand be stayed, and thine eye, yea thy pure eye, behold from the eternal heavens the wrongs of thy people and of thy servants, and thine ear be penetrated with their cries?

Yea, O Lord, how long shall they suffer these wrongs and unlawful oppressions, before thine heart shall be softened toward them, and thy bowels be moved with compassion toward them?

Remember thy suffering saints, O our God; and thy servants will rejoice in thy name forever. (D&C 121:1-3, 6.)

And then came the answer in a revelation to the Prophet:

My son, peace be unto thy soul; thine adversity and thine afflictions shall be but a small moment;

And then, if thou endure it well, God shall exalt thee on high; thou shalt triumph over all thy foes.

Thy friends do stand by thee, and they shall hail thee again with warm hearts and friendly hands. (D&C 121:7-9.)

See the promise? And then the Lord gave this mild chastisement:

Thou art not yet as Job; thy friends do not contend against thee, neither charge thee with transgression, as they did Job.

And they who do charge thee with transgression, their hope shall be blasted, and their prospects shall melt away as the hoar frost melteth before the burning rays of the rising sun. (D&C 121:10-11.)

Another time the Lord indicated to the Prophet that "the ends of the earth shall inquire after thy name, and fools shall have thee in derision, and hell shall rage against thee; While the pure in heart, and the wise, and the noble, and the virtuous, shall seek counsel, and authority, and blessings constantly from under thy hand." (D&C 122:1-2.) Then the Lord uttered this significant statement:

And if thou shouldst be cast into the pit, or into the hands of murderers, and the sentence of death passed upon thee; if thou be cast into the deep; if the billowing surge conspire against thee; if fierce winds become thine enemy; if the heavens gather blackness, and all the elements combine to hedge up the way; and above all, if the very jaws of hell shall gape open the mouth wide after thee, know thou, my son, that all these things shall give thee experience, and shall be for thy good.

The Son of Man hath descended below them all. Art thou greater than he? (D&C 122:7-8.)

God help us to be grateful for our blessings and to never be guilty of the sin of ingratitude. "And he who receiveth all things with thankfulness shall be made glorious; and the things of this earth shall be added unto him, even an hundred fold, yea, more."

22

Scouting—Builder of Men

We love the youth of America. Our boys and girls, young men and women—these are our greatest assets. We have confidence in them. We know that they need the understanding, wisdom, and counsel of age. They are the trustees of posterity; the future of our country will soon rest in their hands. Our common purpose is to help prepare them to be worthy trustees, to help them fit themselves for the responsibilities of the future.

I am grateful for the privilege that has been mine to work with boys and young men in one of America's greatest character-building programs—Scouting.

Some fifty years ago I became an assistant Scoutmaster in a little country town in southern Idaho. What a challenge it was to work with and to lead twenty-four boys in the first Scout troop in this little rural community. Talk about rewards for effort! Every day of my life has been enriched by that association and service. I have been rewarded tenfold.

Such satisfaction cannot be purchased at any price; it must be earned through service and devotion. What a glorious thing it is to have even a small part in helping to build boys into men, real men. And that is the purpose of Scouting—to build men.

I would to God that every boy of Scout age in America could have the benefits and the blessings of the great Scout program. It is truly a noble program; it is a builder of character, not only in the boys, but also in the men who provide the leadership. And character, after all, is the priceless thing we build in this life and take with us into the next. Scouting is essentially a spiritual program; it is established, as is our government and its Constitution, upon a deeply spiritual foundation.

In the first part of the Scout Oath we declare, "On my honor, I will do my best to do my duty to God and my country and to obey the Scout Law." Scouting emphasizes duty to God, reverence for sacred things, observance of the Sabbath, maintenance of the standards of the church with which the boy is affiliated. As each boy repeats that pledge, usually at every Scout meeting or function, and he says aloud in the presence of those whose friendship he values most highly, "On my honor, I will do my best to do my duty to God," it cannot help but make a deep and lasting impression upon him. It becomes the foundation upon which a noble character is built. The oath also pledges duty to country, and that too is basically spiritual.

How grateful we should be to God and our country that we have been born in a land that is free, a land of plenty, a land of freedom. Some two hundred thousand persons were given life in the world during the past twenty-four hours. Only about one in twenty was born in the United States; a far larger portion were born behind the iron curtain. Many of those born in Asia or Africa have only about one chance in four of living more than a year; and if they survive babyhood, they may have only about a fifty-fifty chance of becoming young adults. Most of them may be sick much or all of their lives from disease. They may suffer from constant hunger and sometimes from horrible famine. How fortunate we are to live in this land, choice above all others. How grateful we should be, and how determined to keep our country free and strong! We must teach our boys these essential truths.

Scouting stresses service to others, and again this has a spiritual base. The Scout pledges to help other people at all times. Was it not the Master who said, "Whosoever will be chief among you, let him be your servant"? (Matthew 20:27.) The slogan "Do a Good Turn Daily" has become emblazoned upon American living beyond its place of origin in the Scout movement. Scouting emphasizes duty to self. How charged with spiritual meaning are the words, "to keep myself physically strong, mentally awake, and morally straight"!

There is a tendency to think of fitness solely in terms of physical strength. But to be truly fit, truly equal to the demands of life, requires much more than bodily strength. It involves the mind and the training of the mind, the emotions, and their use and control. Yes, and it involves the soul and the spiritual growth too. And that is why Scouting challenges our youth to be physically strong, mentally awake, and morally straight.

It seems to me that the most successful program of complete youth fitness ever known to man was described in fourteen words. They are the words of the beloved disciple Luke in the New Testament. He uses just one sentence to cover a period of eighteen years—the eighteen years in which the Savior of the world, after returning to Nazareth from Jerusalem, prepared himself for his public life: "And Jesus increased in wisdom and stature, and in favour with God and man." (Luke 2:52.) There is the ideal of any program of youth fitness, to help our youth increase in wisdom and stature and in favor with God and man. It covers everything: physical fitness, mental fitness, social fitness, emotional fitness, spiritual fitness.

The Scout Law is fundamentally spiritual. The points

of the law are expressions of virtues, of ideals; they are the basis of sound character; they are the attributes from which the greatness of America has been derived; they are the characteristics that will determine the future of this nation. If they are adhered to, America will surely fulfill its destiny. If these virtues, these ideals and attributes, are lost, America too will be lost. These virtues of trustworthiness, loyalty, bravery, helpfulness, kindness, obedience, cleanliness, reverence, and all the rest are what the past progress of America and the world is built upon.

Sometimes, in the hurly-burly of living, we forget this great truth. If we ourselves forget, how can we impress it upon our youth? Let us recall a few historic instances showing the importance of the virtues exemplified in the Scout Law.

In 1492 Christopher Columbus set sail from Spain in three small ships with eighty-seven men. For seventy days they sailed across the uncharted sea. As early as the seventeenth day the men began to murmur in fear. From the twentieth day on, Columbus was hard put to restrain them from mutiny, but when we read the log that he kept, we are struck by the force of three words appearing again and again at the end of the day's events: "We sailed on." What courage, what trustworthiness, what faith these words reveal!

Some four and a half centuries after Columbus, Admiral Richard Byrd displayed these same qualities in the exploration of the North and South Poles. In March 1934, Byrd isolated himself in the wastes of Antarctica in a little nine-by-thirteen-foot hut buried in the snow. There he planned to remain during the six-month-long night making weather observations. He took this task on himself. He would not order any of his men to do it. On May 28, fumes from the stove nearly killed him. Though he was critically ill, he refused to send an SOS to the main camp at Little

America, 123 miles away. He preferred to die rather than call any of the men to make the dangerous journey during that treacherous season of constant night.

But this was not his closest call with death. That came one day when he went outside to check the instruments in the midst of a raging blizzard. When he sought to get back inside the hut, he found the trap door frozen. He pulled and yanked, exerting all of his strength. It was like trying to pull open a locked bank vault. The door was frozen solid. He tried to scrape off some of the snow around the edges. He threw himself on the door, trying to break the ice by the pressure of his body. He pulled, tugged, pushed, pounded, yanked, until he was worn out. Now he was terribly cold, even through his heavy clothing. His fingers were numb, losing feeling. He was alone in the vast Antarctica, the frozen wild wastelands.

The wind tore at him, screaming like ten thousand triumphant devils. He was about to panic. Ten minutes more in the cold and it would be too late! With the mighty effort of his will, he resisted panic; he prayed. Suddenly he remembered—a shovel! The other day when he was checking the instruments, he had left a shovel outside. He crawled around. It had snowed a great deal in the past two days. Where was the shovel? He slipped and fell, and as he crashed, he struck something hard. He seized it; it was the shovel.

Now, back to the trap door of the hut! Somehow he got back. Somehow he wedged the handle of the shovel under the handle of the trap door. His hands were almost useless now. He threw his body across the handle of the shovel and, God be praised, the ice cracked and the door opened. With the last of his dwindling strength he forced it open enough for him to tumble through the opening and down inside the hut. This was the bravery, the trustworthiness, the faith of the explorer.

That same bravery, trustworthiness, and faith will be needed in our time by those who will explore the space age.

Scouting teaches these virtues. "A Scout is kind. A Scout is helpful." Do we ourselves sometimes forget what these virtues have meant to all mankind?

There was born in France in 1822 a boy described by his teacher as "the meekest, smallest, and least promising pupil in my class." But he gave to mankind some of its greatest boons because he was helpful. He became a chemist. When a mysterious disease attacked the silkworms of France and threatened the silk business with ruin, he was invited to investigate.

Meantime, tragedy struck at the family. One of his children died; then another; then a third. Working eighteen hours a day, he drained his strength and suffered a stroke. His powers of speech were paralyzed, but even as he lay there paralyzed in body, he was active in mind, and the solution to the silkworm disease suddenly came to him.

He fought his way back. He regained his power to speak, learning to talk all over again. Eventually his research saved the silk industry, not only of France, but also of all the silk-producing countries. He saved another industry by discovering that heat would kill bacteria without spoiling the product. Thus pasteurization was born, a process in daily use all over this country, particularly in the dairy industry.

Louis Pasteur's primary objective in life was helping man to serve God through serving mankind. His name is great in agriculture. He developed a vaccine for anthrax, a fatal cattle disease, and also for chicken cholera. His germ theory revolutionized medicine to understand surgery, which in those days was practically signing one's own death warrant. Pasteur discovered that this was because of microbes getting into open wounds. Some doctors scoffed, "What does this chemist know about medicine?" But in two years, in the first hospital where the germ theory was applied, post-surgery fatalities dropped from ninety percent to fifteen percent. He conquered hydrophobia. Once, in order to get his material for his experiment, it was necessary for him to suck saliva through a tube from the threatening jaws of a mad dog. Calmly he faced a possible horrible death. Then he said, "Well, gentlemen, we can now proceed with the experiment." What a noble soul and what a truly great example to hold not only before our boys, but also before ourselves!

Here is another example from recent times and daily lives. In a southern community a baby fell into a well. The hole was sixty feet deep and only thirteen inches across. A boy could go down, a man could not. Elbert Gray volunteered. He was let down on the end of a rope. Sharp rocks cut his face and his bare feet. He reached the baby and managed to grab its shirt, but the cramped position kept him from getting a good hold. The men above the well pulled him up, and he volunteered to go down again, this time head first so he could take hold of the child with both hands. Shaking with cold, blood pouring from his numerous cuts, he brought the baby back. He was awarded a bronze medal, symbol for heroism, by the Carnegie Fund Hero Commission.

There are many examples in the great program of Scouting of boys who have exhibited the same spirit of helpfulness, of service.

Our youth need to develop qualities of leadership. They need to learn the value of staying power—stick-to-it-iveness. They need to learn devotion to duty—the devotion to duty that keeps a good doctor on the job right around the clock in an emergency; the devotion to duty that leads a scientist or a teacher to persevere in a low-paying position in public service because that is where his maximum contribution can be made.

They need to learn to be tolerant of people but in-
tolerant of untruth, of laziness, of immorality. There is a
type of broadmindedness prevalent today that tolerates
just about anything short of outright murder. It isn't
broadmindedness at all—it's moral apathy, or maybe
moral cowardice.

Yes, what examples we have to follow; what models
to imitate! Whether one studies the Scout Oath, the Scout
Law, the Scout Motto, or the Scout Slogan, they all add
up to America's finest character-building program.

How fortunate are those who may participate in it
and have their lives enriched thereby—boys and men alike.
They with whom Scouting is concerned are made of eternal stuff; theirs is a divine destiny. Godlike men, men of
character, men of truth, men of courage, men of goodwill
—there, then, is our challenge.

Ours is not a boy problem; it is a man problem. Our
boys want Scouting; we want them to have it. Our problem is in leadership. Our great need is to provide the leadership to meet the demands of the boys. Through Scouting
we can help them develop real character; we can teach
them cooperation; we can help them develop qualities of
leadership; we can teach them the value of staying power.

It is not for us to moan about juvenile delinquency
and other problems of our youth. Let us rather use all
possible time and energy in trying to help youth—through
Scouting, 4-H Clubs, the Future Farmers of America,
church, school, and community organizations. Youth need
inspired leaders to help them to be honest with themselves; to guide youth safely along life's pathway is the
noblest work of all.

We need to give them something wholesome to do.
Only a warm heart can kindle warmth in another. Young
people ask for a fair chance to succeed. Let us help provide
wholesome challenges and opportunities, and they will

complete the job of becoming well-adjusted, useful citizens. To awaken the youth of this land and to rekindle in the hearts of its leaders the high ideals of Scouting is to render one of the greatest of all services to our country. To guide right the millions of eager, yearning, active youth who are enrolled in Scouting and the many more who might be added is the mightiest of obligations.

To win their confidence is one of the greatest responsibilities and privileges of life.

Let's mobilize men, hundreds of them, who love boys; who believe in them; who not only have the technical skills, but who will inspire them, because boys need inspiration even more than they need information. Boys are hero-worshipers; they are great idealists; they love to follow one whom they regard as their ideal, their pal, their champion.

Let's get men who are boys' men; who can appeal to them and inspire them to want to live right; who believe that it is best to be good—not goody-good, but happy, full of life, full of vigor; who want them to play and have a clean, wholesome time in life. It pays to live a good life. Scouting can help to emphasize and impress this fact upon the boys of today, the men of tomorrow, and us as men. Can we ignore such a challenge? Are we so busy and self-centered that we cannot take time out to help build a bridge for that boy? Scouting offers us that challenge. It is a tremendous test of leadership, devotion, and courage. Is that nobility within us going to rise up in majesty and answer to the call?

I have faith in the manhood of America; we will not let our boys down. Upon the character of our boys depends America's future. They are our hope. Scouting, as a great spiritual character-building program, needs to grow as never before. America must be kept strong and free. May God bless us in this task of building men, real men.

23

Fitness—A Total Concept

It has been said that our young people are becoming soft, that they are demanding harder and harder butter on softer and softer bread. I for one do not believe it. The youth of this land, choice above all other lands, are the trustees of posterity. A century and a half ago the German poet Goethe said: "The destiny of any nation, at any given time, depends on the opinions of its young men [and women] under five-and-twenty."

Our common purpose is to help our young men and women fit themselves for the responsibilities of the future.

Physical well-being is not only a priceless asset to one's self—it is a heritage to be passed on. With good health, all other activities of life are greatly enhanced. A clean mind in a healthy body enables one to render far more effective service to others. It helps one provide more vigorous leadership. It gives our every experience in life more zest and more meaning. Robust health is a noble and worthwhile attainment.

For much of his youth, Theodore Roosevelt was frail and sickly, so much so that he was privately tutored and could not take part in the rough and tumble games of boys his own age. But Teddy Roosevelt was a resolute character. He deliberately set out to build up his body, and he stuck to it. In a sense he made himself over. He made himself fit. And he went down into the annals of history as a great exponent of the strenuous life—the youngest of all our Presidents and certainly one of the most vigorous, robust, energetic men ever to occupy the White House.

Times have changed greatly since Theodore Roosevelt was President, but the need for fitness is no less urgent.

I am grateful that many elements in my own background have particularly stressed youth fitness. My boyhood was spent in an area where family and church play leading roles in the cultural, recreational, and spiritual development of young people. Most of us were reared on farms or in small villages. Work and physical activity were the accepted and commonplace daily routine. We all realize that these conditions are not universal and normal today for many youth, especially those growing up in large cities.

There is a tendency to think of fitness solely in terms of the physical, in terms of bodily strength. It involves the mind and the training of the mind, the emotions and their use and control—yes, and it involves the soul and spiritual growth, too.

The ideal of any program of youth fitness is to help our youth increase in wisdom and stature and in favor with God and man. (See Luke 2:52.) This covers everything—physical fitness, mental fitness, social fitness, emotional fitness, spiritual fitness.

I like to think of youth as a kind of savings bank. We put in our experiences of all kinds, the things we see and learn, the things we do in the home, in church, in school, at work, at recreation; and all the rest of our lives we keep drawing on that savings bank of experience and knowledge. The wonderful fact is that the more we draw on the account, the larger it seems to grow.

There are some savings that all of our youth ought to have in their accounts. They ought to have some basic knowledge, some basic principles, to fit them for life.

They must realize, first, that they have a duty to God. This includes reverence for sacred things, the observance of the Sabbath, the maintenance of the standards of the church with which they are affiliated, faith that they can reach out and tap that Unseen Power.

General Omar N. Bradley, who once served as the U.S. Army's Chief of Staff, on one occasion said:

> With the monstrous weapons man already has, humanity is in danger of being trapped in this world by its moral adolescence. Our knowledge of science has clearly outstripped our capacity to control it.
>
> We have too many men of science; too few men of God. We have grasped the mystery of the atom and rejected the Sermon on the Mount. Man is stumbling blindly through a spiritual darkness while toying with the precarious secrets of life and death.
>
> The world has achieved brilliance without wisdom, power without conscience. Ours is a world of nuclear giants and ethical infants. We know more about war than we know about peace, more about killing than we know about living.

Those are startling, shocking words from a great military leader.

Second to their duty to God, youth should realize their duty to our country. They should love and honor the Constitution of the United States, the basic concepts and principles upon which this nation has been established. Yes, they need to develop a love for our free institutions.

Third, they should realize their duty to serve others. To serve others willingly and unselfishly is one of the greatest virtues. They should learn cooperation. Not everybody can lead, but everybody can cooperate. More perhaps than anything else, that's what we need in the world today—the ability to work together and serve one another in peace and harmony.

Fourth, they have a duty to themselves. They need to

develop in themselves the finest characteristics of mankind: inward peace, faith, humility, integrity, charity, courage, thrift, cooperation, and an ability for good hard work—all ingredients of a sterling character.

Fitness demands our recognizing that the individual is responsible for his deeds and misdeeds. Fitness demands our understanding that you can't build a worthwhile life without principles and convictions that you are willing to fight for. Fitness demands our knowing that "nothing worth building was ever founded on quicksand; no State ever carved from putty; no enduring society or satisfactory life built on laziness, selfishness, and irresponsibility." (Elizabeth M. Hill, "Don't Call Me Broadminded," *Reader's Digest,* January 1951.)

Fitness, then, is a total concept. It involves the whole person—body, mind, and spirit.

We need to focus attention on, and lend full support to, all worthy youth programs. Those which are nongovernment-sponsored are especially worthy of our help and leadership. Scouting activities are a fine example of such programs. I particularly appreciate what Scouting has meant to my own family, my two sons being Eagle Scouts. Let us use all possible time and energy in trying to help youth through church, school, and community recreation, and other constructive programs. Youth needs hope, not despair; visions, not clouds; models, not critics; inspired leaders to help them to be honest with themselves. To help guide youth safely along life's pathway is the noblest work of all.

Many years ago a good friend, William H. Danforth, wrote a little book that has since inspired thousands of Americans. This small book, *I Dare You,* was in our library at home and it influenced me—as it has influenced our sons and daughters—in a way that is wholly good. This is what it said:

I Dare You, young man, you who come from a home of poverty —I dare you to have the qualities of a Lincoln.

I Dare You, heir of wealth and proud ancestry, with your generations of worthy stock, your traditions of leadership—I dare you to achieve something that will make the future point to you with even more pride than the present is pointing to those who have gone before you.

I Dare You, young mother, to make your life a masterpiece upon which that little family of yours can build. Strong women bring forth strong men.

I Dare You, young executive, to shoulder more responsibility joyously, to launch out into the deep, to build magnificently.

I Dare You, young author, to win the Nobel prize.

I Dare You, young researcher, to become a Microbe Hunter.

I Dare You, barefoot boy on the farm, to become a Master Farmer—A Hunger Fighter.

I Dare You, whoever you are, to share with others the fruits of your daring. Catch a passion for helping others and a richer life will come back to you!

That is the challenge we need to present to our youth.

Let us seek to inspire them to fit themselves for service —to emulate in their own fields, and even to surpass, the achievements of other young people who have dared to pioneer.

Cyrus McCormick, for example, invented the reaper at the age of twenty-two.

Isaac Newton worked out the laws of motion and gravitation by the time he was twenty-four.

John Keats wrote some of the most magnificent poetry in the English language before he was twenty-five.

Charles Lindbergh flew across the Atlantic Ocean, solo, in a single engine plane, and he too was only twenty-five.

Eli Whitney invented the cotton gin as a youngster of twenty-eight.

Thomas Edison applied for his patent on the phonograph when he was thirty and for the incandescent lamp when he was thirty-two.

Thomas Jefferson wrote the Declaration of Independence at thirty-three.

And Mozart, acclaimed by some as the greatest musical composer of all time, wrote all of his immortal works before he was thirty-five.

What youth need and ask today falls into eight categories:

1. Action or activity toward some useful purpose—not enforced confinement.

2. Satisfaction from productive and useful accomplishment—not just empty praise or winning a prize.

3. A chance to learn and serve through apprenticeship or adult-like tasks in preparation for life—not make-believe or busy-work.

4. Adults who serve as good examples—not hypocritical pretenders.

5. Bodies that are developed to their best physical potential.

6. Minds that are developed through practical, real-life experience as well as by academic exercise and study.

7. Camping and out-of-doors experiences that result in an appreciation of nature and living things.

8. Personal standards and ideals that are based on lasting and satisfying spiritual values.

Yes, the future of our nation rests with our youth and with those who, by their devotion to the problems of youth, serve them and all mankind. God bless and speed us in this good work.

24

Strengthening the Family

My plea is to strengthen our families. It has been truly stated that "salvation is a family affair, and the family unit is the most important organization in time or in eternity."

The Church was created in large measure to help the family, and long after the Church has performed its mission, the celestial patriarchal order will still be functioning. This is why President Joseph F. Smith said: "To be a successful father or a successful mother is greater than to be a successful general or a successful statesman," and President David O. McKay added: "When one puts business or pleasure above his home, he, that moment, starts on the downgrade to soul weakness." And this is why President Harold B. Lee said, "The Church must do more to help the home carry out its divine mission."

President Joseph Fielding Smith stated that "never in the history of the . . . Church, have there been so many temptations, so many pitfalls, so many dangers, to lure away the members of the Church from the path of duty and from righteousness, as we find today." (*Take Heed to Yourselves*, Deseret Book, 1966, p. 127.) He also said: "This world is not growing better . . . wickedness is increasing." (Ibid., p. 207.)

Never has the devil been so well organized, and never in our day has he had so many powerful emissaries working for him. We must do everything in our power to strengthen and safeguard the home and family.

The adversary knows "that the home is the first and most effective place for children to learn the lessons of life: truth, honor, virtue, self-control; the value of education, honest work, and the purpose and privilege of life. Nothing can take the place of home in rearing and teaching children, and no other success can compensate for failure in the home." (Letter of President David O. McKay, *Family Home Evening Manual,* 1968-69, p. iii.)

Today the undermining of the home and family is on the increase, with the devil anxiously working to displace the father as the head of the home and create rebellion among the children. The Book of Mormon describes this condition when it states, "And my people, children are their oppressors, and women rule over them." (2 Nephi 13:12.) And then these words follow—and consider these words seriously when you think of those political leaders who are promoting birth control and abortion: "O my people, they who lead thee cause thee to err and destroy the way of thy paths." Let me warn the sisters in all seriousness that you who submit yourselves to an abortion or to an operation that precludes you from safely having additional healthy children are jeopardizing your exaltation and your future membership in the kingdom of God.

Parents are directly responsible for the righteous rearing of their children, and this responsibility cannot be safely delegated to relatives, friends, neighbors, the school, the church, or the state.

"I appeal to you parents, take nothing for granted about your children," said President J. Reuben Clark, Jr. "The great bulk of them, of course, are good, but some of us do not know when they begin to go away from the path of truth and righteousness. Be watchful every day and hour. Never relax your care, your solicitude. Rule kindly in the spirit of the gospel and the spirit of the priesthood, but rule, if you wish your children to follow the right path." Permissive parents are part of the problem.

As a watchman on the tower, I feel to warn you that one of the chief means of misleading our youth and destroying the family unit is our educational institutions. President Joseph F. Smith referred to false educational ideas as one of the three threatening dangers among our Church members. There is more than one reason why the Church is advising our youth to attend colleges close to their homes where institutes of religion are available. It gives the parents the opportunity to stay close to their children, and if they become alerted and informed, these parents can help expose some of the deceptions of men like Sigmund Freud, Charles Darwin, John Dewey, Karl Marx, John Keynes, and others.

Today there are much worse things that can happen to a child than not getting a full education. In fact, some of the worst things have happened to our children while attending colleges led by administrators who wink at subversion and amorality.

Said Karl G. Maeser, "I would rather have my child exposed to smallpox, typhus fever, cholera, or other malignant and deadly diseases than to the degrading influence of a corrupt teacher. It is infinitely better to take chances with an ignorant but pure-minded teacher than with the greatest philosopher who is impure."

Vocational education, correspondence courses, establishment in a family business are being considered for their children by an increasing number of parents.

The tenth plank in Karl Marx's Manifesto for destroying our kind of civilization advocates the establishment of "free education for all children in public schools." There were several reasons why Marx wanted government to run the schools. Dr. A. A. Hodge pointed out one of them when he said:

> It is capable of exact demonstration that if every party in the State has the right of excluding from public schools whatever he does not believe to be true, then he that believes most must give way to him that believes least, and then he that believes least must give way to him that believes absolutely nothing, no matter in how small a minority the atheists or agnostics may be. It is self-evident that on this scheme, if it is consistently and persistently carried out in all parts of the country, the United States system of national popular education will be the most efficient and widespread instrument for the propagation of atheism which the world has ever seen.

After the tragic prayer decision was made by the U.S. Supreme Court, President David O. McKay stated, "The Supreme Court of the United States severs the connecting cord between the public schools of the United States and the source of divine intelligence, the Creator, himself." (*Relief Society Magazine*, December 1962, p. 878.)

Does that make any difference to you? Can't you see why the demand of conscientious parents is increasing the number of private Christian- and Americanist-oriented schools?

Today, Brigham Young University is the largest private school in the United States. Parents from far and near are looking to BYU as never before.

Now, whether your child attends this type of school or not, it is important that you stay close to your children and review, daily, if possible, what they have learned in school, and go over their textbooks.

President Joseph Fielding Smith stated that in public schools you cannot get a textbook, anywhere that he knows of, on the "ologies" that doesn't contain nonsense. (*Take Heed to Yourselves*, p. 32.)

I know one noble father who reviews with his children regularly what they have been taught, and if they have been taught any falsehoods; then the children and the father together research out the truth. If your children are required to put down on exams the falsehoods that have been taught, then perhaps they can follow President Joseph Fielding Smith's counsel of prefacing their answer with the words "teacher says," or they might say "you taught" or "the textbook states."

If your children are taught untruths on evolution in the public schools or even in our Church schools, provide them with a copy of President Joseph Fielding Smith's excellent rebuttal in his book *Man, His Origin and Destiny*.

Recently some parents paid for space in a newspaper to run an open letter to the school principal of their son. The letter stated in part:

> You are hereby notified that our son, (_____), is not allowed by his undersigned parents to participate in, or be subject to, instruction in any training or education in sex, human biological development, attitude development, self-understanding, personal and family life, or group therapy, or sensitivity training, or self-criticism, or any combination or degree thereof, without the consent of the undersigned by express written permission. . . .
>
> We intend to retain and exercise our parental rights to guide our child in the areas of morality and sexual behavior without any interference or contradiction imposed by school personnel.
>
> [Our son] has been taught to recognize the format of sensitivity training, group therapy, self-criticism, etc., as it is being broadly applied, lowering the standards of morality and replacing American individual responsibility with dependency on, and conformity to, the "herd consensus" concept of collectivism.
>
> He has been instructed to promptly remove himself from any class in which he is exposed to the aforementioned indoctrination and to report to us any such disregard of this letter.

The Lord knew that in the last days Satan would try to destroy the family unit. He knew that by court edict, pornography would be allowed to prosper.

How grateful we should be that God inspired his prophet over a half century ago to institute the weekly family home evening program. This is the vanguard for getting parents to assume the responsibility of instructing their children. An increasing number of faithful Saints are holding more than one home evening a week and are adding to or deleting from the family home evening manual as the Spirit dictates.

Designed to strengthen and safeguard the family, the Church family home evening, one night each week, is to be set apart for fathers and mothers to gather their sons and daughters around them in the home. Prayer is offered, hymns and other songs are sung, scripture is read, family topics are discussed, talent is displayed, principles of the gospel are taught, and often games are played and home-made refreshments served.

Now here are the promised blessings for those who will hold a weekly home evening: "If the Saints obey this counsel, we promise that great blessings will result. Love at home and obedience to parents will increase. Faith will be developed in the hearts of the youth of Israel, and they will gain power to combat the evil influences and temptations which beset them." (First Presidency, April 27, 1915, in *Improvement Era*, vol. 18, pp. 733-34.)

Now what of the entertainment that is available to our young people today? Are you being undermined right in your home through your TV, radio, slick magazines, rock records? Much of the rock music is purposely designed to push immorality, narcotics, revolution, atheism, and nihilism, through language that often has a double meaning and with which many parents are not familiar.

Parents who are informed can warn their children of the demoralizing loud, raucous beat of rock music, which deadens the senses and dulls the sensibilities—the jungle rhythm which inflames the savagery within.

Said President J. Reuben Clark, Jr.:

I would have you reflect for a moment upon the fact that a tremendous amount of the modern art, of the modern literature and music, and the drama that we have today is utterly demoralizing— utterly. . . . Your music—well, I do not know how far above the tom-tom of the jungle it is, but it is not too far. . . . These things you must watch. They all have their effects on the children. Make your home life as near heaven-like as you can. (*Relief Society Magazine*, December 1952, p. 798.)

Youth leaders, are you holding aloft our standards, or have you compromised them for the lowest common denominator in order to appease the deceived or vile within the Church? Are the dances and music in your cultural halls virtuous, lovely, praiseworthy, and of good report, or do they represent a modern Sodom with short skirts, loud, beat, strobe lights, and darkness?

Will our youth leaders accept the standards set for young John Wesley by his mother? Hear her sound counsel:

Would you judge of the lawfulness or unlawfulness of pleasure? Take this rule: Now note whatever weakens your reason, impairs the tenderness of your conscience, obscures your sense of God, takes off your relish for spiritual things, whatever increases the authority of the body over the mind, that thing is sin to you, however innocent it may seem in itself.

Have we, as Moroni warned, "polluted the holy church of God"? (Mormon 8:38.) The auxiliaries of the Church are to be a help, not a hindrance, to parents and the priesthood as they strive to lead their families back to God. Do any of us wear or display the broken cross, anti-Christ sign, that is the adversary's symbol of the so-called peace movement?

Today because some parents have refused to become informed and then stand up and inform their children, they are witnessing the gradual physical and spiritual destruction of their posterity. If we would become like God, knowing good and evil, then we had best find out what is undermining us, how to avoid it, and what we can do about it.

It is time that the hearts of us fathers are turned to our children and the hearts of the children are turned to the fathers, or we shall both be cursed. Working mothers should remember that their children usually need more of mother than of money.

As conditions in the world get progressively worse, it is crucial that the family draw closer together in righteousness and that family solidarity be established. As one has said, "There are too many pulls away from the home today. We should seriously consider whether or not too many activities and other interests take too much time and attention from our families, from our children, from those whom the Lord God gave us to love, to nourish, to teach, and to help through life."

> The stick-together families are happier by far
> Than the brothers and the sisters who take separate
>   highways are.
> The gladdest people living are the wholesome folks
>   who make
> A circle at the fireside that no power on earth can
>   break,
> And the finest of conventions ever held beneath the
>   sun
> Are the little family gatherings when the busy day
>   is done.
>
> There are rich folk, there are poor folk, who
>   imagine they are wise,
> And they're very quick to shatter all the little
>   family ties.
> Each with strangers likes to wander, and with
>   strangers likes to play.

But it's bitterness they harvest, and it's empty joy
    they find,
For the children that are wisest are the stick-together
    kind.

There are some who seem to fancy that for gladness
    they must roam,
That for smiles that are the brightest they must
    wander far from home,
That the strange friend is the true friend, and they
    travel far astray,
And they waste their lives in striving for a joy that's
    far away;
But the gladdest sort of people, when the busy day
    is done,
Are the brothers and the sisters who together share
    their fun.

It's the stick-together family that wins the joys of
    earth,
That hears the sweetest music and that finds the
    finest mirth;
It's the old home roof that shelters all the charm
    that life can give;
There you find the gladdest playground, there the
    happiest spot to live.
And, O weary, wandering brother, if contentment
    you would win,
Come you back unto the fireside and be comrade
    with your kin.

                (Adapted from a poem by Edgar A. Guest)

Let's strengthen the family. Family and individual
prayers morning and evening can invite the blessings of the
Lord on our households. Mealtime provides a wonderful
time to review the activities of the day and to not only feed
the body but to feed the spirit as well, with members of the

family taking turns reading the scriptures, particularly the Book of Mormon. Nighttime is a great time for the busy father to go to the bedside of each of his children, to talk with them, answer their questions, and tell them how much they are loved. In such homes there is no generation gap. This deceptive phrase is another tool of the devil to weaken the home and family. Children who honor their parents and parents who love their children can make a home a haven of safety and a little bit of heaven.

Does this poem describe your family gatherings?

> We are all here:
>   Father, mother
>   Sister, brother,
> All who hold each other dear.
> Each chair is filled, we are all at home.
> Tonight, let no cold stranger come;
> It must be often thus around
> Our old familiar hearth we're found.
> Bless, then, the meeting and the spot,
> For once be every care forgot;
> Let gentle peace assert her power,
> And kind affection rule the hour,
> We're all—all here.

(Adapted from a poem by Charles Sprague)

God bless us to strengthen our families by avoiding the crafty designs of the adversary and by following the noble ways of the Lord so that in due time we can report to our Heavenly Father in his celestial home that we are all there, father, mother, sister, brother, all who hold each other dear. Each chair is filled, we are all back home.

25

Three Threatening Dangers

Some years ago President Joseph F. Smith, a prophet of the Lord, warned that "there are at least three dangers that threaten the Church within." (*Gospel Doctrine*, p. 312.) He also counseled the authorities of the Church to warn the people unceasingly against them. These dangers are:

Flattery of prominent men in the world,

False educational ideas,

Sexual impurity.

I should like to comment briefly on these three dangers.

First, the flattery of prominent men in the world:

The Master warned, "Woe unto you, when all men shall speak well of you! for so did their fathers to the false prophets." (Luke 6:26.)

As Latter-day Saints we have been driven, mobbed, misunderstood, and maligned. We have been a peculiar people. Now we are faced with world applause. It has been a welcome change but can we stand acceptance? Can we meet the danger of applause? In the hour of a man's success, applause can be his greatest danger.

There is, of course, nothing wrong with being honored

by men if one is being honored for a good thing, if one comes to these honors through righteous living, and if, while holding these honors, one lives honorably. One should strive to have wide influence for good.

However, virtue is not the only basis for being singled out and promoted. As the world gets more wicked, a possible way to attain worldly success may be to join the wicked. The time is fast approaching when it will require great courage for Latter-day Saints to stand up for their peculiar standards and doctrine—all of their doctrine, including the more weighty principles such as the principle of freedom. Opposition to this weighty principle of freedom caused many of our brothers and sisters in the preexistence to lose their first estate in the war in heaven.

We are far removed from the days of our forefathers who were persecuted for their peculiar beliefs. Some of us seem to want to share their reward but are ofttimes afraid to stand up for principles that are controversial in our generation. We need not solicit persecution, but neither should we remain silent in the presence of overwhelming evil, for this makes cowards of men. We should not go out of the path of duty to pick up a cross there is no need to bear, but neither should we sidestep a cross that clearly lies within the path of duty.

We are in the world, and I fear some of us are getting too much like the world. Rather than continue as a peculiar people, some are priding themselves on how much they are like everybody else, when the world is getting more wicked. The Lord, as he prayed for his apostles, said, ". . . the world hath hated them, because they are not of the world, even as I am not of the world." (John 17:14.) As Latter-day Saints, we too have been called out of the world.

Some things are changeless—priceless. We must anchor ourselves to the eternal verities of life, for life is eternal. The honors of men more often than not are fleeting.

Anxious to run after the honors of office or succumb to the pressures of public glamour and worldly acclaim, some of us are no longer willing to stand up for all the principles of the gospel. We seek to justify our unrighteousness by claiming that if only we can get title or position, then think of the good we can do. Hence we lose our salvation en route to those honors. We sometimes look among our numbers to find one to whom we can point who agrees with us, so we can have company to justify our apostasy. We rationalize by saying that some day the Church doctrine will catch up with our way of thinking.

Seeking the applause of the world, we like to be honored by the men whom the world honors. But therein lies real danger, for ofttimes, in order to receive those honors, we must join forces with and follow those same devilish influences and policies that brought some of those men to positions of prominence.

More and more the honors of this world are being promoted by the wicked for the wicked. We see this in publicity and awards that are given to movies, literature, art, journalism, etc. We find in our own newspapers widely read columnists who advocate one-world socialism, who have been consistently caught in falsehoods, and who continually parrot the communist line. Less and less we see the virtuous rewarded by the world, and when they are, ofttimes it almost seems to be done insidiously in order to get us to swallow the many evils for which the wicked are even more profusely honored.

Yes, President Joseph F. Smith was right. Today we are being plagued within by the flattery of prominent men in the world.

Second, false educational ideas:

During the past several years many of our institutions of learning have been turning out an increasing number of students schooled in amorality, relativity, and atheism—

students divested of a belief in God, without fixed moral principles or an understanding of our constitutional republic and our capitalistic, free enterprise economic system. This follows a pattern that was established years ago at some of our key colleges that produced many of the teachers and leaders in the educational field across the country today.

The fruits of this kind of teaching have been tragic, not only to the souls of the individuals involved, but also to the parents and even to our country.

When a survey was recently made among students asking which they would prefer, nuclear war or surrender to the communists, those campuses scored highest for surrender who had been most permeated by these cowardly teachings of false economic principles, atheism, and amorality. On one very liberal college campus 90 percent favored surrender. Other surveys on moral standards are equally alarming. More disturbing is the fact that the more college courses the students take on these campuses, the worse their thinking seems to become. Freshmen who have just left home or work do not seem as fully permeated with the brainwashing as do the seniors.

Some alumni of various schools have expressed concern. One alumnus from Yale wrote a book a few years ago entitled *God and Man at Yale*. Another group from Harvard established the Veritas Foundation and wrote a book, *Keynes at Harvard*, explaining the degree to which the destructive Fabian economic philosophy has permeated educational institutions and government. Concerned educators have begun to write books. Professor E. Merrill Root authored *Collectivism on the Campus* and *Brainwashing in the High Schools*. Dr. Max Rafferty wrote *Suffer Little Children* and *What They Are Doing to Your Children*.

In school history textbooks of recent years, some of the greatest phrases in American history have been dropped.

This Week magazine surveyed history books issued before 1920 and since 1920. Patrick Henry's famous words, "Give me liberty or give me death," appeared in twelve out of the fourteen earlier texts, but in only two out of forty-five recent texts. Perhaps this might help explain the percentage of students who are willing to surrender to communism.

The whole process can be quite insidious. Young people know that the best jobs are available to college graduates. They want to do well at school. When exam time comes, they must give back to the teacher what the teacher wants. Now, under the guise of academic freedom—which some apparently feel is freedom to destroy freedom—some teachers reserve to themselves the privilege of teaching error, destroying faith in God, debunking morality, and depreciating our free economic system. If questions reflecting the teacher's false teachings appear on the exam, how will the student answer who believes in God and morality and our Constitution? One student put on his exam paper what he knew the professor wanted to see, but then the student added a little P.S., which said, "Dear Professor So-and-so: I just want you to know I don't believe one word of what I just wrote above."

These kinds of professors are not concerned about the truth or even giving both sides of a question that only has one right answer. They weigh the scales on the side of falsehood. If they can see there is another side, it usually gets but passing and belittling reference. To give the impression that they are objective, these professors often invite someone to present a different point of view in one lecture, while the professor spends the whole semester pointing out the other side.

Now truth, if given as much time and emphasis as error, will invariably prove itself. And if our young students could have as much time studying the truth as they and some of their professors have had time to study error, then there would be no question of the outcome. The problem arises when under the pressure of a heavy course of study and the necessity of parroting back what certain professors have said, the student does not have the time or take the time to learn the truth. If he does not learn the truth, some day he will suffer the consequences. Many an honest student, after graduation, has had to do some unlearning and then fresh learning of basic principles that never change and that he should have been taught initially.

These false educational ideas are prevalent in the world, and we have not entirely escaped them among teachers in our own system. There are a few teachers within the Church who, while courting apostasy, still want to remain members of the Church, for being members makes them more effective in misleading the Saints. But their day of judgment is coming, and when it does come, for some of them it would have been better, as the Savior said, that a millstone had been put around their necks and they had drowned in the depths of the sea, than to have led away any of the youth of the Church.

The Lord has stated that his church will never again be taken from the earth because of apostasy. But he has also stated that some members of his church will fall away. There has been individual apostasy in the past, it is going on now, and there will be an even increasing amount in the future. While we cannot save all the flock from being deceived, we should, without compromising our doctrine, strive to save as many as we can. For as President J. Reuben Clark, Jr., said, "We are in the midst of the greatest exhibition of propaganda that the world has ever seen." (*Conference Report,* October 1941, p. 16.)

Parents, stay close to your children; you cannot delegate your responsibility to the educators no matter how competent they may be. Parents have a duty to train their children, to talk over their problems with them, to discuss what they are learning at school. And it is neither wise nor safe to leave the determination of our educational system and policies exclusively to the professional educators.

Students, study the writings of the prophets. Fortunately, a consistent position has been taken over the years by the prophets of the Church on vital issues facing this nation. Pray for inspiration and knowledge. Counsel with your parents. Let Sunday be the day to fill up your spiritual batteries for the week by reading good Church books, particularly the Book of Mormon. Take time to meditate. Don't let the philosophies and falsehoods of men throw you. Hold on to the iron rod. Learn to sift. Learn to discern error through the promptings of the Spirit and your study of the truth.

Yes, false educational ideas are a serious threat today.

Third, sexual immorality:

Sexual immorality is a viper that is striking not only in the world, but in the Church today. Not to admit it is to be dangerously complacent or is like putting one's head in the sand. In the category of crimes, only murder and denying the Holy Ghost come ahead of illicit sexual relations, which we call fornication when it involves an unmarried person, or the graver sin of adultery when it involves one who is married. I know the laws of the land do not consider unchastity as serious as God does, nor punish as severely as God does, but that does not change its abominableness. In the eyes of God, there is but one moral standard for men and women. In the eyes of God, chastity will never be out of date.

The natural desire for men and women to be together is from God. But such association is bounded by his laws. Those things properly reserved for marriage, when taken within the bonds of marriage, are right and pleasing before God and fulfill the commandment to multiply and replenish the earth. But those same things when taken outside the bonds of marriage are a curse.

No sin is causing the loss of the Spirit of the Lord

among our people more today than sexual promiscuity. It is causing our people to stumble, damning their growth, darkening their spiritual powers, and making them subject to other sins.

Recently a young man commented that if he quit reading books, watching TV, seeing movies, reading newspapers and magazines, and going to school, there was a chance he might live a clean life. And this explains, in large part, the extent to which this insidious evil has spread, for the world treats this sin flippantly. These evil forces build up your lust and then fail to tell of the tragic consequences. In so many movies the hero is permitted to get away with crime so long as he can joke about it, or explain he was powerless to do anything, or else the close of the movie shows forth one minimal virtue that is supposed to cover over the grossest of sin. Many of our prominent national magazines pander to the baser side, then try to cover for themselves by including other articles too.

So garbled in values have our morals become that some youth would not dare touch a cigarette, but freely engage in petting. Both are wrong, but one is infinitely more serious than the other.

Parents should give their children specific instructions on chastity at an early age, for both their physical and their moral protection.

May I suggest some steps to avoid the pitfalls of immorality:

1. Avoid late hours and weariness. The Lord said to retire to your bed early (D&C 88:124), and there are good reasons for that. Some of the worst sins are committed after midnight by tired heads. Officers in the wards and stakes, branches and missions, should not keep our people, especially our youth, up late at night even for wholesome recreation.

2. Keep your dress modest. Short skirts are not pleas-

ing to the Lord, but modesty is. Girls, do not be an entice-
ment for your downfall because of your immodest and
tight-fitting clothes.

3. Have good associates or don't associate at all. Be
careful in the selection of your friends. If in the presence
of certain persons you are lifted to nobler heights, you are
in good company. But if your friends or associates encourage base thoughts, then you had best leave them.

4. Avoid necking and petting like a plague, for
necking and petting are the concession that precedes the
complete loss of virtue.

5. Have a good physical outlet of some sport or exercise. Overcome evil with good. You can overcome many evil
inclinations through good physical exertion and healthful
activities. A healthy soul, free of the body- and spirit-
dulling influences of alcohol and tobacco, is in better condition to overthrow the devil.

6. Think clean thoughts. Those who think clean
thoughts do not do dirty deeds. You are responsible before
God not only for your acts but also for controlling your
thoughts. So live that you would not blush with shame if
your thoughts and acts should be flashed on a screen in
your church. The old adage is still true that you sow
thoughts and you reap acts, you sow acts and you reap
habits, you sow habits and you reap a character, and your
character determines your eternal destiny. "As [a man]
thinketh in his heart, so is he." (Proverbs 23:7.)

7. Pray. There is no temptation placed before you that
you cannot shun. Do not allow yourself to get in positions
where it is easy to fall. Listen to the promptings of the
Spirit. If you are engaged in things where you do not feel
you can pray and ask the Lord's blessings on what you are
doing, then you are engaged in the wrong kind of activity.

Yes, avoid late hours; dress modestly; seek good associates; avoid necking and petting; have a good physical

outlet; think good thoughts; pray. May the Lord bless us as a people. We have taken upon us sacred covenants. We must be faithful. We are in the world, it is true, but we must not partake of the evils of the world. Let us ever be on guard against the flattery of prominent men in the world, false educational ideas, and sexual impurity.

26

Satan's Thrust—Youth

It has been well said that "there comes a time when the general defilement of a society becomes so great that the rising generation is put under undue pressure and cannot be said to have a fair choice between the Way of Light and the Way of Darkness." (Hugh Nibley, *An Approach to the Book of Mormon,* Deseret Book, 1957, p. 117.)

We live in a wicked world. Never in our memory have the forces of evil been arrayed in such deadly formation. The devil is well organized. Never in our day has he had so many emissaries working for him. Through his many agents, his satanic majesty has proclaimed his intentions to destroy one whole generation of our choice young people.

Evidence of the dastardly work of evil forces is increasingly evident. On every side we see the sad and heart-rending results. The devil-inspired destructive forces are present in our literature, in our art, in the movies, on the radio, in our dress, in our dances, on the TV screen, and even in our modern, so-called popular music. Satan uses many tools to weaken and destroy the home and family and especially our young people. Today, as never before, it seems the devil's thrust is directed at our youth.

A letter from a concerned father, a well-informed teacher of youth, about the evil effects of some popular music is one of many:

> Music creates atmosphere. Atmosphere creates environment. Environment influences behavior. What are the mechanics of this process?
>
> *Rhythm* is the most physical element in music. It is the only element in music that can exist in bodily movement without benefit of sound. A mind dulled by drugs or alcohol can still respond to the beat.
>
> *Loudness* adds to muddling the mind. Sound magnified to the threshold of pain is of such physical violence as to block the higher processes of thought and reason. (And turning down the volume of this destructive music does not remove the other evils.) . . .
>
> *Repetition* to the extreme is another primitive rock device. . . .
>
> *Gyrations,* a twin to rock rhythm, are such that even clean hands and a pure heart cannot misinterpret their insinuations. . . .
>
> *Darkness* [and dimmed lights] is another facet of the rock scene. It is a black mass that deadens the conscience in a mask of anonymity. Identity lost in darkness shrinks from the normal feelings of responsibility.
>
> *Strobe lights* split the darkness in blinding shafts that reduce resistance like the lights of an interrogator's third degree or the swinging pendulum of the hypnotist who would control your behavior. . . .
>
> The whole psychedelic design is a swinging door to drugs, sex, rebellion, and Godlessness. Combined with the screaming obscenities of the lyrics, this mesmerizing music has borne the fruit of filth. Leaders of the rock society readily proclaim their degeneracy. . . .
>
> And the most diabolical deceit of this infamy is that it denies evil to be an absolute. Our religion is one of absolutes and cannot be rationalized into a relativistic philosophy of the "liberal Mormons." We cannot safely rationalize away righteousness.
>
> What could be more misguided than fear that "if rock music were not endorsed by our leaders, we may lose many young people." (MIA Music Committee.) Even now we are losing them to the songs of Satan, drugs, sex, riot, and apostasy. We could be well reminded by a message from the *Mormon Miracle* pageant: "Moroni knew that you cannot compromise with evil. If you do, evil always wins." (Richard Nibley, excerpts from letter.)

This letter from a father, teacher of youth, and member of a college music department, although analytical, expresses the concern of many other parents and youth leaders.

The Church must not compromise standards before popular demands. Surely tobacco, coffee, and alcohol users have been alienated by uncompromising standards as much as today's rocking miniskirts.

Never has the Church had a finer group of young people. They are choice spirits—sent to earth in this most challenging and important period of the world. Charged with the great responsibility of building up the kingdom of God on earth, they have an awesome challenge.

This great and momentous responsibility and challenge comes at a most difficult time. Never have the forces of evil been so insidious, widespread, and enticing. Everywhere there seems to be a cheapening, weakening, downgrading of all that is fine, good, and uplifting—all aimed at our youth, while many of their parents are lulled away into a false security as they enjoy their comfortable complacency.

All is not well in Zion. The inspired Book of Mormon prophets saw this day and, as watchmen on the towers, issued grave warnings, such as this one:

For behold, at that day shall he [the devil] rage in the hearts of the children of men, and stir them up to anger against that which is good.

And others will he pacify, and lull them away into carnal security, that they will say: All is well in Zion; yea, Zion prospereth, all is well —and thus the devil cheateth their souls, and leadeth them away carefully down to hell.

And behold, others he flattereth away, and telleth them there is no hell; and he saith unto them: I am no devil, for there is none —and thus he whispereth in their ears, until he grasps them with his awful chains, from whence there is no deliverance. . . .

Therefore, wo be unto him that is at ease in Zion!

Wo be unto him that crieth: All is well!

Yea, wo be unto him that hearkeneth unto the precepts of men, and denieth the power of God, and the gift of the Holy Ghost! (2 Nephi 28:20-22, 24-26.)

The Lord, through a modern prophet, has given us a solemn charge:

> Verily I say unto you all: Arise and shine forth, that thy light may be a standard for the nations. (D&C 115:5.)
> For Zion must increase in beauty, and in holiness; her borders must be enlarged; her stakes must be strengthened; yea, verily I say unto you, Zion must arise and put on her beautiful garments. (D&C 82:14.)
> Wherefore, lift up your hearts and rejoice, and gird up your loins, and take upon you my whole armor, that ye may be able to withstand the evil day, having done all, that ye may be able to stand. (D&C 27:15.)

We love the youth of the Church and we know the Lord loves them. There isn't anything the Church wouldn't do that's right to help our young people—to save them. They are our future. We have faith in them. We want them to be successful in their chosen fields. We want them to be exalted in the celestial kingdom.

We say to them, you are eternal beings. Life *is* eternal. You cannot do wrong and feel right. It pays to live the good, wholesome, joy-filled life. Live so you will have no serious regrets—no heartaches. Live so you can reach out and tap that Unseen Power, without which no man or woman can do his or her best.

There must needs be opposition in all things. Freedom of choice is a God-given eternal principle. To escape Satan's snares and booby traps by following the Lord is our assignment. It is not an easy one.

Using life as a laboratory, we can observe and study the lives of others as we might through a microscope. Observe that the man of God is a happy man. The hedonist, who proclaims "Do your thing," who lives for sinful, so-called pleasure, is never happy. Behind his mask of mock gaiety lurks the inevitable tragedy of eternal death.

Haunted by its black shadow, he trades the useful, happy life for the bleak forgetfulness of drugs, alcohol, sex, and rock.

A study of Satan's method can alert us to his seductions. In his cunning he knows where and how to strike. It is in youth when his victims are most vulnerable. Youth is the springtime of life when all things are new. Youth is the spirit of adventure and awakening. It is a time of physical emerging when the body can attain the vigor and good health that may scorn the caution of temperance. Youth is a time of timelessness when the horizons of age often seem too distant to be noticed. Thus, the "now" generation forgets that the present will soon be the past that looks to a life left in waste or a past rich in works. These are the ingredients in youth that make Satan's plan of "play now and pay later" so irresistible. Yes, the devil uses many, many tools.

A state of confusion is an effective environment for Satan. There is much confusion today. He employs several methods to create it. One is the distortion of definitions. To describe a drug experience he uses the term "mind expanding" rather than the more accurate description of "reality shrinking."

Freedom, a word of noble tradition, is a favorite confuser. Riots, bombings, arson, and killings are committed in the name of freedom. Obscenities test the freedom of speech. Pornography, drugs, and immorality are claimed to be manifestations of personal freedom, along with miniskirts and nudity. License and anarchy are products of these false freedoms.

A confusion of definitions includes pornography. A child can identify it, yet some of the supposedly great legal minds of our time cannot define it.

Tolerance is a word valuable in the service of Satan. Alexander Pope warned 200 years ago that:

> Vice is a monster of so frightful mien
> As to be hated needs but to be seen;
> Yet seen too oft, familiar with her face,
> We first endure, then pity, then embrace.
> —"An Essay on Man"

Ridicule works well in collaboration with confusion. To confuse youth in its searching years, the cynic defends his degeneracy by ridiculing his critics with confusing metaphors. The words of the rock recording "I Couldn't Get High," then "High on the Mountain Top" must be stricken from our songbooks. Scoffing in this manner may bring an easy laugh and a reassurance that all is well in Zion, but it is diabolically dishonest.

The philosophy of relativism attacks the eternal principles of truth. The relativist will say, "If one sees filthy implications in a popular song, it is because he has a dirty mind." The logic of this philosophy finds its fallacy in the word implications. No filth is implied in many of the lyrics. It is proclaimed.

If there are any doubts as to the insidious evil of rock, you can judge by its fruits. The well-publicized perversions of its practitioners alone are enough to condemn its influence. Its ultimate achievement is that contemporary phenomenon, the mammoth rock music festival. As these diseased celebrations mount into the hundreds, they infect youth by the hundreds of thousands. And where is there today a rock festival that is not also a drug festival, a sex festival, and a rebellion festival? (Richard Nibley.)

The Spirit of the Lord blesses that which edifies and leads men to Christ. Would his Spirit bless with its presence these festering festivals of human degradation cured in LSD, marijuana, and "speed"? Would he be pleased by the vulgar display of unashamed nudity and immorality? The speech of the rock festival is often obscene. Its music, crushing the sensibilities in a din of primitive idolatry, is in glorification of the physical to the debasement of the spirit. In the long panorama of man's history, these youthful rock music festivals are among Satan's greatest successes. The legendary orgies of Greece and Rome cannot compare to the monumental obscenities found in these cesspools of drugs, immorality, rebellion, and pornophonic sound. The famed Woodstock festival was a gigantic manifestation of a sick nation. Yet the lurid movie and rock recordings of its unprecedented filth were big business in our own mountain home.

The Lord said, "For my soul delighteth in the song of the heart; yea, the song of the righteous is a prayer unto me. . . ." (D&C 25:12.) It was pleasing unto the Lord where in Third Nephi in the great Book of Mormon we read: ". . . they did break forth, all as one, in singing, and praising their God. . . ." (3 Nephi 4:31.) It was pleasing unto Satan when, in First Nephi, Lehi's children and the "sons of Ishmael and also their wives began to make themselves merry, insomuch that they began to dance, and to sing, and to speak with much rudeness. . . ." (1 Nephi 18:9.)

And now a music scholar points to—

a new direction in the rock-drug culture [which is] hailed by many ministers and the music industry as a silver lining in the clouds of gold. Religious rock is climbing up the "Top Ten" charts. The growing resistance to the rock-drug scene is being diverted by this wholesome-appearing retreat from the new morality. But a review of religious rock materials unmasks an insidiously disguised anti-Christ. By reducing revealed religion to mythology, rock assumes the mantle of righteousness while rejecting the reality of sin. Without sin the new morality can continue in its Godless revel behind the pretense of religious robes. By reversing the roles of Jesus and Judas, one fast-selling album fits perfectly the warning of Isaiah [5:20]: "Woe unto them that call evil good, and good evil; that put darkness for light, and light for darkness." (Richard Nibley.)

Little wonder that the leadership of the Church felt impelled to speak out against this sacrilegious, apostate deception by calling this wickedness to the attention of the members of the Church in a special item in the Church *Priesthood Bulletin* of August 1971.

Yes, we live in the best of times when the restored gospel of Jesus Christ brings hope to all the world. And the worst of times, for Satan is raging. With relentless vigor he plunges in the harvest.

How can we thwart his designs? The thirteenth Article of Faith of the Church contains an important key: ". . . If there is anything virtuous, lovely, or of good report or praiseworthy, we seek after these things."

But will we really seek? To seek requires effort.

The record bins that beckon our young people with

their colorful and often off-color jackets bury many master-works that are virtuous or lovely under a vast bulk of crass commercialism.

The magnetism of TV and radio is in the accessibility of their mediocrity. Lovely is not an adjective to describe most of their products. The inventors of these wonders were inspired by the Lord. But once their good works were introduced to the world, the power of darkness began to employ them for our destruction. In each medium—the phonograph, motion pictures, radio, and television—the evolution of decline from the inventor's intentions can be easily traced.

May I quote from a musician who for many years has observed the influence of music on behavior:

> Satan knows that music hath charms to sooth or *stir* the savage beast. That music has power to create atmosphere has been known before the beginning of Hollywood. Atmosphere creates environment, and environment influences behavior—the behavior of Babylon or of Enoch.
>
> Parents who retch at the radio and records reverberating in psychedelic revolt would do well to inventory their own record collection before complaining. If it is small, undiversified, and unused, the complaint must rest on the parent. Seeds of culture are best sown in the fertile ground of infant imitation. No amount of criticizing in the teen years can substitute for the young years of example that are lost. A parent who lost his chance to be a hero-image left a gap for a teen hero. (Richard Nibley.)

Most of these heroes who are being glamorized today are no longer noble, accomplished, humble, or righteous. From reports in books, magazines, and newspapers—especially the youth sections—we learn that they are lewd, obscene, immoral, avaricious, and in some cases even cruel. It is the very life-style we are here to avoid that is paraded before our young people by their celebrated peers. To deflect the admiration of youth from these examples of the ugly life, we must start young. The care and feeding of children must include equal concern for their emotional lives as well as their physical, spiritual, and intellectual lives.

For young people to be *in* the world but not *of* the world has never been more difficult than today. But this burden must be shared by the parents. The family home evening is an important barrier to the works of Satan. Our church youth program must protect our youth against every evil influence and should fill a vacuum left by rejecting worldly enticements. And, of course, a great panacea for all problems and personal doubts: prayer—private and family prayer, night and morning.

The critical and complaining adult will be less effective than the interested and understanding. Love and understanding are only effective when they are genuine, and to be genuine, they must be motivated by love. We must love our young people, whether they are in righteousness or in error. In this way we can give them a chance to discern and to learn. But we must also give them a fair choice. Today many are not succeeding.

Yes, "There comes a time when the general defilement of a society becomes so great that the rising generation is put under undue pressure and cannot be said to have a fair choice between the Way of Light and the Way of Darkness."

God grant that we as parents and leaders of youth may have the power and the good common sense to give them "a fair choice."

27

Destructive Precepts of Men

One of the grand promises that the Lord made when he restored his church in these latter days was that the Church should never again be taken from the earth nor given to another people. This is reassuring, for no matter how much individual apostasy we may see occur among Church members, the Church itself shall endure and remain intact. Our task, then, is to see that we personally endure to the end in faithful fellowship with the Church.

The Lord distinguishes between the Church and its members. He said he was well pleased with the restored church, speaking collectively, but not individually. (D&C 1:30.) During his ministry on earth, the Lord spoke of the gospel net drawing in fish. The good fish, he said, were gathered into vessels, while the bad were cast away.

It is important to realize that while the Church is made up of mortals, no mortal is the Church. Judas, for a period of time, was a member of the Church—in fact, one of its apostles—but the Church was not Judas.

Sometimes we hear someone refer to a division in the Church. In reality, the Church is not divided. It simply means that there are some who, for the time being at least, are members of the Church but not in harmony with it. These people have a temporary membership and influence in the Church; but unless they repent, they will be missing when the final membership records are recorded.

It is well that our people understand this principle, so they will not be misled by those apostates within the Church who have not yet repented or been cut off. But there is a cleansing coming. The Lord says that his vengeance shall be poured out "upon the inhabitants of the earth. . . . And upon my house shall it begin, and from my house shall it go forth, saith the Lord; First among those among you, saith the Lord, who have professed to know my name and have not known me. . . ." (D&C 112:24-26.) I look forward to that cleansing; its need within the Church is becoming increasingly apparent.

The Lord strengthened the faith of the early apostles by pointing out Judas as a traitor, even before this apostle had completed his iniquitous work. So also in our day the Lord has told us of the tares within the wheat that will eventually be hewn down when they are fully ripe. But until they are hewn down, they will be with us, amongst us. The hymn entitled "Though in the Outward Church Below" contains this thought:

> Though in the outward Church below
> Both wheat and tares together grow,
> Ere long will Jesus weed the crop
> And pluck the tares in anger up. . . .
>
> We seem alike when here we meet;
> Strangers may think we are all wheat;
> But to the Lord's all-searching eyes,
> Each heart appears without disguise.
>
> The tares are spared for various ends,
> Some for the sake of praying friends,

Others the Lord, against their will,
Employs, his counsel to fulfill.

But though they grow so tall and strong,
His plan will not require them long;
In harvest, when he saves his own,
The tares shall into hell be thrown.
                                    —*Hymns,* no. 102

Yes, within the Church today there are tares among the wheat and wolves within the flock. As President J. Reuben Clark, Jr., stated: "The ravening wolves are amongst us, from our own membership, and they, more than any others, are clothed in sheep's clothing because they wear the habiliments of the priesthood. . . . We should be careful of them. . . ." (*Conference Report,* April 1949, p. 163.)

The wolves amongst our flock are more numerous and devious today than when President Clark made this statement.

President David O. McKay said that "the Church is little, if at all, injured by persecution, and calumnies from ignorant, misinformed, or malicious enemies. A greater hindrance to its progress comes from faultfinders, shirkers, commandment-breakers, and apostate cliques within its own ecclesiastical and quorum groups." (*Conference Report,* October 1967, p. 9.)

Not only are there apostates within our midst, but there are also apostate doctrines that are sometimes taught in our classes and from our pulpits and that appear in our publications. And these apostate precepts of men cause our people to stumble. As the Book of Mormon, speaking of our day, states: ". . . they have all gone astray save it be a few, who are the humble followers of Christ; nevertheless, they are led, that in many instances they do err because they are taught by the precepts of men." (2 Nephi 28:14.)

Let us consider some of the precepts of men that may and do cause some of the humble followers of Christ to err.

Christ taught that we should be in the world but not of it. Yet there are some in our midst who are not so much concerned about taking the gospel into the world as they are about bringing worldliness into the gospel. They want us to be in the world and of it. They want us to be popular with the world even though a prophet has said that this is impossible, for all hell would then want to join us.

Through their own reasoning and a few misapplied scriptures, they try to sell us the precepts and philosophies of men. They do not feel the Church is progressive enough —they say that it should embrace the social and socialist gospel of apostate Christendom.

They are bothered that the First Presidency believes that "the social side of the Restored Gospel is only an incident of it; it is not the end thereof." (Letter of the First Presidency to Dr. Lowry Nelson, July 17, 1947.)

They attack the Church for not being in the forefront of the so-called civil rights movement. They are embarrassed over some Church doctrine, and as Lehi foretold, the scoffing of the world over this and other matters will cause some of them to be ashamed and they shall fall away. (See 1 Nephi 8:28.)

Unauthorized to receive revelation for the Church, but I fear still anxious to redirect the Church in the way they think it should go, some of them have taken to publishing their differences with the Church, in order to give their heretical views a broader and, they hope, a more respectable platform.

Along this line it would be well for all of us to remember these words of President George Q. Cannon:

A friend . . . wished to know whether we . . . considered an honest difference of opinion between a member of the Church and the Authorities of the Church was apostasy. . . . We replied that we had not stated that an honest difference of opinion between a member of the Church and the Authorities constituted apostasy, for we could conceive of a man honestly differing in opinion from the Authorities of the Church and yet not be an apostate; but we could not conceive of a man publishing those differences of opinion and seeking by arguments, sophistry, and special pleading to enforce them upon the people to produce division and strife and to place the acts and counsels of the Authorities of the Church, if possible, in a wrong light and not be an apostate, for such conduct was apostasy as we understood the term. (*Gospel Truth*, Deseret Book Co., 1974, vol. 2, pp. 276-77.)

The world teaches birth control. Tragically, many of our sisters subscribe to its pills and practices when they could easily provide earthly tabernacles for more of our Father's children. We know that every spirit assigned to this earth will come, whether through us or someone else. There are couples in the Church who think they are getting along just fine with their limited families but who will someday suffer the pains of remorse when they meet the spirits that might have been part of their posterity. The first commandment given to man was to multiply and replenish the earth with children. That commandment has never been altered, modified, or cancelled. The Lord did not say to multiply and replenish the earth if it is convenient, or if you are wealthy, or after you have gotten your schooling, or when there is peace on earth, or until you have four children. The Bible says, "Lo, children, are an heritage of the Lord: . . . Happy is the man that hath his quiver full of them. . . ." (Psalm 127:3, 5.) We believe God is glorified by having numerous children and a program of perfection for them. So also will God glorify that husband and wife who have a large posterity and who try to raise them up in righteousness.

The precepts of men would have you believe that by limiting the population of the world, we can have peace and plenty. That is the doctrine of the devil. Small numbers do not insure peace; only righteousness does. After all, there were only a handful of men on the earth when Cain interrupted the peace of Adam's household by slaying Abel. On the other hand, the whole city of Enoch was peaceful; and it was taken into heaven because it was made up of righteous people.

And so far as limiting the population in order to provide plenty is concerned, the Lord answered that falsehood in the Doctrine and Covenants when he said:

"For the earth is full, and there is enough and to spare; yea, I prepared all things, and have given unto the children of men to be agents unto themselves." (D&C 104:17.)

A major reason why there is famine in some parts of the world is because evil men have used the vehicle of government to abridge the freedom that men need to produce abundantly.

True to form, many of the people who desire to frustrate, through worldwide birth control, God's purposes of giving mortal tabernacles to his spirit children are the very same people who support the kinds of government that perpetuate famine. They advocate an evil to cure the results of the wickedness they support.

The world worships the learning of man. They trust in the arm of flesh. To them, men's reasoning is greater than God's revelations. The precepts of man have gone so far in subverting our educational system that in many cases a higher degree today, in the so-called social sciences, can be tantamount to a major investment in error. Very few men build firmly enough on the rock of revelation to go through this kind of indoctrination and come out untainted. Unfortunately, of those who succumb, some use their higher degree to get teaching positions even in our Church Educational System, where they spread the falsehoods they have been taught. President Joseph F. Smith was right when he said that false educational ideas would be one of these threats to the Church within. (*Gospel Doctrine*, pp. 312-13.)

Another threat, and he said it is the most serious of the three, would be sexual impurity. Today we have both of these threats combined in the growing and increasingly amoral program of sex education in the schools.

President Clark said in regard to this matter:

Many influences (more than ever before in my lifetime) are seeking to break down chastity with its divinely declared sanctity. . . .

In schoolrooms the children are taught what is popularly called "the facts of life." Instead of bringing about the alleged purpose of the teaching, that is, strengthening of the morals of youth, this teaching seems to have had directly the opposite effect. The teaching seems merely to have whetted curiosity and augmented appetite. . . . (*Relief Society Magazine,* December 1952, p. 793.)

. . . A mind engrossed in sex is not good for much else. . . .

Already the schools have taught sex facts *ad nauseam.* All their teachings have but torn away the modesty that once clothed sex; their discussions tend to make, and sometimes seem to make, sex animals of our boys and girls. The teachings do little but arouse curiosity for experience. . . .

A work on chastity can be given in one sentence, two words: Be chaste! That tells everything. You do not need to know all the details of the reproductive processes in order to keep clean. . . . (*Conference Report,* October 1949, p. 194.)

Our *Church News* editorials have warned us about sex education in the schools. As the April 1, 1967, editorial stated: "Sex education belongs in the home. . . . Movements to place sex education in nearly all grades of public schools can end only in the same result which came to Sweden."

In answer to inquiries that have been received by the First Presidency about sex education in the schools, they have made the following statement: "We believe that serious hazards are involved in entrusting to the schools the teaching of this vital and important subject to our children. This responsibility cannot wisely be left to society, nor the schools; nor can the responsibility be shifted to the Church. It is the responsibility of parents to see that they fully perform their duty in this respect."

When you make a close study of the Sex Information

and Education Council of the United States (known as SIECUS), which is the major organization pushing sex education in the schools, and read their literature and learn of their amoral leadership, you can better appreciate why the Church is opposed to sex education in the schools, whether it is called family living program or by any other name. I commend the parents who have worked to keep it out of their schools and those who have pushed it out or are attempting to do so. They must love their children.

Let us consider another precept of men: One of the tragedies of the Korean War was the fact that the enemy was able to brainwash some of our men. Those methods, highly refined and deviously developed, have been introduced on a broad scale into our own country by some behavioral scientists through a program commonly called sensitivity training. While claiming otherwise, the overall effect of this training has been to break down personal standards, encourage immorality, reduce respect for parents, and make well minds sick.

The heart of the training involves trying to get each member of a group to self-criticize and confess as much as possible to the group. Now any informed holder of the priesthood knows that this is directly contrary to the word of the Lord as contained in the Doctrine and Covenants, section 42, verses 88-92. Only when a person has sinned against many people is he to make a public confession.

"If any shall offend in secret, he or she shall be rebuked in secret, that he or she may have opportunity to confess in secret to him or her whom he or she has offended, and to God, that the church may not speak reproachfully of him or her." (D&C 42:92.)

As President Brigham Young put it, ". . . if you have sinned against your God, or against yourselves, confess to God, and keep the matter to yourselves, for I do not want to know anything about it." (Discourses of Brigham Young, Deseret Book, 1943, p. 158.)

But some sensitivity training doesn't stop there. They usually want each person to tell the group about all of their innermost feelings, their personal secrets, their fears, their repressed desires. They have even conducted nudity sessions as a means of supposedly breaking down inhibitions. They want the group to know each other's vulgar thoughts and lustful ideas, their hates, envies, jealousies. But this flies in the face of the counsel of our prophets, one of whom has said, ". . . all such evils you must overcome by suppression. That is where your control comes in. Suppress that anger! Suppress that jealousy, that envy! They are all injurious to the spirit. . . ." (David O. McKay, *Gospel Ideals,* Improvement Era, 1953, p. 356.)

In these sensitivity sessions one's standards, religion, family, and friends may be subjected to brutal and prolonged attack by the group. And when it's all over, if you've confessed all and had your values and ideals smashed, you may doubt if there is much worth believing or defending, and your loyalties may now have been realigned away from your family and church toward the group —for on them you may now feel very dependent, and you may be more anxious to get their consensus on a position and their approval than to find out what's right and do it.

When General William F. Dean was released from a Korean communist prison camp, the young Chinese psychologists who had been trying to break him said: "General, don't feel bad about leaving us. You know, we will soon be with you. We are going to capture your country." Asked how, they replied: "We are going to destroy the moral character of a generation of your young Americans, and when we have finished you will have nothing with which to really defend yourselves against us."

And so the precepts of men are at work on our youth in so many ways. Said President Clark, ". . . a tremendous amount of the modern art, of the modern literature and music, and the drama that we have today is utterly demoralizing—utterly." (*Relief Society Magazine,* December 1952, p. 792.)

Have you been listening to the music that many young folks are hearing today? Some of it is nerve-jamming in nature and much of it has been deliberately designed to promote revolution, dope, immorality, and a gap between parent and child. And some of this music has invaded our Church cultural halls.

Have you noticed some of our Church dances lately? Have they been praiseworthy, lovely, and of good report? "I doubt," said President McKay, "whether it is possible to dance most of the prevalent fad dances in a manner to meet LDS standards." And what about modesty in dress? When was the last time you saw a high school girl wearing a dress that covered her knees? The courageous address of President Spencer W. Kimball a few years ago entitled "A Style of Our Own" is certainly applicable today. (See *Faith Precedes the Miracle,* Deseret Book, 1972, p. 161.)

What kind of magazines come into your home? With perhaps one or two exceptions, I would not have any of the major national slick magazines in my home. As President Clark so well put it. ". . . take up any national magazine, look at the ads and, if you can stand the filth, read some of the stories—they are, in their expressed and suggestive standards of life destructive of the very foundations of our society." (*Conference Report,* April 1951, p. 79.)

Now hear this test proposed by President George Q. Cannon:

> If the breach is daily widening between ourselves and the world . . . we may be assured that our progress is certain, however slow. On the opposite hand, if our feeling and affections, our appetites and desires, are in unison with the world around us and freely fraternize with them . . . we should do well to examine ourselves. Individuals in such a condition might possess a nominal position in the Church but would be lacking the life of the work, and, like the foolish virgins who slum-

bered while the bridegroom tarried, they would be unprepared for his coming. . . . (*Millennial Star,* October 5, 1861 [vol. 23], pp. 645-46.)

To repeat again from the Book of Mormon, ". . . they have all gone astray save it be a few, who are the humble followers of Christ; nevertheless, they are led, that in many instances they do err because they are taught by the precepts of men." (2 Nephi 28:14.)

May we cherish God's revelations more than man's reasoning and choose to follow the prophets of the Lord rather than the precepts of men.

28

Prepare Ye

A revelation of the Lord to Joseph Smith, the Prophet, at a conference of the Church January 2, 1831, reads as follows: ". . . if ye are prepared ye shall not fear." (D&C 38: 30.)

In section 1 of the Doctrine and Covenants we read these words: "Prepare ye, prepare ye for that which is to come." (D&C 1:12.) Further in this same revelation are these warning words: "I the Lord, knowing the calamity which should come upon the inhabitants of the earth. . . ." (D&C 1:17.)

What are some of the calamities for which we are to prepare? In section 29 the Lord warns us of "a great hailstorm sent forth to destroy the crops of the earth." (D&C 29:16.) In section 45 we read of "an overflowing scourge; for a desolating sickness shall cover the land." (D&C 45: 31.) In section 63 the Lord declares he has "decreed wars upon the face of the earth." (D&C 63:33.)

In Matthew, we learn of "famines, and pestilences, and earthquakes. . . ." (Matthew 24:7.) The Lord declared that these and other calamities shall occur. These particular prophecies seem not to be conditional. The Lord, with his foreknowledge, knows that they will happen. Some will come about through man's manipulations; others through the forces of nature and nature's God, but that they will come seems certain. Prophecy is but history in reverse—a divine disclosure of future events.

Yet, through all of this, the Lord Jesus Christ has said: ". . . if ye are prepared ye shall not fear."

What, then, is the Lord's way to help us prepare for these calamities? The answer is also found in section 1 of the Doctrine and Covenants, wherein he says: "Wherefore, I the Lord, knowing the calamity which should come upon the inhabitants of the earth, called upon my servant Joseph Smith, Jun., and spake unto him from heaven, and gave him commandments; And also gave commandments to others. . . ." (D&C 1:17-18.) He has also said: "Search these commandments, for they are true and faithful, and the prophecies and promises which are in them shall all be fulfilled." (D&C 1:37.)

Here then is the key—look to the prophets for the words of God, which will show us how to prepare for the calamities that are to come. For the Lord, in that same section, states: "What I the Lord have spoken, I have spoken, and I excuse not myself; and though the heavens and the earth pass away, my word shall not pass away, but shall all be fulfilled, whether by mine own voice or by the voice of my servants, it is the same." (D&C 1:38.)

Again, the Lord warned those who will reject the inspired words of his representatives: ". . . and the day cometh that they who will not hear the voice of the Lord, neither the voice of his servants, neither give heed to the words of the prophets and apostles, shall be cut off from among the people." (D&C 1:14.)

The present-day Church welfare program was instituted by revelation from God to his mouthpiece, the prophet and earthly President of The Church of Jesus

Christ of Latter-day Saints. It was inaugurated by the First Presidency at a general conference of the Church held in October 1936.

At the April 1937 general conference of the Church, President J. Reuben Clark, Jr., of the First Presidency, asked: "What may we as a people and as individuals do for ourselves to prepare to meet this oncoming disaster, which God in his wisdom may not turn aside from us?" He then set forth these inspired basic principles of the Church welfare program:

First, and above and beyond everything else, let us live righteously. . . .

Let us avoid debt as we would avoid a plague; where we are now in debt, let us get out of debt; if not today, then tomorrow.

Let us straitly and strictly live within our incomes, and save a little.

Let every head of every household see to it that he has on hand enough food and clothing, and, where possible, fuel also, for at least a year ahead. You of small means put your money in foodstuffs and wearing apparel, not in stocks and bonds; you of large means will think you know how to care for yourselves, but I may venture to suggest that you do not speculate. Let every head of every household aim to own his own home, free from mortgage. Let every man who has a garden spot, garden it; every man who owns a farm, farm it. (*Conference Report*, April 1937, p. 26.)

For the righteous, the gospel provides a warning before a calamity, a program for the crises, a refuge for each disaster.

The Lord has said that "the day cometh, that shall burn as an oven. . ." (Malachi 4:1), but he assures us that "he that is tithed shall not be burned. . ." (D&C 64:23). He has warned us of famines, but the righteous will have listened to prophets and stored at least a year's supply of survival food.

The Lord has set loose the angels to reap down the earth (see *Discourses of Wilford Woodruff*, p. 251), but those

who obey the Word of Wisdom along with the other commandments are assured "that the destroying angel shall
pass by them, as the children of Israel, and not slay them."
(D&C 89:21.)

The Lord desires his Saints to be free and independent
in the critical days ahead. But no man is truly free who is
in financial bondage. "Think what you do when you run
in debt," said Benjamin Franklin; "you give to another
power over your liberty." ". . . pay thy debt and live," said
Elisha. (2 Kings 4:7.) And in the Doctrine and Covenants
the Lord says, ". . . it is my will that you shall pay all your
debts." (D&C 104:78.)

For over one hundred years we have been admonished
to store up grain. "Remember the counsel that is given,"
said Elder Orson Hyde, " '. . . Store up all your grain.' and
take care of it! . . . And I tell you it is almost as necessary
to have bread to sustain the body as it is to have food for the
spirit; for the one is as necessary as the other to enable us
to carry on the work of God upon the earth." (*Journal of
Discourses,* vol. 5, p. 17.) He also said: "There is more salvation and security in wheat, than in all the political schemes
of the world. . . ." (*JD*, vol. 2, p. 207.)

As to the foodstuffs which should be stored, the
Church has left that decision primarily to the individual
members. Some excellent suggestions are available from
the Church Welfare Committee. "All grain is good for the
food of man" (D&C 89:16), the Lord states, but he particularly singles out wheat. Dry, whole, hard grains, when
stored properly, can last indefinitely, and their nutritional
value can be enhanced through sprouting, if desired.

It would be well if every family had on hand grain
for at least a year. And may I remind you that it generally
takes several times as much land to produce a given amount
of food when grains are fed to livestock and we consume

the meat. Let us be careful not to overdo beef cattle and other livestock projects on our welfare farms.

From the standpoint of food production, storage, handling, and the Lord's counsel, wheat should have high priority. Water, of course, is essential. Other basics could include honey or sugar, legumes, milk products or substitutes, and salt or its equivalent. The revelation to store food may be as essential to our temporal salvation today as boarding the ark was to the people in the days of Noah.

President Harold B. Lee wisely counseled:

> Perhaps if we think not in terms of a year's supply of what we ordinarily would use, and think more in terms of what it would take to keep us alive in case we didn't have anything else to eat, that last would be very easy to put in storage for a year . . . just enough to keep us alive if we didn't have anything else to eat. We wouldn't get fat on it, but we would live; and if you think in terms of that kind of annual storage rather than a whole year's supply of everything that you are accustomed to eat which, in most cases, is utterly impossible for the average family, I think we will come nearer to what President Clark advised us way back in 1937. (*Ensign*, September 1973, p. 71.)

There are blessings in being close to the soil, in raising your own food, even if it is only a garden in your yard and/ or a fruit tree or two. Man's material wealth basically springs from the land and other natural resources. Combined with his human energy and multiplied by his tools, this wealth is assured and expanded through freedom and righteousness. Those families will be fortunate who, in the last days, have an adequate supply of each of these particulars.

Concerning human energy, we can be grateful for the Word of Wisdom, which tells us it is possible to "run and not be weary, and . . . walk and not faint." (D&C 89:20.) The Lord has advised us to "retire to thy bed early, that ye may not be weary; arise early, that your bodies and your minds may be invigorated." (D&C 88:124.) He has also counseled, "Do not run faster or labor more than you have strength. . . ." (D&C 10:4.)

Healthful foods, proper rest, adequate exercise, and a clean conscience can prepare us to tackle the trials that lie ahead.

Concerning clothing, we should anticipate future needs, such as extra work clothes and clothes that would supply warmth during winter months when there may be shortages or lack of heating fuel. Leather and bolts of cloth could be stored, particularly for families with younger children who will outgrow and perhaps outwear their present clothes.

"The day will come," said President Wilford Woodruff, "when, as we have been told, we shall all see the necessity of making our own shoes and clothing and raising our own food. . . ." (*Discourses of Wilford Woodruff*, p. 166.)

In a message to the Saints in July 1970, President Joseph Fielding Smith stated that the pioneers "were taught by their leaders to produce, as far as possible, all that they consumed. . . . This is still excellent counsel." (*Improvement Era*, July 1970, p. 3.)

Wood, coal, gas, oil, kerosene, and even candles are among those items which could be reserved as fuel for warmth, cooking, and light or power. Some may be used for all of these purposes and certain ones would have to be stored and handled cautiously. It would also be well to have on hand some basic medical supplies to last for at least a year.

Men should seek honorable employment and do their work well in order to provide for their own. Those who can perform useful skills with their hands will be in increasing demand. Handymen, farmers, builders, tailors, gardeners, and mechanics can and will provide a real blessing to their families and their fellowmen.

The Saints have been advised to pay their own way

and maintain a cash reserve. Recent history has demonstrated that in difficult days it is reserves with intrinsic value that are of most worth, rather than reserves the value of which may be destroyed through inflation. It is well to remember that continued government deficits cause inflation; inflation is used as an excuse for ineffective price controls; price controls lead to shortages; artificial shortages inevitably are used as an excuse to implement rationing. When will we learn these basic economic principles?

". . . when we really get into hard times," said President Clark, "where food is scarce or there is none at all, and so with clothing and shelter, money may be no good for there may be nothing to buy, and you cannot eat money, you cannot get enough of it together to burn to keep warm, and you cannot wear it." (*Church News,* November 21, 1953, p. 4.)

The strength of the Church welfare program lies in every family following the inspired direction of the Church leaders to be self-sustaining through adequate preparation. God intends for his saints to so prepare themselves "that the church may stand independent above all other creatures beneath the celestial world." (D&C 78:14.)

"How on the face of the earth could a man enjoy his religion," said Elder George A. Smith many years ago, "when he had been told by the Lord how to prepare for a day of famine, when, instead of doing so, he had fooled away that which would have sustained him and his family." (*JD*, vol. 12, p. 142.)

And President Brigham Young said:

If you are without bread, how much wisdom can you boast, and of what real utility are your talents, if you cannot procure for yourselves and save against a day of scarcity those substances designed to sustain your natural lives? . . . If you cannot provide for your natural lives, how can you expect to have wisdom to obtain eternal lives? (*JD*, vol. 8, p. 68.)

When will all these calamities strike? We do not know the exact time, but it appears that it may be in the not-too-distant future. Those who are prepared now have the continuing blessings of early obedience, and they are ready. Noah built his ark before the flood came, and he and his family survived. Those who waited to act until after the flood began were too late.

Let us not be dissuaded from preparing because of a seeming prosperity today, or a so-called peace.

I have seen the ravages of inflation. I shall never forget Germany in the early 1920s. In December 1923 in Cologne, Germany, I paid six billion marks for breakfast. That was just 15 cents in American money. Today, the real inflation concern is in America and several other nations.

I know that the Church welfare program is inspired of God. I have witnessed with my own eyes the ravages of hunger and destitution as, under the direction of the President of the Church, I spent a year in war-torn Europe at the close of World War II, without my family, distributing food, clothing, and bedding to our needy members. I have looked into the sunken eyes of Saints in almost the last stages of starvation. I have seen faithful mothers carrying their children, three and four years of age, who were unable to walk because of malnutrition. I have seen a hungry woman turn down food for a spool of thread. I have seen grown men weep as they ran their hands through the wheat and beans sent to them from Zion—America.

Thanks be to God for a prophet for this inspired program, and for Saints who so managed their stewardship that they could provide for their own and still share with others. What a marvelous way to become a savior on Mount Zion!

"The time is about ripe," said President Lee, "for the demonstration of the power and efficacy of the Lord's Plan which He designed as 'a light to the world, and to be a standard for my people, and for the Gentiles to seek to it.' " (*Church News*, December 20, 1947, p. 7; see also D&C 45:9.) May we ever remember the Lord's promise: ". . . if ye are prepared ye shall not fear."

Let us live the gospel fully, and may we recognize the infallibility of God's inspired word—whether by his "own voice" or the "voice of [his] my servants, it is the same." The days ahead are sobering and challenging. Oh, may we be prepared spiritually and temporally!

SECTION THREE

COUNTRY

"Yes, I love this nation. To me it is not just another nation, not just a member of the family of nations. It is a great and glorious nation with a divine mission, brought into being under the inspiration of heaven. It is truly a land choice above all others. . . .

"I am grateful that the God of heaven saw fit to put his stamp of approval upon the Constitution to indicate that it had come into being through wise men whom he raised up unto this very purpose."

—ADDRESS AT BRIGHAM YOUNG UNIVERSITY
DECEMBER 4, 1973

29

The Twelfth Article of Faith

When the Prophet Joseph Smith outlined the Articles of Faith, he set forth in clear, unmistakable terms the foundations of our worship and of our relationships with one another. In view of the troubled times which the nations of the earth are experiencing at present, it is well for us as members of the Lord's kingdom to understand clearly our responsibilities and obligations respecting governments and laws as declared in the Twelfth Article of Faith: "We believe in being subject to kings, presidents, rulers, and magistrates, in obeying, honoring, and sustaining the law."

In it is a declaration requiring obedience, loyalty to, and respect for duly constituted laws and the officials administering those laws. In justifying such loyal compliance, however, the Lord also promulgated certain safeguards and conditions which must be observed if freedom and liberty are to be preserved and enjoyed. These are emphasized primarily in the 98th and 134th sections of the Doctrine and Covenants. How I wish these fundamental concepts were emblazoned on the hearts of all our people!

It seems to me there are two thoughts with regard to

governments and laws which might profitably be considered at this time. One relates to the people who administer the laws and the other to the laws themselves. Concerning our public officials, the Lord has counseled: "Nevertheless, when the wicked rule the people mourn. Wherefore, honest men and wise men should be sought for diligently, and good men and wise men ye should observe to uphold; otherwise whatsoever is less than these cometh of evil." (D&C 98:9-10.)

These admonitions, in my humble judgment, are just as binding upon the Latter-day Saints as are the law of tithing, the Word of Wisdom, and baptism. We should seek out honest men and wise men to hold political office in our respective governments. This is the will of the Lord as spoken by revelation.

Many people have had cause for serious reflection of late as they have observed the rise and fall of once glorious and powerful nations. Why, they ask, have nations which have contributed so richly to the fields of literature, music, and the arts and sciences permitted selfish, ambitious men to rise to great power as has been evidenced in several European nations? One of the important reasons, as I have observed it firsthand, is the fact that the citizens generally failed to carry out the admonition which the Lord has given the Latter-day Saints: to seek out their good and wise men to serve as their leaders in political capacities. Men without faith in eternal principles were permitted to rise to power.

We must not think it cannot happen here. We must be eternally vigilant as Latter-day Saints and inspire in the lives of our children a love for eternal principles and a desire to seek out honorable men—the best possible—to stand at the head of our political governments, local, state, and federal. Only in this way can we safeguard the liberties which have been vouchsafed to us as our inalienable rights.

Unless we do so, we may very easily lose them because of our indifference, because of our failure to exercise our franchise, because we permit men who are unworthy to rise to positions of political power.

Not only should we seek humble, worthy, courageous leadership; but we should also measure all proposals having to do with our national or local welfare by four standards:

First, is the proposal, the policy, or the idea being promoted right as measured by the gospel of Jesus Christ? I assure you it is much easier for one to measure a proposed policy by the gospel of Jesus Christ if he has accepted the gospel and is living it.

Second, is it right as measured by the Lord's standard of constitutional government, wherein he says: "And that law of the land which is constitutional, supporting that principle of freedom in maintaining rights and privileges, belongs to all mankind, and is justifiable before me"? (D&C 98:5.) Whether we live under a divinely inspired constitution, as in the United States, or under some other form of government, the Lord's standard is a safe guide.

Third, we might well ask, is it right as measured by the counsel of the living oracles of God? It is my conviction that these living oracles are not only authorized, but are also obligated to give counsel to this people on any subject that is vital to the welfare of this people and to the up-building of the kingdom of God. So that measure should be applied.

Fourth, what will be the effect upon the morale and the character of the people if this or that policy is adopted? After all, as a church, we are interested in building men and women and in building character, because character is the one thing we make in this world and take with us into the next. It must never be sacrificed for expediency.

May we do our duty as citizens and as members of the Church to see to it that the right kind of people are elected to public office, so that the rich blessings that we now enjoy and that have been promised to us may be realized in all the days to come. May we likewise use wisdom and care as we evaluate various proposals and programs, so men everywhere may come to know the joy of living under wise laws honorably administered by men and women intent upon preserving and strengthening man's free agency and ennobling his character.

30

The Proper Role of Government

Men in the public spotlight are constantly asked to express opinions on a myriad of government proposals and projects. "What do you think of TVA?" "What is your opinion of Medicare?" "How do you feel about urban renewal?" The list is endless. All too often, answers to these questions seem to be based, not upon any solid principle, but upon the popularity of the specific government in question. Seldom are men willing to oppose a popular program if they themselves wish to be popular—especially if they seek public office.

Such an approach to vital political questions of the day can only lead to public confusion and legislative chaos. Decisions of this nature should be based upon and measured against certain basic principles regarding the proper role of government. If principles are correct, then they can be applied to any specific proposal with confidence.

Are there not, in reality, underlying, universal principles with reference to which all issues must be resolved whether the society be simple or complex in its mechanical organization? It seems to me we could relieve ourselves of most of the bewilderment which so unsettles and distracts us by subjecting each situation to the simple test of right and wrong. Right and wrong as moral principles do not change. They are applicable and reliable determinants whether the situations with which we deal are simple or complicated. There is always a right and wrong to every question which requires our solution. (Albert E. Bowen, *Conference Report,* October 1944, p. 153.)

Unlike the political opportunist, the true statesman values principle above popularity, and he works to create popularity for those political principles which are wise and just.

I should like to outline in clear, concise, and straightforward terms the political principles to which I subscribe. These are the guidelines which determine, now and in the future, my attitudes and actions toward all domestic proposals and projects of government. These are the principles which, in my opinion, proclaim the proper role of government in the domestic affairs of the nation.

[I] believe that governments were instituted of God for the benefit of man; and that he holds men accountable for their acts in relation to them, both in making laws and administering them, for the good and safety of society.

[I] believe that no government can exist in peace, except such laws are framed and held inviolate as will secure to each individual the free exercise of conscience, the right and control of property, and the protection of life.

[I] believe that all men are bound to sustain and uphold the respective governments in which they reside, while protected in their inherent and inalienable rights by the laws of such governments; and that sedition and rebellion are unbecoming every citizen thus protected, and should be punished accordingly; and that all governments have a right to enact such laws as in their own judgments are best calculated to secure the public interest; at the same time, however, holding sacred the freedom of conscience. (D&C 134:1-2, 5.)

It is generally agreed that the single most important function of government is to secure the rights and freedoms of individual citizens. But what are those rights? And what is their source? Until these questions are answered, there is little likelihood that we can correctly determine *how* government can best secure them.

Thomas Paine, back in the days of the American Revolution, explained that "rights are not gifts from one man to another, nor from one class of men to another. . . . It is impossible to discover any origin of rights otherwise than in the origin of man; it consequently follows that rights appertain to man in right of his existence, and must therefore be equal to every man."

The great Thomas Jefferson asked: "Can the liberties of a nation be thought secure when we have removed their only firm basis, a conviction in the minds of the people that these liberties are of the gift of God? That they are not to be violated but with his wrath?" (*Notes on Virginia,* 1781, Query XVIII.)

Starting at the foundation of the pyramid, let us first consider the origin of those freedoms we have come to know as human rights. There are only two possible sources. Rights are either God-given as part of the divine plan or they are granted by government as part of the political plan. Reason, necessity, tradition, and religious convictions all lead me to accept the divine origin of these rights. If we accept the premise that human rights are granted by government, then we must be willing to accept the corollary that they can be denied by government. I, for one, shall never accept that premise. As the French political economist, Frederick Bastiat, phrased it so succinctly, "Life, liberty, and property do not exist because men have made laws. On the contrary, it was the fact that life, liberty, and property existed beforehand that caused men to make laws in the first place." (*The Law,* 1850, p. 6.)

I support the doctrine of separation of church and state as traditionally interpreted to prohibit the establishment of an official national religion. But I am opposed to the doctrine of separation of church and state as currently interpreted to divorce government from any formal recognition of God. The current trend strikes a potentially fatal blow at the concept of the divine origin of our rights and unlocks the door for an easy entry of future tyranny. If Americans should ever come to believe that their rights and freedoms are instituted among men by politicians and bureaucrats, then they will no longer carry the proud inheritance of their forefathers, but will grovel before their masters seeking favors and dispensations—a throwback to the feudal system of the Dark Ages. We must ever keep in mind the inspired words of Thomas Jefferson, as found in the Declaration of Independence:

> We hold these truths to be self-evident: that all men are created equal; that they are endowed by their Creator with certain inalienable rights; that among these are life, liberty, and the pursuit of happiness. That to secure these rights, governments are instituted among men, deriving their just powers from the consent of the governed. . . .

Since God created man with certain inalienable rights, and man, in turn, created government to help secure and safeguard those rights, it follows that man is superior to government and should remain master over it, not the other way around. Even the nonbeliever can appreciate the logic of this relationship.

Leaving aside, for a moment, the question of the divine origin of rights, it is obvious that a government is nothing more nor less than a relatively small group of citizens who have been hired, in a sense, by the rest of us to perform certain functions and discharge certain responsibilities which have been authorized. It stands to reason that the government itself has no innate power or privilege to do anything. Its only source of authority and power is from the people who have created it. This is made clear in the Preamble to the Constitution of the United States, which reads: "We the people . . . do ordain and establish this Constitution for the United States of America. . . ."

The important thing to keep in mind is that the people who have created their government can give to that government only such powers as they themselves have in the first place. Obviously, they cannot give that which they do not possess. So the question boils down to this: What powers properly belong to each and every person in the absence of and prior to the establishment of any organized governmental form? A hypothetical question? Yes, indeed! But it is a question that is vital to an understanding of the principles that underlie the proper function of government.

As James Madison, sometimes called the father of the Constitution, said, "If men were angels, no government would be necessary. If angels were to govern men, neither external nor internal controls on government would be necessary." (*The Federalist,* no. 51.)

In a primitive state, there is no doubt that each man would be justified in using force, if necessary, to defend himself against physical harm, against theft of the fruits of his labor, and against enslavement of another. This principle was clearly explained by Bastiat:

> Each of us has a natural right—from God—to defend his person, his liberty, and his property. These are the three basic requirements of life, and the preservation of any one of them is completely dependent upon the preservation of the other two. For what are our faculties but the extension of our individuality? And what is property but an extension of our faculties? (*The Law,* p. 6.)

Indeed, the early pioneers found that a great deal of their time and energy was being spent doing all three—defending themselves, their property, and their liberty—in what properly was called the lawless West. In order for man to prosper, he cannot afford to spend his time constantly guarding his family, his fields, and his property against attack and theft, so he joins together with his neighbors and hires a sheriff. At this precise moment, government is born. The individual citizens delegate to the sheriff their unquestionable right to protect themselves. The sheriff now does for them only what they had a right to do for themselves—nothing more. Quoting again from Bastiat:

> If every person has the right to defend—even by force—his person, his liberty, and his property, then it follows that a group of men have the right to organize and support a common force to protect these rights constantly. Thus the principle of collective right—its reason for existing, its lawfulness—is based on individual right.

So far so good. But now we come to the moment of truth. Suppose pioneer "A" wants another horse for his wagon. He doesn't have the money to buy one, but since pioneer "B" has an extra horse, he decides that he is entitled to share in his neighbor's good fortune. Is he entitled to take his neighbor's horse? Obviously not. If his neighbor wishes to give it or lend it, that is another question. But so long as pioneer "B" wishes to keep his property, pioneer "A" has no just claim to it.

If "A" has no proper power to take "B's" property, can he delegate any such power to the sheriff? No. Even if everyone in the community desires that "B" give his extra horse to "A," they have no right individually or collectively to force him to do it. They cannot delegate a power they themselves do not have. This important principle was clearly understood and explained by John Locke nearly 300 years ago: "For nobody can transfer to another more power than he has in himself, and nobody has an absolute arbitrary power over himself, or over any other, to destroy his own life, or take away the life or property of another." (*Two Treatises of Civil Government*, 1690, Book 2, no. 135.)

This means, then, that the proper function of government is limited only to those spheres of activity within which the individual citizen has the right to act. By deriving its just powers from the governed, government becomes primarily a mechanism for defense against bodily harm, theft, and involuntary servitude. It cannot claim the power to redistribute the wealth or force reluctant citizens to perform acts of charity against their will. Government is created by man. No man possesses such power to delegate. The creature cannot exceed the creator.

In general terms, therefore, the proper role of government includes such defensive activities as maintaining national military and local police forces for protection against loss of life, loss of property, and loss of liberty at the hands of either foreign despots or domestic criminals. It also includes those powers necessarily incidental to the protective functions, such as:

1. The maintenance of courts where those charged with crimes may be tried and where disputes between citizens may be impartially settled.

2. The establishment of a monetary system and a standard of weights and measures so that courts may render money judgments, taxing authorities may levy taxes, and citizens may have a uniform standard to use in their business dealings.

My attitude toward government is succinctly expressed by the following provision taken from the Alabama Constitution: "That the sole object and only legitimate end of government is to protect the citizen in the enjoyment of life, liberty, and property, and when the government assumes other functions it is usurpation and oppression." (Article I, section 35.)

An important test I use in passing judgment upon an act of government is this: If it were up to me as an individual to punish my neighbor for violating a given law, would it offend my conscience to do so? Since my conscience will never permit me to physically punish my fellowman unless he has done something evil or unless he has failed to do something that I have a moral right to require him to do, I will never knowingly authorize my agent, the government, to do this on my behalf.

I realize that when I give my consent to the adoption of a law, I specifically instruct the police—the government —to take either the life, liberty, or property of anyone who disobeys that law. Furthermore, I tell them that if anyone resists the enforcement of the law, they are to use any means necessary—yes, even putting the law-breaker to death or putting him in jail—to overcome such resistance. These are extreme measures but unless laws are enforced, anarchy results.

As John Locke explained many years ago:

> The end of law is not to abolish or restrain, but to preserve and enlarge freedom. For in all the states of created beings, capable of laws, *where there is no law there is no freedom.* For liberty is to be free from restraint and violence from others, which cannot be where there is no law; and is not, as we are told, "a liberty for every man to do what he lists." For who could be free, when every other man's humour might domineer over him? But a liberty to dispose and order freely as he lists his person, actions, possessions, and his whole property within the allowance of those laws under which he is, and therein not to be subject to the arbitrary will of another, but freely follow his own. (*Two Treatises,* Book 2, no. 57.)

I believe we Americans should use extreme care before lending our support to any proposed government program. We should fully recognize that government is no plaything. As George Washington warned, "Government is not reason, it is not eloquence—it is force! Like fire, it is a dangerous servant and a fearful master!" It is an instrument of force, and unless our conscience is clear that we would not hesitate to put a man to death, put him in jail, or forcibly deprive him of his property for failing to obey a given law, we should oppose it.

Another standard I use in determining what law is good and what is bad is the Constitution of the United States. I regard this inspired document as a solemn agreement between the citizens of this nation that every officer of government is under a sacred duty to obey. As Washington stated so clearly in his immortal Farewell Address:

> The basis of our political systems is the right of the people to make and to alter their constitutions of government.—But the constitution which at any time exists, until changed by an explicit and authentic act of the whole people is sacredly obligatory upon all. The very idea of the power and the right of the people to establish government presuppose the duty of every individual to obey the established government. (September 17, 1796.)

I am especially mindful that the Constitution provides that the great majority of the legitimate activities of government are to be carried out at the state or local level. This is the only way in which the principle of self-government can be made effective. As James Madison said before the adoption of the Constitution, "We rest all our political experiments on the capacity of mankind for self-government." (*The Federalist,* no. 39.) Thomas Jefferson made this interesting observation: "Sometimes it is said that man cannot be trusted with the government of himself. Can he, then, be trusted with the government of others? Or have we found angels in the forms of kings to govern him? Let history answer this question." (*Inaugural Address,* March 4, 1801.)

It is a firm principle that the smallest or lowest level that can possibly undertake the task is the one that should do so. First, the community or city. If the city cannot handle it, then the county. Next, the state; and only if no smaller unit can possibly do the job should the federal government be considered. This is merely the application to the field of politics of that wise and time-tested principle of never asking a larger group to do that which can be done by a smaller group. And so far as government is concerned, the smaller the unit and the closer it is to the people, the easier it is to guide it, to correct it, to keep it solvent, and to keep our freedom. Thomas Jefferson understood the principle very well and explained it this way:

> The way to have good and safe government, is not to trust it all to one, but to divide it among the many, distributing to every one exactly the functions he is competent to. Let the national government be entrusted with the defense of the nation, and its foreign and federal relations; the State governments with the civil rights, law, police, and administration of what concerns the State generally; the counties with the local concerns of the counties, and each ward direct the interests within itself. It is by dividing and subdividing these republics from the great national one down through all its subordinations, until it ends in the administration of every man's farm by himself; by placing under every one what his own eye may superintend, that all will be done for the best. What has destroyed liberty and the rights of man in every government which has ever existed under the sun? The generalizing and concentrating all cares and powers into one body. (Letter to Joseph C. Cabell, February 2, 1816.)

It is well to remember that the people of the states of this republic created the federal government. The federal government did not create the states.

A category of government activity that today not only requires the closest scrutiny, but that also poses a grave danger to our continued freedom, is the activity *not* within the proper sphere of government. No one has the authority to grant such powers as welfare programs, schemes for redistributing the wealth, and activities that coerce people into acting in accordance with a prescribed code of social planning. There is one simple test. Do I as an individual have a right to use force upon my neighbor to accomplish this goal? If I do have such a right, then I may delegate that power to my government to exercise on my behalf. If I do not have that right as an individual, then I cannot delegate it to government, and I cannot ask my government to perform the act for me.

To be sure, there are times when this principle of the proper role of government is most annoying and inconvenient. If I could only *force* the ignorant to provide for themselves, or the selfish to be generous with their wealth! But if we permit government to manufacture its own authority out of thin air and to create self-proclaimed powers not delegated to it by the people, then the creature exceeds the creator and becomes master. Beyond that point, where shall the line be drawn? Who is to say "this far, but no further"? What clear principle will stay the hand of government from reaching further and yet further into our daily lives? We shouldn't forget the wise words of President Grover Cleveland, that "though the people support the Government the Government should not support the people." (*Messages and Papers of the Presidents*, vol. 8, p. 557.) We should also remember, as Frederick Bastiat reminded us, that "nothing can enter the public treasury for the benefit of one citizen or one class unless other citizens and other classes have been forced to send it in." (*The Law*, p. 30.)

As Bastiat pointed out over a hundred years ago, once government steps over this clear line between the protective or negative role into the aggressive role of redistributing the wealth and providing so-called benefits for some of its citizens, it then becomes a means for what he accurately described as legalized plunder. It becomes a lever of unlimited power, which is the sought-after prize of unscrupulous individuals and pressure groups, each seeking to control the machine to fatten his own pockets or to benefit its favorite charities—all with the other fellow's money, of course.

Listen to Bastiat's explanation of this "legal plunder":

When a portion of wealth is transferred from the person who owns it—without his consent and without compensation, and whether by force or by fraud—to anyone who does not own it, then I say that property is violated; that an act of plunder is committed. . . .

How is this legal plunder to be identified? Quite simply. See if the law takes from some persons what belongs to them, and gives it to other persons to whom it does not belong. See if the law benefits one citizen at the expense of another by doing what the citizen himself cannot do without committing a crime. . . . (*The Law*, p. 21, 26.)

As Bastiat observed, and as history has proven, each class or special interest group competes with the others to throw the lever of governmental power in their favor, or at least to immunize itself against the effects of a previous thrust. Labor gets a minimum wage, so agriculture seeks a price support. Consumers demand price controls, and industry gets protective tariffs. In the end, no one is much further ahead, and everyone suffers the burdens of a gigantic bureaucracy and a loss of personal freedom. With each group out to get its share of the spoils, such governments historically have mushroomed into total welfare states. Once the process begins, once the principle of the protective function of government gives way to the aggressive or redistributive function, then forces are set in motion that drive the nation toward totalitarianism. "It is impossible," Bastiat correctly observed, ". . . to introduce into society . . . a greater evil than this: the conversion of the law into an instrument of plunder." (*The Law*, p. 12.)

Students of history know that no government in the history of mankind has ever created any wealth. People who work create wealth. James R. Evans, in his inspiring book *The Glorious Quest*, gives this simple illustration of legalized plunder:

Assume, for example, that we were farmers, and that we received a letter from the government telling us that we were going to get a thousand dollars this year for ploughed up acreage. But rather than the normal method of collection, we were to take this letter and collect $69.71 from Bill Brown, at such and such an address, and $82.47 from Henry Jones, $59.80 from a Bill Smith, and so on down the line; that these men would make up our farm subsidy.

Neither you nor I, nor would 99 per cent of the farmers, walk up and ring a man's doorbell, hold out a hand and say, "Give me what you've earned even though I have not." We simply wouldn't do it because we would be facing directly the violation of a moral law, "Thou shalt not steal." In short, we would be held accountable for our actions.

The free creative energy of this choice nation "created more than 50% of all the world's products and possessions in the short span of 160 years. The only imperfection in the system is the imperfection in man himself."

The last paragraph in this remarkable Evans book—which I commend to all—reads:

No historian of the future will ever be able to prove that the ideas of individual liberty practiced in the United States of America were a failure. He may be able to prove that we were not yet worthy of them. The choice is ours. (Chicago: Charles Haelberg and Company.)

According to Marxist doctrine, a human being is primarily an economic creature. In other words, his material well-being is all important; his privacy and his freedom are strictly secondary. The Soviet constitution reflects this philosophy in its emphasis on security: food, clothing, housing, medical care—the same things that might be considered in a jail. The basic concept is that the government has full responsibility for the welfare of the people and, in order to discharge that responsibility, must assume control of all their activities. It is significant that in actuality the Russian people have few of the rights supposedly guaranteed to them in their constitution, while the American people have them in abundance even though they are not guaranteed. The reason, of course, is that material gain and economic security simply cannot be guaranteed by any government. They are the result and reward of hard work and industrious production. Unless the people bake one loaf of bread for each citizen, the government cannot guarantee that each will have one loaf to eat. Constitutions can be written, laws can be passed, and imperial decrees can be issued, but unless the bread is produced, it can never be distributed.

Why, then, do Americans bake more bread, manufacture more shoes, and assemble more TV sets than Russians do? They do so precisely because our government does *not* guarantee these things. If it did, there would be so many accompanying taxes, controls, regulations, and political manipulations that the productive genius that is America's would soon be reduced to the floundering level of waste and inefficiency now found behind the iron curtain. As Henry D. Thoreau explained:

> This government never of itself furthered any enterprise, but by the alacrity with which it got out of its way. *It* does not keep the country free. *It* does not settle the West. *It* does not educate. The character inherent in the American people has done all that has been accomplished; and it would have done somewhat more, if the government had not sometimes got in its way. For government is an expedient by which men would fain succeed in letting one another alone; and, as has been said, when it is most expedient, the governed are most let alone by it. (*Civil Disobedience*, 1849.)

In 1801 Thomas Jefferson, in his First Inaugural Address, said:

> With all these blessings, what more is necessary to make us a happy and prosperous people? Still one thing more, fellow citizens—a wise and frugal government, which shall restrain men from injuring one another, which shall leave them otherwise free to regulate their own pursuits of industry and improvement, and shall not take from the mouth of labor the bread it had earned.

The principle behind this American philosophy can be reduced to a rather simple formula:

1. Economic security for all is impossible without widespread abundance.

2. Abundance is impossible without industrious and efficient production.

3. Such production is impossible without energetic, willing, and eager labor.

4. This is not possible without incentive.

5. Of all forms of incentive, the freedom to attain a reward for one's labors is the most sustaining for most people. Sometimes called the profit motive, it is simply the right to plan and to earn and to enjoy the fruits of your labor.

6. This profit motive diminishes as government controls, regulations, and taxes increase to deny the fruits of success to those who produce.

7. Therefore, any attempt through governmental intervention to redistribute the material rewards of labor can only result in the eventual destruction of the productive base of society, without which real abundance and security for more than the ruling elite is quite impossible. (See G. Edward Griffin, *The Fearful Master*, 1964, p. 128.)

We have before us currently a sad example of what happens to a nation which ignores these principles. Former FBI agent Dan Smoot succinctly pointed this out as follows:

> England was killed by an idea: the idea that the weak, indolent, and profligate must be supported by the strong, industrious, and frugal —to the degree that tax consumers will have a living standard comparable to that of taxpayers; the idea that government exists for the purpose of plundering those who work to give the product of their labor to those who do not work.
>
> The economic and social cannibalism produced by this communist-socialist idea will destroy any society which adopts it and clings to it as a basic principle—any society. (Broadcast no. 649, January 29, 1968.)

Nearly two hundred years ago, Adam Smith, the Englishman, who understood these principles very well, published his great book *The Wealth of Nations*, which contains this statement:

> The natural effort of every individual to better his own condition when suffered to exert itself with freedom and security, is so powerful a principle, that it is alone, and without any assistance, not

only capable of carrying on the society to wealth and prosperity, but of surmounting a hundred impertinent obstructions with which the folly of human laws too often incumbers its operations; though the effect of these obstructions is always more or less either to encroach upon its freedom, or to diminish its security. (Book 4, chapter 5.)

On the surface this may sound heartless and insensitive to the needs of those less fortunate individuals who are found in any society, no matter how affluent. "What about the lame, the sick, and the destitute?" is an often-voiced question. Most other countries in the world have attempted to use the power of government to meet this need. Yet, in every case, the improvement has been marginal at best and has resulted, in the long run, in creating more misery, more poverty, and certainly less freedom than when government first stepped in. As Henry Grady Weaver wrote in his excellent book *The Mainspring of Human Progress:*

> Most of the major ills of the world have been caused by well-meaning people who ignored the principle of individual freedom, except as applied to themselves, and who were obsessed with fanatical zeal to improve the lot of mankind-in-the-mass through some pet formula of their own. . . . The harm done by ordinary criminals, murderers, gangsters, and thieves is negligible in comparison with the agony inflicted upon human beings by the professional "do-gooders," who attempt to set themselves up as gods on earth and who would ruthlessly force their views on all others—with the abiding assurance that the end justifies the means. (The Foundation for Economic Education, 1953, p. 313.)

By comparison, America traditionally has followed Jefferson's advice of relying on individual action and charity. The result is that the United States has fewer cases of genuine hardship per capita than any other country in the entire world or throughout all history. Even during the depression of the 1930s, Americans ate and lived better than most people in other countries do today.

In reply to the argument that just a little bit of socialism is good so long as it doesn't go too far, it is tempting to say that, in like fashion, just a little bit of theft or a little bit of cancer is all right too! History proves that the growth of the welfare state is difficult to check before it comes to its full flower of dictatorship. But let us hope that this time around, the trend can be reversed. If not, then we will see the inevitability of complete socialism, probably within our lifetime.

Three factors may make a difference. First, there is sufficient historical knowledge of the failures of socialism and of the past mistakes of previous civilizations. Second, there are modern means of rapid communication to transmit these lessons of history to a large literate population. And third, there is a growing number of dedicated men and women who, at great personal sacrifice, are actively working to promote a wider appreciation of these concepts. The timely joining together of these three factors may make it entirely possible for us to reverse the trend.

This brings up the next question: How is it possible to cut out the various welfare-state features of our government that have already fastened themselves like cancer cells onto the body politic? Isn't drastic surgery already necessary, and can it be performed without endangering the patient? In answer, it is obvious that drastic measures *are* called for. No half-way or compromise actions will suffice. Like all surgery, it will not be without discomfort and perhaps even some scar tissue for a long time to come. But it must be done if the patient is to be saved, and it can be done without undue risk.

Obviously, not all welfare-state programs currently in force can be dropped simultaneously without causing tremendous economic and social upheaval. To try to do so would be like finding oneself at the controls of a hijacked airplane and attempting to return it by simply cutting off the engines in flight. It must be flown back, lowered in altitude, gradually reduced in speed, and brought in for a smooth landing. Translated into practical terms, this means that the first step toward restoring the limited concept of government should be to freeze all welfare-state programs at their present level, making sure that no new ones are added. The next step would be to allow all present programs to run out their term with absolutely no renewal. The third step would involve the gradual phasing-out of those programs which are indefinite in their term. In my opinion, the bulk of the transition could be accomplished within a ten-year period and virtually completed within twenty years. Congress would serve as the initiator of this phase-out program, and the President would act as the executive in accordance with traditional constitutional procedures.

As I summarize what I have attempted to cover, try to visualize the structural relationship between the six vital concepts that have made America the envy of the world. I have reference to the foundation of the *divine origin of rights, limited government,* and pillars of *economic freedom and personal freedom,* which result in *abundance,* followed by *security and the pursuit of happiness.*

America was built upon a firm foundation and created over many years from the bottom up. Other nations, impatient to acquire equal abundance, security, and pursuit of happiness, rush headlong into that final phase of construction without building adequate foundations or supporting pillars. Their efforts are futile. And even in our country, there are those who think that, because we now have the good things in life, we can afford to dispense with the foundations that have made them possible. They want to remove any recognition of God from governmental institutions. They want to expand the scope and reach of government that will undermine and erode our economic and personal freedoms. The abundance that is ours, the carefree existence that we have come to accept as a matter of course, can be toppled by these foolish experimenters and power seekers. By the grace of God, and with his help, we shall fence them off from the foundations of our liberty and then begin our task of repair and construction.

As a fitting summary to this discussion, I present a declaration of principles that have recently been prepared by a few American patriots, and to which I wholeheartedly subscribe.

As an independent American for constitutional government I declare that:

1. I believe that no people can maintain freedom unless their political institutions are founded upon faith in God and belief in the existence of moral law.

2. I believe that God has endowed men with certain inalienable rights as set forth in the Declaration of Independence and that no legislature and no majority, however great, may morally limit or destroy these; that the sole function of government is to protect life, liberty, and property, and anything more than this is usurpation and oppression.

3. I believe that the Constitution of the United States was prepared and adopted by men acting under inspiration from Almighty God; that it is a solemn compact between the peoples of the states of this nation that all officers of government are under duty to obey; that the eternal moral laws expressed therein must be adhered to or individual liberty will perish.

4. I believe it a violation of the Constitution for government to deprive the individual of either life, liberty, or property except for these purposes:

   a. To punish crime and provide for the administration of justice;

   b. To protect the right and control of private property;

c. To wage defensive war and provide for the nation's defense;

d. To compel each one who enjoys the protection of government to bear his fair share of the burden of performing the above functions.

5. I hold that the Constitution denies government the power to take from the individual either his life, liberty, or property except in accordance with moral law; that the same moral law which governs the actions of men when acting alone is also applicable when they act in concert with others; that no citizen or group of citizens has any right to direct their agent, the government, to perform any act that would be evil or offensive to the conscience if that citizen were performing the act himself outside the framework of government.

6. I am hereby resolved that under no circumstances shall the freedoms guaranteed by the Bill of Rights be infringed. In particular I am opposed to any attempt on the part of the federal government to deny the people their right to bear arms, to worship, and to pray when and where they choose, or to own and control private property.

7. I consider ourselves at war with international communism, which is committed to the destruction of our government, our right of property, and our freedom; that it is treason as defined by the Constitution to give aid and comfort to this implacable enemy.

8. I am unalterably opposed to socialism, either in whole or in part, and regard it as an unconstitutional usurpation of power and a denial of the right of private property for government to own or operate the means of producing and distributing goods and services in competition with private enterprise, or to regiment owners in the legitimate use of private property.

9. I maintain that every person who enjoys the protection of his life, liberty, and property should bear his fair

share of the cost of government in providing that protection; that the elementary principles of justice set forth in the Constitution demand that all taxes imposed be uniform; and that each person's property or income be taxed at the same rate.

10. I believe in honest money, the gold and silver coinage of the Constitution, and a circulating medium convertible into such money without loss. I regard it as a flagrant violation of the explicit provisions of the Constitution for the federal government to make it a criminal offense to use gold or silver coin as legal tender or to issue irredeemable paper money.

11. I believe that each state is sovereign in performing those functions reserved to it by the Constitution, and it is destructive of our federal system and the right of self-government guaranteed under the Constitution for the federal government to regulate or control the states in performing their functions or to engage in performing such functions itself.

12. I consider it a violation of the Constitution for the federal government to levy taxes for the support of state or local government; that no state or local government can accept funds from the federal government and remain independent in performing its functions, nor can the citizens exercise their rights of self-government under such conditions.

13. I deem it a violation of the right of private property guaranteed under the Constitution for the federal government to forcibly deprive the citizens of this nation of their property through taxation or otherwise, and make a gift thereof to foreign governments or their citizens.

14. I believe that no treaty or agreement with other countries should deprive our citizens of rights guaranteed them by the Constitution.

15. I consider it a direct violation of the obligation

imposed upon it by the Constitution for the federal government to dismantle or weaken our military establishment below that point required for the protection of the states against invasion, or to surrender or commit our men, arms, or money to the control of foreign or world organizations or governments.

These things I believe to be the proper role of government. We have strayed far afield. We must return to basic concepts and principles—to eternal verities. There is no other way. The storm signals are up. They are clear and ominous.

As Americans—citizens of the greatest nation under heaven—we face difficult days. Never since the days of the Civil War has this choice nation faced such a crisis.

In closing I wish to refer you to the words of the patriot Thomas Paine, whose writings helped so much to stir into a flaming spirit the smoldering embers of patriotism during the days of the American Revolution:

> These are the times that try men's souls. The summer soldier and the sunshine patriot will in this crisis, shrink from the service of his country; but he that stands it now, deserves the love and thanks of man and woman. Tyranny, like hell, is not easily conquered; yet we have this consolation with us, that the harder the conflict, the more glorious the triumph. What we obtain too cheap, we esteem too lightly; 'tis dearness only that gives everything its value. Heaven knows how to put a proper price upon its goods; and it would be strange indeed, if so celestial an article as freedom should not be highly rated. (*The American Crisis*, no. 1, 1776.)

President Theodore Roosevelt warned that "the things that will destroy America are prosperity at any price, peace at any price, safety first instead of duty first, and love of soft living, and the get-rich-quick theory of life."

I intend to keep fighting. My personal attitude is one of resolution—not resignation.

I have faith in the American people. I pray that we will never do anything that will jeopardize in any manner our priceless heritage. If we live and work so as to enjoy the approbation of a Divine Providence, we cannot fail. Without that help we cannot long endure.

So I urge all Americans to put their courage to the test. Be firm in our conviction that our cause is just. Reaffirm our faith in all things for which true Americans have always stood.

I urge all Americans to arouse themselves and stay aroused. We must not make any further concessions to communism at home or abroad. We do not need to. We should oppose communism from our position of strength, for we are not weak.

"We are not cowards," said Ted Dealey of the Dallas *Morning News*, "and will not wallow in the sloughs of degradation. We do not want to be lulled to sleep any more. We are awake and angry and intend to remain so."

There is much work to be done. The time is short. Let us begin—in earnest—now, and may God bless our efforts, I humbly pray.

31
Survival of the American Way of Life

The phrase "survival of the American way of life" carries a somewhat different connotation to various groups even within the United States. Probably to no other group will it bring a more significant meaning in terms of farms of America than to those who operate our farms and ranches. As one who has been reared among them, served them, and been served by them, I declare that our rural people are today the strongest bulwark we have against all that is aimed not only at weakening, but also at the very destruction of our American way of life. It seems that man must get his feet into the soil to keep sane. In any event, no other segment of our population knows so well that "as ye sow, so shall ye reap." America and the world must learn this eternal truth. Failure to do so can bring only disappointment, suffering, and desperation.

It is not surprising that we should turn our thoughts to a consideration of those factors which will determine in large measure our future success and happiness as a nation through the preservation of the American way of life. What, then, is the American way of life? What are its fruits? Do we really want our free enterprise system to survive?

If you could have spent a recent year with me in war-torn Europe, that which you would have seen would have given the answers. It is heartrending to see people who have lost their freedom of choice—their free agency—and who feel no security; who have no homes they can call their own; who own no property; whose hearts are filled with hatred, distrust, and fear of the future.

The outlook for free enterprise in the world has never seemed so uncertain as now. A world survey by the New York *Times* shows that nationalization is growing rapidly, especially outside the western hemisphere. Many nations have a mixed economy brought about by an increase in state control and a corresponding weakening of the private enterprise system. Under various forms of socialism and communism, the growth of governmental restrictions and nationalization goes on apace. The seriousness of the situation demands careful reflection by all interested in the preservation and perpetuation of our system of individual free enterprise, predicated, as it is, on a democratic capitalistic economy under a republican form of government.

The New York *Times* also printed the results of a survey of twenty-two nations, made by correspondents—and of all the countries, Canada appeared to be the only one in which private enterprise "can be said to be functioning today with anything like the freedom from governmental controls that obtains in the United States."

Millions of people today have become slaves to the state. The dignity and value of the individual, except as a tool of government, have vanished in many parts of the world. We have experienced in years past in many nations, including America, the slavery of person to person. We fought two great wars to settle these issues in our own land. The first was a fight for national freedom; the second was a fight for freedom of person from person. The current question, and one that has brought and is bringing so much sorrow and misery to people in many parts of Europe, is that of slavery of the individual to the state.

Should we as American citizens be concerned? We need not think it cannot happen here.

Fortunately, the founding fathers of this great land, under the benign influence of a kind Providence, established a solid foundation aimed at guaranteeing a maximum of individual freedom, happiness, and well-being. "We hold these truths to be self-evident," they said in the Declaration of Independence, "that all men are created equal; that they are endowed by their Creator with certain inalienable rights; that among these are life, liberty, and the pursuit of happiness. That to secure these rights, governments are instituted among men, deriving their just powers from the consent of the governed." This inspired document proclaims clearly that governments should be established on such principles as "seem most likely to effect" the "safety and happiness" of the people. The Constitution of the United States, which Gladstone has described as "the most wonderful work ever struck off at a given time by the brain and purpose of man," was aimed to "establish justice, insure domestic tranquillity, provide for the common defense, promote the general welfare, and secure the blessings of liberty to ourselves and our posterity."

In these sacred documents are embodied eternal principles that no man, group of men, or nation has the right to withhold from others. Here is our basis for freedom of individual achievement. Our Constitution with its Bill of Rights guarantees to all our people the greatest freedom ever enjoyed by the people of any great nation. This system guarantees freedom of individual enterprise, freedom to own property, freedom to start one's own business and to operate it according to one's own judgment so long as the enterprise is honorable.

The individual has power to produce beyond his needs, to provide savings for the future protection of himself and family. He can live where he wishes and pick any job he wants and select any educational opportunity. He is, to a high degree, free through his own hard work and wise management to make a profit, to invest in any enterprise he may choose, and to leave a part of his accumulation to be inherited by others as they may, in large measure, determine. He may enjoy the sacred rights of freedom of speech, freedom of assembly, freedom of the press, and freedom of worship. To this American entrepreneur his home is his castle, and in the event that he is accused of an offense against the laws established by the people, he has the right of trial by a jury made up of his own fellow citizens.

All these and more, embodied in written documents that cannot be changed easily and quickly to suit the whim of some would-be dictator, are our heritage under the American way of life. Here is freedom guaranteed by the limitation of government through a written constitution. Do we recognize and fully appreciate the priceless value of this legacy? Now, while the world is in commotion and turmoil over ideologies and political philosophies, is a good time to reflect upon the past. It is a good time to draw a few comparisons—to take stock.

Under these principles of freedom and enterprise America has become the richest nation under heaven and has grown to be the most powerful and influential nation in the world, using an economy based upon freedom of individual achievement. Here has been established the most highly developed industrial system in the world, together with the technological equipment, human and otherwise, to support it.

Our republic has now been an operating unit for almost two centuries. During that period we have developed a productive plant and a way of life that have given the highest standard of living for the masses known to the civilized world. In the long run, a nation enjoys in the form of goods and services only what it produces. We have established an all-time record of production.

Within the past century we have received a huge increase in net output per man-hour. These vast gains in human welfare have lessened human toil. At the time of the Civil War the average work week was seventy hours. In America the inventive genius provides horse-drawn and tractor-drawn equipment, and one family can cultivate 50, 100, 200, or even 400 acres and more. A man working by hand has the physical force of one-tenth of a horse. A man with a ten-horsepower tractor has ninety times that much power. American ingenuity under freedom of choice has harnessed tremendous amounts of mineral energy to do physical work. Most occupations in the United States today require more horse sense than horsepower. Under our free enterprise system there are good reasons to believe that the technological progress of the past will continue in the future, perhaps at an accelerated rate.

Our free enterprise system also allows for all necessary flexibility. No other economic program responds so readily to changes in wartime and peacetime demands. Witness what happened after the fall of France in 1940, when the President asked Congress for 50,000 planes to strengthen America's defense in a dangerous world. Other nations and some of our people cried, "Impossible! We haven't the plants, money, or materials." What was the answer of America's free enterprise system? By June 1945, 297,000 war planes had been produced, nearly 100,000 of them bombers.

No fair-minded person contends that the private enterprise system is perfect. It is operated by human beings who are full of imperfections. Many of us deplore the fact that a few of our corporate entities seem to lack that social consciousness proportionate to their power and the privileges granted them by the state. Some businesses apparently still fail to recognize that there are social and spiritual values as well as profits that should be considered in their operations.

Neither do our needs always correspond to our demands under the free enterprise system. For example, the American male still prefers steak and potatoes and apple pie to a better balanced diet. Many American families often prefer housing below a decency level to the "indecency" of getting along without a family car. As a nation we have spent twice as much money for liquor and tobacco as for medical care, about the same for movies as for the support of the churches, and almost as much for beauty parlor services as for private social welfare. Whether wise or unwise, these decisions on the part of individuals as to how they spend their money are the result of free consumer choice, which is a part of the free enterprise system.

With all of its weaknesses, our free enterprise system has accomplished in terms of human welfare that which no other economic or social system has even approached. Our freedom of individual opportunity permits us to draw upon our natural resources and upon the total brain and brawn power of the nation in a most effective manner. This freedom of individual choice inspires competition. Competition inspires shrewd and efficient management, which is conducive to the production of the best product possible at the lowest price.

Are we to discard a system that has produced so much simply because it has not worked perfectly? We all admit there are abuses. One should not condemn an entire system because of the abuses of a handful of those who do not play the game according to established rules. We often refer to the family unit as the very basis of civilized society, and yet all will agree that family life is not perfect—divorces are too frequent, some homes are unhappy—but our objective is not to throw the family overboard, but rather to work for the improvement of family relations. Even the churches of America are not perfect, but no sane American would recommend that the churches be discredited and discarded. We all recognize religion as the basis of true character-building for which the world is starving.

The evidence clearly indicates that our most cherished rights and interests are all a part of the American way of life. Can communism, socialism, fascism, or any other coercive system provide these priceless blessings which flow to us as a part of our American way of life? The common denominator of all these coercive systems is the curtailment of individual liberty. Surely we will all agree that our Constitution provides the basis for the only economic system acceptable to true Americans.

Although we all cherish the material blessings which flow from the American system of individual achievement, it would be folly for us to close our eyes to certain challenging and dangerous trends that are in evidence and that strike at its very foundation. As Americans, far removed from the struggles which won for us our freedom, we are inclined to take the inevitable blessings of freedom for granted. It has been seven generations since the adoption of the American Constitution. Many in America today seem to have forgotten the cost and the value of freedom.

In addition, during the past few years, particularly, loud voices have been calling attention to the weaknesses of private enterprise without pointing out its virtues. We have been teaching our people to depend upon government instead of relying upon their own initiative as did our pioneer forefathers. Our freedom to work out our individual destinies has been abridged. We have been looking upon government as something apart from us and have failed to realize that we, the people, are the government.

We have also been making individual success unpopular. There has been a tendency to refer to men who have cash to invest in tools and equipment for the use of workers as "coupon clippers," "economic royalists," "capitalists," and "profiteers"—as though there were something inherently bad in it. Evidence of this fact is found in the writings and discussions of our high school and college students, the majority of whom, it is reported, believe private enterprise is a failure, although they don't have a clear understanding of what private enterprise is. With them, as with many adults, there is a vague notion that it is some unfair system which tends to give special advantage to big corporations and wealthy individuals. This attitude is encouraged by certain textbook writers who hold the idea, in many cases, that a government-planned economy is the remedy for all of our economic ills and the weaknesses in our American way of life, to which they readily point without referring to the beneficent fruits of the system.

We are rearing a generation that does not seem to understand the fundamentals of our American way of life, a generation that is no longer dedicated to its preservation. A long-range educational program beginning with the adult level is, of course, the only answer. Our people, both before and after they arrive at the age of the right of the ballot, should understand what it is that has made America great. We can only appreciate freedom if we understand the comparative fruits thereof. It was Jefferson who said: "The price of freedom is eternal vigilance." It is one thing to win freedom; its preservation is equally important. If reference is made continually to weaknesses of the private enterprise system without any effort to point out its virtues and the comparative fruits of this and other systems, the tendency in this country will be to demand that the government take over more and more of the economic and social responsibilities and make more of the decisions for the people. This can result in but one thing: slavery of the individual to the state. This seems to be the trend in the world today. The issue is whether the individual exists for the state or the state for the individual.

In a democracy the real danger is that we may slowly slide into a condition of slavery of the individual to the state rather than entering this condition by a sudden revolution. The loss of our liberties might easily come about, not through the ballot box, but through the death of incentive to work, to earn, and to save. Such a condition is usually brought about by a series of little steps which, at the time, seem justified by a variety of reasons and which may on the surface appear to be laudable as to intent. It has been pointed out that the more basic reasons offered by would-be planned economy advocates are "the desire to change and control others, the search for security, and the desire of individuals or groups to improve their own economic status or that of others by means of direct governmental intervention."

Europe today is evidence of the fact that one of the most common routes toward serfdom is followed by those in search of economic security. Never has there been so much apparent interest in security. Many programs so labeled have wide appeal. In order to appraise properly any so-called governmental security plan, however, we must look behind its name. Many so-called progressive programs are attractively labeled, and if we are to preserve our freedom and liberty, we must constantly analyze the nature of issues and programs and ignore labels that have been attached to them.

Equality is also a favorite term. Most people believe themselves to be below the average in income; therefore they feel they stand to gain through equalization via governmental intervention. All would like to equalize with those who are better off than they themselves. They fail to realize that incomes differ, and will always differ, because people differ in their economic drive and ability. The evidence clearly indicates that government has been unable to prevent inequality of incomes and, further, that equalization efforts usually stifle initiative and retard progress to the extent that the real incomes of everyone are lowered.

Many of our problems and dangers center in the issues of so-called fair prices, wages, and profits and the relationship between management and labor. We must realize that it is just as possible for wages to be too high as it is for prices and profits to be excessive. There is a tendency, of course, for almost everyone to feel that his share is unfair, whether it is or not. An effort to adjust apparent inequities often calls for government subsidies. Too often these are authorized without asking, "Who will pay for them?" Much of our program of letting the government pay for it can be described as "an attempt to better yourself by increasing your pay to yourself and then sending yourself the bill."

The only safe and solid answer is the mechanism of a free market operating in an enterprise and free competition. Here everyone has a chance to cast his vote in the election that will decide what is a fair price, fair wage, and fair profit, and what should be produced and in what quantities. To contradict the justice of that decision is to contradict the whole concept of justice by the democratic process. All will agree that the democratic processes and the free market—both parts of our American way of life— are not perfect, but they are believed to have fewer faults and to do a better job than any other known device. A sure way to take a shortcut to serfdom is to discard the sovereign rights of all the people in either the political or the economic realm.

We must remember that government assistance and control are essentially political provisions, and that experience has demonstrated that, for that reason, they are not sufficiently stable to warrant their utilization as a foundation for sound economic growth under a free enterprise system. The best way—the American way—is still maximum freedom for the individual guaranteed by a wise government that establishes and enforces the rules of the game. History records that eventually people get the form of government they deserve. Good government, which guarantees the maximum of freedom, liberty, and development to the individual, must be based upon sound principles, and we must ever remember that ideas and principles are either sound or unsound in spite of those who hold them. Freedom of achievement has achieved and will continue to produce the maximum of benefits in terms of human welfare.

Our way of life is based upon eternal principles. It rests upon a deep spiritual foundation established by inspired instruments of an all-wise Providence.

32

Civic Standards for the Faithful Saints

In the fall of 1971 I was invited by Baron von Blomberg, president of the United Religious Organization, to represent the Church as a guest of the king of Persia at the twenty-five hundredth anniversary of the founding of the Persian Empire by Cyrus the Great.

King Cyrus lived more than five hundred years before Christ and figured in prophecies of the Old Testament mentioned in 2 Chronicles and the book of Ezra, and by the prophets Ezekiel, Isaiah, and Daniel. The Bible states how "the Lord stirred up the spirit of Cyrus king of Persia." (2 Chronicles 36:22.) Cyrus restored certain political and social rights to the captive Hebrews, gave them permission to return to Jerusalem, and directed that Jehovah's temple should be rebuilt.

Parley P. Pratt, in describing the Prophet Joseph Smith, said that he had "the boldness, courage, temperance, perseverance and generosity of a Cyrus." (*Autobiography of Parley Parker Pratt,* Deseret Book, 1938, p. 46.)

President Wilford Woodruff said:

Now I have thought many times that some of those ancient kings that were raised up, had in some respects more regard for the carrying

out of some of these principles and laws, than even the Latter-day
Saints have in our day. I will take as an ensample Cyrus. . . . To trace
the life of Cyrus from his birth to his death, whether he knew it or
not, it looked as though he lived by inspiration in all his movements.
He began with that temperance and virtue which would sustain any
Christian country or any Christian king. . . . Many of these principles
followed him, and I have thought many of them were worthy, in many
respects, the attention of men who have the Gospel of Jesus Christ.
(*Discourses of Wilford Woodruff,* pp. 315-16.)

God, the Father of us all, uses the men of the earth,
especially good men, to accomplish his purposes. It has
been true in the past, it is true today, it will be true in the
future.

Elder Orson F. Whitney of the Council of the Twelve
said:

Perhaps the Lord needs such men on the outside of His Church
to help it along. They are among its auxiliaries, and can do more good
for the cause where the Lord has placed them, than anywhere else. . . .
Hence, some are drawn into the fold and receive a testimony of the
truth; while others remain unconverted . . . the beauties and glories
of the gospel being veiled temporarily from their view, for a wise purpose. The Lord will open their eyes in His own due time. God is using
more than one people for the accomplishment of His great and marvelous work. The Latter-day Saints cannot do it all. It is too vast, too
arduous for any one people. . . . We have no quarrel with the Gentiles.
They are our partners in a certain sense. (*Conference Report,* April 1928,
p. 59.)

This would certainly have been true of Colonel Thomas L. Kane, a true friend of the Saints in their dire need. It
was true of General Doniphan, who, when ordered by his
superior to shoot Joseph Smith, said, "It is cold blooded
murder, I will not obey your order . . . and if you execute
these men, I will hold you responsible before an earthly
tribunal, so help me God." (Joseph Fielding Smith, *Essentials in Church History,* Deseret Book, 1971 ed., p. 201.)

We honor these partners because their devotion to

correct principles overshadowed their devotion to popularity, party, or personalities.

We honor our founding fathers of this republic for the same reason. God raised up these patriotic partners to perform their mission, and he called them "wise men." (See D&C 101:80.) The First Presidency acknowledged that wisdom when they gave us the guideline a few years ago of supporting political candidates "who are truly dedicated to the Constitution in the tradition of our Founding Fathers." (*Deseret News,* November 2, 1964.) That tradition has been summarized in the book *The American Tradition* by Clarence Carson.

The Lord said that "the children of this world are in their generation wiser than the children of light." (Luke 16:8.) Our wise founders seemed to understand, better than most of us, our own scripture that states that "it is the nature and disposition of almost all men, as soon as they get a little authority . . . they will immediately begin to exercise unrighteous dominion." (D&C 121:39.)

To help prevent this, the founders knew that our elected leaders should be bound by certain fixed principles. Said Thomas Jefferson: "In questions of power, then, let no more be heard of confidence in man, but bind him down from mischief by the chains of the Constitution." (Draft of the Kentucky Resolutions of 1798.)

These wise founders, our patriotic partners, seemed to appreciate more than most of us the blessings of the boundaries that the Lord set within the Constitution, for he said, "And as pertaining to law of man, whatsoever is more or less than this, cometh of evil." (D&C 98:7.)

In God the founders trusted, and in his Constitution— not in the arm of flesh. "O Lord," said Nephi, "I have trusted in thee, and I will trust in thee forever. I will not put my trust in the arm of flesh; . . . cursed is he that putteth his trust in man or maketh flesh his arm." (2 Nephi 4:34.)

President J. Reuben Clark, Jr., put it well when he said:

> God provided that in this land of liberty, our political allegiance shall run not to individuals, that is, to government officials, no matter how great or how small they may be. Under His plan our allegiance and the only allegiance we owe as citizens or denizens of the United States, runs to our inspired Constitution which God himself set up. So runs the oath of office of those who participate in government. A certain loyalty we do owe to the office which a man holds, but even here we owe just by reason of our citizenship, no loyalty to the man himself. In other countries it is to the individual that allegiance runs. This principle of allegiance to the Constitution is basic to our freedom. It is one of the great principles that distinguishes this "land of liberty" from other countries. (*Stand Fast by Our Constitution*, Deseret Book, 1962, p. 189.)

"Patriotism," said Theodore Roosevelt, "means to stand by the country. It does not mean to stand by the President or any other public official save exactly to the degree in which he himself stands by the country. . . .

"Every man who parrots the cry of 'stand by the President' without adding the proviso 'so far as he serves the Republic' takes an attitude as essentially unmanly as that of any Stuart royalist who championed the doctrine that the King could do no wrong. No self-respecting and intelligent free man could take such an attitude." (Theodore Roosevelt, *Works*, vol. 21, pp. 316, 321.) As Latter-day Saints we should pray for our civic leaders and encourage them in righteousness.

". . . to vote for wicked men, it would be sin," said Hyrum Smith. (*Documentary History of the Church*, vol. 6, p. 323.)

And the Prophet Joseph Smith said, ". . . let the people of the whole Union, like the inflexible Romans, whenever they find a *promise* made by a candidate that is not *practiced* as an officer, hurl the miserable sycophant from his exaltation. . . ." (*DHC,* vol. 6, p. 207.)

Joseph and Hyrum's trust did not run to the arm of flesh, but to God and correct eternal principles. "I am the greatest advocate of the Constitution of the United States there is on the earth," said the Prophet Joseph Smith. (*DHC,* vol. 6, p. 56.)

The warning of President Joseph Fielding Smith is most timely: "Now I tell you it is time the people of the United States were waking up with the understanding that if they don't save the Constitution from the dangers that threaten it, we will have a change of government." (*Conference Report,* April 1950, p. 159.)

Another guideline given by the First Presidency was "to support good and conscientious candidates, of either party, who are aware of the great dangers" facing the free world. (*Deseret News,* November 2, 1964.)

Fortunately we have materials to help us face these threatening dangers in the writings of President David O. McKay and other Church leaders. Some other fine sources by LDS authors attempting to awaken and inform us of our duty are: *Prophets, Principles, and National Survival* (Jerreld L. Newquist), *Many Are Called But Few Are Chosen* (H. Verlan Andersen), and *The Elders of Israel and the Constitution* (Jerome Horowitz).

But the greatest handbook for freedom in this fight against evil is the Book of Mormon.

This leads me to the second great civic standard for the Saints. For in addition to our inspired Constitution, we have the scriptures.

Joseph Smith said that the Book of Mormon was the "keystone of our religion" and the "most correct" book on earth. (*DHC,* vol. 6, p. 56.) This most correct book on earth states that the downfall of two great American civilizations came as a result of secret conspiracies whose desire was to overthrow the freedom of the people. "And they have caused the destruction of this people of whom I am now speaking," says Moroni, "and also the destruction of the people of Nephi." (Ether 8:21.)

Now undoubtedly Moroni could have pointed out many factors that led to the destruction of the people, but notice how he singled out the secret combinations, just as the Church today could point out many threats to peace, prosperity, and the spread of God's work, but it has singled out as the greatest threat the Godless conspiracy. There is no conspiracy theory in the Book of Mormon—it is a conspiracy fact.

Then Moroni speaks to us in this day and says, "Wherefore, the Lord commandeth you, when ye shall see these things come among you that ye shall awake to a sense of your awful situation, because of this secret combination which shall be among you. . . ." (Ether 8:24.)

The Book of Mormon further warns that "whatsoever nation shall uphold such secret combinations, to get power and gain, until they shall spread over the nation, behold they shall be destroyed. . . ." (Ether 8:22.)

This scripture should alert us to what is ahead unless we repent, because there is no question but that as people of the free world, we are increasingly upholding many of the evils of the adversary today. By court edict godless conspirators can run for government office, teach in our schools, hold office in labor unions, work in our defense plants, serve in our merchant marines, etc. As a nation, we are helping to underwrite many evil revolutionaries in our country.

Now we are assured that the Church will remain on the earth until the Lord comes again—but at what price? The Saints in the early days were assured that Zion would be established in Jackson County, but look at what their unfaithfulness cost them in bloodshed and delay.

President Clark warned us that "we stand in danger of losing our liberties, and that once lost, only blood will bring them back; and once lost, we of this church will, in order to keep the Church going forward, have more sacrifices to make and more persecutions to endure than we have yet known. . . ." (*CR*, April 1944, p. 116.) He also stated that if the conspiracy "comes here it will probably come in its full vigor and there will be a lot of vacant places among those who guide and direct, not only this government, but also this Church of ours." (*CR*, April 1952, p. 80.)

Now the third great civic standard for the Saints is the inspired word of the prophets—particularly the living president, God's mouthpiece on the earth today. Keep your eye on the captain and judge the words of all lesser authority by his inspired counsel.

The story is told how Brigham Young, driving through a community, saw a man building a house and told him to double the walls. Shortly afterward a flood came through that town, resulting in much destruction, but this man's walls stood. While putting the roof on his house, he was heard singing, "We thank thee, O God, for a prophet!"

Joseph Smith taught that "a prophet was a prophet only when he was acting as such." (*DHC*, vol. 5, p. 265.)

Suppose a leader of the Church were to tell you that you were supporting the wrong side of a particular issue. Some might immediately resist this leader and his counsel or ignore it, but I would suggest that you first apply the fourth great civic standard for the faithful Saints. That standard is to live for, to get, and then to follow the promptings of the Holy Spirit.

A number of years ago, because of a statement that appeared to represent the policy of the Church, a faithful member feared he was supporting the wrong candidate for public office. Humbly he took the matter up with the Lord.

324 GOD, FAMILY, COUNTRY

Through the Spirit of the Lord he gained the conviction of the course he should follow, and he dropped his support of this particular candidate. This good brother, by fervent prayer, got the answer that in time proved to be the right course.

We urge all men to read the Book of Mormon and then ask God if it is true. And the promise is sure that they may know of its truthfulness through the Holy Ghost, "and by the power of the Holy Ghost [men] may know the truth of all things." (Moroni 10:5.)

We need the constant guidance of that Spirit. We live in an age of deceit. "O my people," said Isaiah in the Book of Mormon, "they who lead thee cause thee to err and destroy the way of thy paths." (2 Nephi 13:12.)

The Lord holds us accountable if we are not wise and are deceived. "For they that are wise," he said, "and have received the truth, and have taken the Holy Spirit for their guide, and have not been deceived—verily I say unto you, they shall not be hewn down and cast into the fire, but shall abide the day." (D&C 45:57.)

And so four great civic standards for the faithful Saints are, first, the Constitution ordained by God through wise men; second, the scriptures, particularly the Book of Mormon; third, the inspired counsel of the prophets, especially the living president, and fourth, the guidance of the Holy Spirit.

God bless us all that we may use these standards and by so doing bless ourselves, our families, our community, our nation, and the world.

33

Christ and the Constitution

Nearly two thousand years ago a perfect man walked the earth: Jesus the Christ. He was the son of a heavenly father and an earthly mother. He is the God of this world, under the Father. He taught men truth, that they might be free. His example and precepts provide the great standard, the only sure way, for all mankind. He became the first and only one who had the power to reunite his body with his spirit after death. By his power all men who have died shall be resurrected. Before him one day we all must stand to be judged by his laws. He lives today and in the not too distant future shall return, in triumph, to subdue his enemies, to reward men according to their deeds, and to assume his rightful role and to rule and reign in righteousness over the entire earth.

Nearly two hundred years ago, some inspired men walked this land of America—not perfect men, but men raised up by the Perfect Man to perform a great work. Foreordained were they, to lay the foundation of this republic, the Lord's base of operations in these latter days. Blessed by the Almighty in their struggle for liberty and independence, the power of heaven rested on these founders as they drafted that great document for governing men, the Constitution of the United States. Like the Ten Commandments, the truths on which the Constitution was based were timeless; and also, as with the Decalogue, the hand of the Lord was in it. They filled their mission well. From them we were endowed with a legacy of liberty—a constitutional republic.

But today the Christian constitutionalist mourns for his country. He sees the spiritual and political faith of his fathers betrayed by wolves in sheep's clothing. He sees the forces of evil increasing in strength and momentum under the leadership of Satan, the archenemy of freedom. He sees the wicked honored and the valiant abused. He senses that his own generation faces Gethsemanes and Valley Forges that may yet rival or surpass the trials of the early apostles and the men of '76. And this gives him cause to reflect on the most basic of fundamentals, the reason for our existence. Once we understand the fundamental purpose for mortality, we may more easily chart a correct course in the perilous seas that are engulfing our nation.

This life is a probation: a probation in which you and I prove our mettle, a probation that has eternal consequences for each of us. And now is our time and season—as every generation has had theirs—to learn our duties and to do them.

The Lord has so arranged things in this life that men are free agents unto themselves to do good or evil. The Lord allows men to go only so far, but the latitude is great enough that some men promote much wickedness and other men much righteousness.

Clearly, there would be little trial of faith if we received our full reward immediately for every goodly deed, or immediate retribution for every sin. But that there will be an eventual reckoning for each, there is no question.

The Lord is displeased with wickedness, and he will

help those who oppose it. But he has given all of us freedom to choose, while reserving for himself our final judgment. And herein lies the hope of all Christian constitutionalists. Why? Because the fight for freedom is God's fight, and free agency is an eternal principle. It existed before this world was formed; it will exist forever. Some men may succeed in denying some aspects of this God-given freedom to their fellowmen, but their success is temporary. Freedom is a law of God, an eternal law. And, like any of God's laws, men cannot break it with impunity. They can only break themselves upon it. So as long as a man stands for freedom, he stands with God. Therefore, any man will be eternally vindicated and rewarded who stands for freedom.

Men receive blessings by obedience to God's laws, and without obedience there is no blessing. Before the final triumphal return of the Lord, the question as to whether we may save our constitutional republic is simply based on two factors: the number of patriots and the extent of their obedience.

That the Lord desires to save this nation that he raised up, there is no doubt. But that he leaves it up to us, with his help, is the awful reality.

There is a time and season for all righteous things, and many of life's failures arise when men neither take the time nor find the season to perform their eternal duties. What, then, in this time and season may best equip us to save our Christian constitutional legacy, while at the same time rescuing our own souls? May I humbly submit six suggestions:

1. *Spirituality.* In the Book of Mormon, sacred to me as scripture, the Lord states that America is a land choice above all others and that it shall remain free so long as the inhabitants worship the God of the land, Jesus Christ.

Certainly spirituality is the foundation upon which any battle against sin and tyranny must be waged. And because this is basically the struggle of the forces of Christ versus antichrist, it is imperative that our people be in tune with the supreme leader of freedom, the Lord our God. Men stay in tune only when their lives are in harmony with God, for apart from God we cannot succeed, but as a partner with God, we cannot fail. We must be in the amoral and immoral world, but not of it.

2. *Balance.* We have many responsibilities, and one cannot expect the full blessings of a kind Providence if he neglects any major duty.

A man has duties to his church, his home, his country, and his profession or job.

Duty to church: Each man, in communication with God, must determine his responsibility to the Church. This becomes a serious consideration in a day when many pulpits are being turned into pipelines of collectivist propaganda, preaching the social gospel and denying basic principles of salvation. The least any Christian can do is to study daily the word of the Lord and seek divine aid through daily prayer. We invite all men to examine prayerfully The Church of Jesus Christ of Latter-day Saints—the Mormon Church—which I testify is the Church of Christ, restored to the earth and led today by a prophet of God.

Duty to home: Fathers, you cannot delegate your duty as the head of the home. Mothers, train up your children in righteousness; do not attempt to save the world and thus let your own fireside fall apart. For many years now the Mormon Church has advised parents to set aside one night a week when the family meets together for an evening at home. At this time family goals and duties are discussed, spiritual guidance given, and recreation enjoyed. To this end the Church has published and distributes, free of charge, a home evening manual with helpful suggestions for each week's activities.

The duty of parents is to be of help to each other and

to their children; then comes their duty to their neighbors, community, nation, and world, in that order. The home is the rock foundation, the cornerstone of civilization. No nation will ever rise above its homes.

Duty to country: No one can delegate his duty to preserve his freedom, for the price of liberty is still eternal vigilance. There are now thousands of businessmen behind the iron curtain who, if they had their lives to live over, would balance their time more judiciously and give more devotion to their civic responsibilities. An ounce of energy in the preservation of freedom is worth a ton of effort to get it back once it is lost.

Duty to job: Every man should provide the necessities of food, clothing, and shelter for his family. As Paul wrote to Timothy: "But if any provide not for his own, and specially for those of his own house, he hath denied the faith, and is worse than an infidel." (1 Timothy 5:8.)

Indolence invites the benevolent straightjacket of the character-destroying welfare state. But a man pays too high a price for worldly success if in his climb to prominence he sacrifices his spiritual, home, and civic responsibilities. How a person should apportion his time among his several duties requires good judgment and is a matter over which each should invite divine assistance.

3. *Courageous action.* I believe that, while we should ask the Lord's blessings on all our doings and should never do anything upon which we cannot ask his blessings, we should not expect the Lord to do for us what we can do for ourselves. I believe in faith and works, and that the Lord will bless more fully the man who works for what he prays for than he will the man who only prays.

Today you cannot effectively fight for freedom and not be attacked, and those who think they can are deceiving themselves. While I do not believe in stepping out of the path of duty to pick up a cross I do not need, a man is a coward who refuses to pick up a cross that clearly lies within his path.

A man must not only stand for the right principles, but he must also fight for them. Those who fight for principle can be proud of the friends they've gained and the enemies they've earned.

4. *Education.* We must each of us do our homework. We must be wise as serpents; for, as the apostle Paul said, we wrestle "against the rulers of the darkness. . . , against spiritual wickedness in high places." (Ephesians 6:12.)

We are going through the greatest, most insidious propaganda campaign of all time. Even the character-destroying "credibility gap" seems to be gaining respectability. We cannot believe all we read, and what we can believe is not all of the same value. We must sift. We must learn by study and prayer.

Study the scriptures and study the mortals who have been most consistently accurate about the most important things. When your freedom and your eternal welfare are at stake, your information had better be accurate.

5. *Health.* To meet and beat the enemy will require clear heads and strong bodies. Hearts and hands grow strong, based on what they are fed. Let us take into our bodies and souls only those things that will make us more effective instruments. We need all the physical, mental, and moral power we can get.

Righteous concern about conditions is commendable when it leads to constructive action. But undue worry is debilitating. When we have done what we can do, then let's leave the rest to God.

Man needs beneficial recreation, a change of pace that refreshes him for heavy tasks ahead. Man also must take time to meditate, to sweep the cobwebs from his mind, so that he might get a more firm grip on the truth and spend less time chasing phantoms and dallying in projects of lesser worth.

Clean hearts and healthful food, exercise, early sleep and fresh air, wholesome recreation and meditation, combined with optimism that comes from fighting for the right and knowing you'll eventually win for keeps—this is the tonic every true Christian patriot needs and deserves.

6. *Be Prepared.* We have a duty to survive, not only spiritually but also physically. Not survival at the cost of principles, for this is the surest way to defeat, but a survival that comes from intelligent preparation. We face days ahead that will test the moral and physical sinews of all of us.

The scriptural parable of the five wise and the five foolish virgins is a reminder that one can wait too long before he attempts to get his spiritual and temporal house in order. Are we prepared?

A man should not only be prepared to protect himself physically, but he should also have on hand sufficient supplies to sustain himself and his family in an emergency. For many years the leaders of the Mormon Church have recommended, with instructions, that every family have on hand at least a year's supply of basic food, clothing, fuel (where possible), and provisions for shelter. This has been most helpful to families suffering temporary reverses. It can and will be useful in many circumstances in the days ahead. We also need to get out of financial bondage, to be debt free.

Now these suggestions regarding spirituality, balance, courageous action, education, health, and preparation are given not only to help equip one for the freedom struggle, but also to help equip one for eternal life.

Those who hesitate to get into this fight because it is controversial fail to realize that life's decisions should be based on principles, not on public opinion polls.

There were men at Valley Forge who weren't sure how the revolution would end, but they were in a much better position to save their own souls and their country than those timid men whose major concern was deciding which side was going to win, or how to avoid controversy.

The basic purpose of life is to prove ourselves, not to be with the majority when it is wrong. Those who hesitate to get into the fight for freedom because they're not sure if we're going to win fail to realize that we will win in the long run, and for good.

Time is on the side of truth, and truth is eternal. Those who are fighting against freedom and other eternal principles of right may feel confident now, but they are shortsighted.

This is still God's world. The forces of evil, working through some mortals, have made a mess of a good part of it. But it is still God's world. In due time, when each of us has had a chance to prove himself—including whether or not we are going to stand up for freedom—God will interject himself, and the final and eternal victory shall be for free agency. And then shall those weak-willed souls on the sidelines and those who took the wrong but temporarily popular course lament their decisions.

Let us get about our business, for any Christian constitutionalist who retreats from this battle jeopardizes his life here and hereafter. Seldom has so much responsibility hung on so few, so heavily; but our numbers are increasing, and we who have been warned have a responsibility to warn our neighbor.

To his disciples, the Lord said that they should be of good cheer, for he had overcome the world—and so he had. And so can we, if we are allied with him. Time is on the side of truth, and the wave of the future is freedom. There is no question of the eventual, final, and lasting triumph of righteousness. The major question for each of us is what part will we play in helping to bring it to pass.

This is a glorious hour in which to live. Generations past and future will mark well our response to our awesome duty. There is a reason why we have been born in this day. Ours is the task to try to live and perpetuate the principles of the Christ and the Constitution in the face of tremendous odds. May we, with God's help, have strength for the battle and fill our mission in honor for God, family, and country.

The Lord declared that "if ye are prepared ye shall not fear." (D&C 38:39). May we prepare, then fear not, I humbly pray.

34

Be Not Deceived

Years ago my great-grandfather, while an investigator, attended a Mormon meeting during which a member had a quarrel with the branch president. When the service was over, Mrs. Benson turned to Ezra T. and asked him what he thought of the Mormons now. I'll always be grateful for his answer. He said he thought the actions of its members in no way altered the truth of Mormonism. That conviction saved him from many a tragedy. Before joining the Church Grandfather was moved by a marvelous prayer of Elder John E. Page of the Council of the Twelve. But later the young convert was greatly shocked by the same young man whose actions reflected his gradual apostasy. Ironically, when Elder Page eventually was excommunicated, Brigham Young selected the young convert, Ezra T. Benson, to fill Elder Page's place in the Council.

Six of the original twelve apostles selected by Joseph Smith were excommunicated. The three witnesses to the Book of Mormon left the Church. Three of Joseph Smith's counselors fell—one even helped plot the Prophet's death.

A natural question that might arise would be, if the Lord knew in advance that these men would fall, as he undoubtedly did, why did he have his prophet call them to such high office? The answer is, to fill the Lord's purposes. For even the Master followed the will of the Father by selecting Judas. President George Q. Cannon suggested an explanation, too, when he stated, "Perhaps it is His own design that faults and weaknesses should appear in high places in order that His Saints may learn to trust in Him and not in any man or men." (*Gospel Truth*, Deseret Book Co., 1974, vol. 1, p. 319.)

And this would parallel Lehi's warning: put not your "trust in the arm of flesh. . . ." (2 Nephi 4:35.)

"The Church," said President David O. McKay, "is little, if at all, injured by persecution and calumnies from ignorant, misinformed, or malicious enemies." (*Treasures of Life*, 1962, p. 385.)

It is from within the Church that the greatest hindrance comes. And so, it seems, it has been. Now the question arises, will we stick with the kingdom and can we avoid being deceived? Certainly this is an important question, for the Lord has said that in the last days the devil will "rage in the hearts of . . . men" (2 Nephi 28:20), and if it were possible he shall "deceive the very elect." (See Joseph Smith 1:5-37.)

Brigham Young said:

> The adversary presents his principles and arguments in the most approved style, and in the most winning tone, attended with the most graceful attitudes; and he is very careful to ingratiate himself into the favour of the powerful and influential of mankind, uniting himself with popular parties, floating into offices of trust and emolument by pandering to popular feeling, though it should seriously wrong and oppress the innocent. Such characters put on the manners of an angel, appearing as nigh like angels of light as they possibly can, to deceive the innocent and the unwary. The good which they do, they do it to bring to pass an evil purpose upon the good and honest followers of Jesus Christ. (*Journal of Discourses*, vol. 11, pp. 238-39.)

Those of us who think "all is well in Zion" (2 Nephi

28:21) in spite of Book of Mormon warnings might ponder the words of Heber C. Kimball, who said:

> Yes, we think we are secure here in the chambers of these ever-lasting hills . . . but I want to say to you, my brethren, the time is coming when we will be mixed up in these now peaceful valleys to that extent that it will be difficult to tell the face of a Saint from the face of an enemy against the people of God. Then is the time to look out for the great sieve, for there will be a great sifting time, and many will fall. For I say unto you there is a test, a Test, a TEST coming. (Orson F. Whitney, *The Life of Heber C. Kimball,* 1888 ed., p. 456-57.)

One of the greatest discourses that I have ever heard or read on how to avoid being deceived was given during the priesthood session of the October 1960 semiannual conference by President Marion G. Romney. I commend it to you for your close study. During the talk Elder Romney stated that there was no guarantee that the devil will not deceive a lot of men who hold the priesthood. Then, after referring to a talk on free agency by President David O. McKay, President Romney stated, "Free agency is the principle against which Satan waged his war in heaven. It is still the front on which he makes his most furious, devious, and persistent attacks. That this would be the case was foreshadowed by the Lord. . . ."

And then, after quoting the scripture from the Pearl of Great Price regarding the war in heaven over free agency (Moses 4:1-4), President Romney continued:

> You see, at the time he was cast out of heaven, his objective was (and still is) "to deceive and to blind men, and to lead them captive at his will." This he effectively does to as many as will not hearken unto the voice of God. His main attack is still on free agency. When he can get men to yield their agency, he has them well on the way to captivity.
>
> We who hold the priesthood must beware concerning ourselves, that we do not fall into the traps he lays to rob us of our freedom. We must be careful that we are not led to accept or support in any way any organization, cause or measure which, in its remotest effect, would jeopardize free agency, whether it be in politics, government, religion,

employment, education, or any other field. It is not enough for us to be sincere in what we support. We must be right! (*Look to God and Live*, Deseret Book Co., 1971, pp. 57-58.)

President Romney then outlined some tests to distinguish the true from the counterfeit. Now this is crucial for us to know, for as President John Taylor said, "Besides the preaching of the Gospel, we have another mission, namely, the perpetuation of the free agency of man and the maintenance of liberty, freedom, and the rights of man." (*JD*, vol. 28, p. 63.)

It was the struggle over free agency that divided us before we came here; it may well be the struggle over the same principle that will deceive and divide us again.

May I suggest three short tests to avoid being deceived, pertaining to both this freedom struggle and all other matters.

1. *What do the standard works have to say about it?* "To the law and to the testimony: if they speak not according to this word, it is because there is no light in them," said Isaiah. (Isaiah 8:20.) This is one of the great truths of Isaiah so important that it was included in the Book of Mormon. There it reads: "To the law and to the testimony; and if they speak not according to this word, it is because there is no light in them." (2 Nephi 18:20.)

We must diligently study the scriptures. Of special importance to us are the Book of Mormon and the Doctrine and Covenants.

The Book of Mormon, Brigham Young said, was written on the tablets of his heart and no doubt helped save him from being deceived. The Book of Mormon has a lot to say about America, freedom, and secret combinations.

The Doctrine and Covenants is important because it contains the revelations which helped lay the foundation of this great latter-day work. It speaks of many things. Section 134, verse 2, states that government should hold inviolate the rights and control of property. This makes important reading in a day when government controls are increasing and people are losing the right to control their own property.

2.   The second guide is: *What do the latter-day presidents of the Church have to say on the subject, particularly the living president?* President Wilford Woodruff related an instance in Church history when Brigham Young was addressing a congregation in the presence of the Prophet Joseph Smith:

> Brother Brigham took the stand, and he took the Bible and laid it down; he took the Book of Mormon, and laid it down; and he took the Book of Doctrine and Covenants, and laid it down before him, and he said, "There is the written word of God to us, concerning the work of God from the beginning of the world, almost, to our day." "And now," said he, "when compared with the living oracles, those books are nothing to me; those books do not convey the word of God direct to us now, as do the words of a Prophet or a man bearing the Holy Priesthood in our day and generation. I would rather have the living oracles than all the writing in the books." That was the course he pursued. When he was through, Brother Joseph said to the congregation: "Brother Brigham has told you the word of the Lord, and he has told you the truth." (*Conference Report*, October 1897, pp. 18-19.)

There is only one man on the earth today who speaks for the Church. That man is the President of the Church. (See D&C 132:7, 21:4.) Because he gives the word of the Lord for us today, his words have an even more immediate importance than those of the dead prophets. When speaking under the influence of the Holy Ghost, his words are scripture. (D&C 68:4.)

The President can speak on any subject he feels is needful for the Saints. As Brigham Young stated: "I defy any man on earth to point out the path a prophet of God should walk in, or point out his duty, and just how far he must go, in dictating temporal or spiritual things. Temporal and spiritual things are inseparably connected, and ever will be." (*JD*, vol. 10, p. 364.) Other officers in the kingdom have fallen, but never the presidents. The words of a living prophet must and ever will take precedence.

President David O. McKay said a lot about our tragic trends toward socialism and communism and the responsibilities of liberty-loving people in defending and preserving our Constitution. Have we read his words and pondered on them?

3. *The third and final test is the Holy Ghost—the test of the Spirit.* By that Spirit we "may know the truth of all things." (Moroni 10:5.) This test can be fully effective only if one's channels of communication with God are clean and virtuous and uncluttered with sin. Said Brigham Young:

> You may know whether you are led by right or wrong, as well as you know the way home; for every principle God has revealed carries its own convictions of its truth to the human mind. . . .
> What a pity it would be if we were led by one man to utter destruction! Are you afraid of this? I am more afraid that this people have so much confidence in their leaders that they will not inquire of themselves of God whether they are led by Him. I am fearful they settle down in a state of blind self-security, trusting their eternal destiny in the hands of their leaders with a reckless confidence that in itself would thwart the purposes of God in their salvation, and weaken that influence they could give to their leaders, did they know for themselves, by the revelations of Jesus, that they are led in the right way. Let every man and woman know, by the whispering of the Spirit of God to themselves, whether their leaders are walking in the path that the Lord dictates, or not. This has been my exhortation continually. (*JD*, vol. 9, pp. 149-50.)

Elder Heber C. Kimball stated, "The time will come when no man or woman will be able to endure on borrowed light." (Orson F. Whitney, *Life of Heber C. Kimball*, 1888 edition, p. 461.)

How, then, can we know if a man is speaking by the Spirit? The Bible, Book of Mormon, and Doctrine and Covenants give us the key. (See D&C 50:17-23; 100:5-8; 2 Nephi 33:1; 1 Corinthians 2:10-11.) President Clark summarized this well when he said:

We can tell when the speakers are moved upon by the Holy Ghost only when we, ourselves, are moved upon by the Holy Ghost. In a way, this completely shifts the responsibility from them to us to determine when they so speak. . . . The Church will know by the testimony of the Holy Ghost in the body of the members, whether the brethren in voicing their views are moved upon by the Holy Ghost; and in due time that knowledge will be made manifest. (*Church News,* July 31, 1954.)

Will this Spirit be needed to check actions in other situations? Yes, and it could be used as a guide and a protector for the faithful in a situation described by President Harold B. Lee:

In the history of the Church there have been times or instances where Counselors in the First Presidency and others in high station have sought to overturn the decision or to persuade the President contrary to his inspired judgment, and always, if you will read carefully the history of the Church, such oppositions brought not only disastrous results to those who resisted the decision of the President, but almost always such temporary persuasions were called back for reconsideration, or a reversal of hasty action not in accordance with the feelings, the inspired feelings, of the President of the Church. And that, I submit, is one of the fundamental things that we must never lose sight of in the building up of the kingdom of God. (*Conference Report,* April 1963, p. 81.

These, then, are the three tests: the standard works, the inspired words of the Presidents of the Church (particularly the living presidents), and the promptings of the Holy Ghost.

Now, in this great struggle for free agency, just think what a power for good we could be in this world if we were united. President McKay reiterated this thought again and again:

Next to being one in worshiping God, there is nothing in this world upon which this Church should be more united than in upholding and defending the Constitution of the United States!

May the appeal of our Lord in his intercessory prayer for unity be realized in our homes, our wards, our stakes, and in our support of the basic principles of our Republic. (*Treasures of Life,* p. 387.)

To that I say Amen and Amen.
President Clark said:

> I wish to say with all the earnestness I possess that when you youth and maidens see any curtailment of these liberties I have named, when you see government invading any of these realms of freedom which you have under our Constitution, you will know that they are putting shackles on your liberty, and that tyranny is creeping upon you, no matter who curtails these liberties or who invades these realms, and no matter what the reason and excuse therefore may be. (*Stand Fast by Our Constitution*, pp. 189-90.)

Now, inasmuch as all these warnings have come through the mouthpieces of the Lord on earth today, there is one major question we should ask ourselves. Assuming we are living a life so we can know, then what does the Holy Ghost have to say about it? We are under obligation to answer this question. God will hold us responsible.

Let us not be deceived in the sifting days ahead. Let us rally together on principle behind the prophet as guided by the promptings of the Spirit. We should continue to speak out for freedom and against socialism and communism. We should continue to come to the aid of patriots, programs, and organizations that are trying to save our Constitution through every legal and moral means possible.

God has not left us in darkness regarding these matters. We have the scriptures ancient and modern. We have a living prophet, and we may obtain the Spirit.

Joseph Smith did see the Father and the Son. The kingdom established through the Prophet's instrumentality will roll forth. We can move forward with it. That we may all do so and be not deceived is my humble prayer.

35

The American Heritage of Freedom

Every member of the priesthood should understand the divine plan designed by the Lord to raise up the first free people in modern times. Here is how scripture says it was achieved:

First: Prophecy is abundant that God deliberately kept the American continent hidden until after the Holy Roman Empire had been broken up and the various nations had established themselves as independent kingdoms. Keeping America hidden until this time was no accident. (2 Nephi 1:6, 8.)

Second: At the proper time, God inspired Columbus to overcome almost insurmountable odds to discover America and bring this rich new land to the attention of the gentiles in Europe. (1 Nephi 13:12.)

Third: God revealed to his ancient American prophets that shortly after the discovery of America there would be peoples in Europe who would desire to escape the persecution and tyranny of the Old World and flee to America. (1 Nephi 13:13-16.)

Fourth: God told his prophets that the kingdoms in Europe would try to exercise dominion over the people who had fled to America, but that in the wars for independence the American settlers would win. (This is a remarkable prophecy in that 2,300 years before the Revolutionary War was fought, God through his prophets predicted who would win it.) (1 Nephi 13:16-19.)

Fifth: The prophets were told that in the latter days when the gentiles came to America, they would establish it as a land of liberty on which there would be no kings. The Lord declared that he would protect the land, and whosoever would try to establish kings either from within or without would perish. (2 Nephi 10:8-14.)

Sixth: Having declared America to be a land of liberty, God undertook to raise up a band of inspired and intelligent leaders who could write a constitution of liberty and establish the first free people in modern times. The hand of God in this undertaking is clearly indicated by the Lord himself in a revelation to the Prophet Joseph Smith in these words: ". . . I established the Constitution of this land, by the hands of wise men whom I raised up unto this very purpose. . . ." (D&C 101:80.)

Seventh: God declared that the United States Constitution was divinely inspired for the specific purpose of eliminating bondage and the violation of the rights and protection which belong to "all flesh." (See D&C 101:77-80.)

Eighth: God placed a mandate upon his people to befriend and defend the constitutional laws of the land and see that the rights and privileges of all mankind are protected. He verified the declaration of the founding fathers, that God created all men free. He also warned against those who would enact laws encroaching upon the sacred rights and privileges of free men. He urged the election of honest and wise leaders and said that evil men and laws were of Satan. (D&C 98:5-10.)

Ninth: God predicted through his prophets that this

great gentile nation, raised up on the American continent in the last days, would become the richest and most powerful nation on the face of the earth; even "above all other nations." (See 1 Nephi 13:15, 30; Ether 2:12.)

Tenth: Concerning the United States, the Lord revealed to his prophets that its greatest threat would be a vast, worldwide "secret combination" which would not only threaten the United States but also seek to "overthrow the freedom of all lands, nations and countries." (Ether 8:25.)

Eleventh: In connection with attack on the United States, the Lord told the Prophet Joseph Smith there would be an attempt to overthrow the country by destroying the Constitution. Joseph Smith predicted that the time would come when the Constitution would hang, as it were, by a thread, and at that time "this people will step forth and save it from the threatened destruction." (*Journal of Discourses,* vol. 7, p. 15.) It is my conviction that the elders of Israel, widely spread over the nation, will at that crucial time successfully rally the righteous of our country and provide the necessary balance of strength to save the institutions of constitutional government.

Twelfth: The Lord revealed to the prophet Nephi that he established the gentiles on this land to be a free people forever, that if they were a righteous nation and overcame the wickedness and secret abominations that would rise in their midst, they would inherit the land forever. (1 Nephi 14:1-2.)

Thirteenth: On the other hand, if the gentiles on this land reject the word of God and conspire to overthrow liberty and the Constitution, then their doom is fixed, and they "shall be cut off from among my people who are of the covenant." (1 Nephi 14:6; 3 Nephi 21:11, 14, 21; D&C 84: 114-115, 117.)

Fourteenth: The great destructive force which was to

be turned loose on the earth and which the prophets for centuries have been calling the "abomination of desolation" is vividly described by those who saw it in vision. Ours is the first generation to realize how literally these prophecies can be fulfilled now that God, through science, has unlocked the secret to thermonuclear reaction.

In the light of these prophecies, there should be no doubt in the mind of any priesthood holder that the human family is headed for trouble. There are rugged days ahead. It is time for every man who wishes to do his duty to get himself prepared—physically, spiritually, and psychologically—for the task which may come at any time, as suddenly as the whirlwind.

Where do we stand today? All over the world the light of freedom is being diminished. Across whole continents of the earth freedom is being totally obliterated.

Never in recorded history has any movement spread its power so far and so fast as has socialistic communism. The facts are not pleasant to review. Communist leaders are jubilant with their success. They are driving freedom back on almost every front.

It is time, therefore, that every American, and especially every member of the priesthood, become informed about the aims, tactics, and schemes of socialistic communism. This becomes particularly important when it is realized that communism is turning out to be the earthly image of the plan which Satan presented in the preexistence. The whole program of socialistic communism is essentially a war against God and the plan of salvation— the very plan which we fought to uphold during "the war in heaven."

Up to now some members of the Church have stood aloof, feeling that the fight against socialistic communism is controversial and unrelated to the mission of the Church or the work of the Lord. But the president of the Church in our day has made it clear that the fight against atheistic communism is a major challenge to the Church and every member in it.

During the general conference of the Church in October 1959, President David O. McKay, in discussing the threat of communism, referred to W. Cleon Skousen's book *The Naked Communist* and said, "I admonish everybody to read that excellent book." He then quoted the following from the flyleaf: "The conflict between communism and freedom is the problem of our time. It overshadows all other problems." (*Conference Report,* October 1959, p. 5.)

The fight against Godless communism is a very real part of the duty of every man who holds the priesthood. It is the fight against slavery, immorality, atheism, terrorism, cruelty, barbarism, deceit, and the destruction of human life through a kind of tyranny unsurpassed by anything in human history. Here is a struggle against the evil, satanical priestcraft of Lucifer. Truly it can be called "a continuation of the war in heaven."

In the war in heaven the devil advocated absolute eternal security at the sacrifice of our freedom. Although there is nothing more desirable to a Latter-day Saint than eternal security in God's presence, and although God knew, as we did, that some of us would not achieve this security if we were allowed our freedom, yet the very God of heaven who has more mercy than us all still decreed no guaranteed security except by a man's own freedom of choice and individual initiative.

Today the devil as a wolf in a supposedly new suit of sheep's clothing is enticing some men, both in and out of the Church, to parrot his line by advocating planned government-guaranteed security programs at the expense of our liberties. Latter-day Saints should be reminded how and why they voted as they did in heaven. If some have decided to change their votes they should repent—throw their support on the side of freedom—and cease promoting this subversion.

When all of the trappings of propaganda and pretense have been pulled aside, the exposed hard-core structure of modern communism is amazingly similar to the ancient Book of Mormon record of secret societies such as the Gadiantons. In the ancient American civilization there was no word which struck greater terror to the hearts of the people than the name of the Gadiantons. It was a secret political party which operated as a murder cult. Its object was to infiltrate legitimate government, plant its officers in high places, and then seize power and live off the spoils appropriated from the people. (It would start out as a small group of dissenters, and by using secret oaths with the threat of death for defectors, it would gradually gain a choke hold on the political and economic life of whole civilizations.)

The object of the Gadiantons, like modern communists, was to destroy the existing government and set up a ruthless criminal dictatorship over the whole land.

One of the most urgent, heart-stirring appeals made by Moroni as he closed the Book of Mormon was addressed to the gentile nations of the last days. He foresaw the rise of a great worldwide secret combination among the gentiles which "seeketh to overthrow the freedom of all lands, nations, and countries." (Ether 8:25.) He warned each gentile nation of the last days to purge itself of this gigantic criminal conspiracy which would seek to rule the world.

The prophets, in our day, have continually warned us of these internal threats in our midst—that our greatest threat from socialistic communism lies within our country. We don't need a prophet—we have one; we need a listening ear. And if we do not listen and heed, then "the day cometh that they who will not hear the voice of the Lord, neither the voice of his servants, neither give heed to the words of the prophets and apostles, shall be cut off from among the people." (D&C 1:14.)

The prophets have said that these threats are among us. The prophet Moroni, viewing our day, said, "Wherefore the Lord commandeth you, when ye shall see these things come among you that ye shall awake to a sense of your awful situation." (Ether 8:24.)

Unfortunately, our nation has not treated the socialistic communist conspiracy as "treasonable to our free institutions," as the First Presidency pointed out in a signed 1936 statement. If we continue to uphold communism by not making it treasonable, our land shall be destroyed, for the Lord has said that "whatsoever nation shall uphold such secret combinations, to get power and gain, until they shall spread over the nation, behold they shall be destroyed." (Ether 8:22.)

Moroni described how the secret combination would take over a country and then fight the work of God, persecute the righteous, and murder those who resisted. Moroni therefore proceeded to describe the workings of the ancient secret combinations so that modern man could recognize this great political conspiracy in the last days. (See Ether 8:23-25.)

Moroni seemed greatly exercised lest in our day we might not be able to recognize the startling fact that the same secret societies which destroyed the Jaredites and decimated numerous kingdoms of both Nephites and Lamanites would be precisely the same form of criminal conspiracy which would rise up among the gentile nations in this day.

The strategems of the leaders of these societies are amazingly familiar to anyone who has studied the tactics of modern communist leaders.

The Lord has declared that before the second coming of Christ it will be necessary to "destroy the secret works of darkness" in order to preserve the land of Zion—the Americas. (See 2 Nephi 10:11-16.)

The worldwide secret conspiracy which has risen up in our day to fulfill these prophecies is easily identified. President McKay left no room for doubt as to what attitude Latter-day Saints should take toward the modern "secret combinations" of conspiratorial communism. In a lengthly statement on communism, he said:

> Latter-day Saints should have nothing to do with secret combinations and groups antagonistic to the constitutional law of the land, which the Lord "suffered to be established," and which "should be maintained for the rights and protection of all flesh according to just and holy principles." (*Gospel Ideals,* Improvement Era, 1953, p. 306.)

There are those who recommend that the clash between communism and freedom be avoided through disarmament agreements. Abolishing our military strength and adopting an unenforceable contract as a substitute to protect us would go down in history as the greatest mistake free men could make in a time of peril.

President McKay declared:

> Force rules in the world today; consequently, our government must keep armies abroad, build navies and air squadrons, create atom bombs to protect itself from the threatened aggression of a nation which seems to listen to no other appeal than compulsion. (Ibid., p. 304.)

This parallels the historic statement by George Washington when he vigorously warned:

> There is a rank due in the United States among the nations that will be totally lost by the reputation of weakness. If we would avoid insult we must be able to repel it, if we would secure the peace, it must be known that we are at all times ready for war. (Speech to Congress, December 3, 1793.)

Some timid, vacillating political leaders proclaim that communism is something we will have to learn to live with. The present communist system, they declare, will continue because *there is no alternate system to replace communism.* The policy of increasing power, of pushing their system outward, and using the communist party, they say, will go on.

Such a negative attitude writes off the hundreds of millions behind the iron curtain as a lost cause. Surely no courageous, liberty-loving citizen will treat the communist secret combination as "something we will have to learn to live with."

There is a more courageous and sounder point of view. President McKay expressed it in these words:

Men will be free. I have hoped for twenty years that the Russian system would break up. There is no freedom under it, and sooner or later the people will rise against it. They cannot oppose those fundamentals of civilization and of God. They can't crush their people always. Men will be free. (*Church News,* November 6, 1957.)

What is the official position of the Church on communism? In 1936 the First Presidency made an official declaration on communism which has never been abrogated. I quote the concluding paragraph: "We call upon all Church members completely to eschew communism. The safety of our divinely inspired constitutional government and the welfare of our Church imperatively demand that communism shall have no place in America." (*Improvement Era,* vol. 39 [1936], p. 488.)

We must ever keep in mind that collectivized socialism is part of the communist strategy. Communism is fundamentally socialism. We will never win our fight against communism by making concessions to socialism. Communism and socialism, closely related, must be defeated on principle. The close relationship between socialism and communism is clearly pointed out by Senator Strom Thurmond of South Carolina in the following letter to the editor of the Washington *Post,* published August 6, 1961:

Both socialism and communism derive from the teachings of

Marx and Engels. In fact, the movements were one until the split over the methods of approach, which resulted after the Russian revolution in 1905. . . . The aim and purpose of both was then and is now world socialism, which communism seeks to achieve through revolution and which socialists seek to achieve through evolution.

The industrial achievements of the U.S. are the result of an economic system which is the antithesis of socialism. Our economic system is called "capitalism" or "private enterprise" and is based on private property rights, the profit motive and competition.

Both communism and socialism seek to destroy our economic system and replace it with socialism; and their success, whether through evolution by socialism or through revolution by communism or a combination, will destroy not only our economic system, but our liberty, including the "civil" aspects as well. . . .

. . . The "common ground" of socialism and communism is a factor to which the American people should be alerted. Without a clear understanding that communism is socialism, the total threat and menace of the cold war can never be comprehended and fought to victory.

When socialism is understood, we will realize that many of the programs advocated, and some of those already adopted in the United States, fall clearly within the category of socialism. What is socialism? It is simply governmental ownership and management of the essential means for the production and distribution of goods.

We must never forget that nations may sow the seeds of their own destruction while enjoying unprecedented prosperity.

The socialistic-communist conspiracy to weaken the United States involves attacks on many fronts. To weaken the American free-enterprise economy that outproduced both its enemies and allies during World War II is a high priority target of the communist leaders. Their press and other propaganda media are therefore constantly selling the principles of centralized or federal control of farms, railroads, electric power, schools, steel, maritime shipping, and many other aspects of the economy—but always in the name of public welfare.

This carries out the strategy laid down by the communist masters. John Strachey, a top official in the Labor Socialist party of Great Britain, in his book entitled *The Theory and Practice of Socialism* said:

> It is impossible to establish communism as the immediate successor to capitalism. It is accordingly proposed to establish socialism as something which we can put in the place of our present decaying capitalism. Hence, communists work for the establishment of socialism as a necessary transition stage on the road to communism.

The paramount issue today is liberty against creeping socialism. It is in this spirit that President McKay stated:

> Communism is antagonistic to the American way of life. Its avowed purpose is to destroy belief in God and free enterprise. . . . The fostering of full economic freedom lies at the base of our liberties. Only in perpetuating economic freedom can our social, political, and religious liberties be preserved. (*Treasures of Life,* pp. 501-502; *Gospel Ideals,* p. 433.)

Again President McKay warned, citing the words of W. C. Mullendore, president of Southern California Edison Company:

> "During the first half of the twentieth century we have traveled far into the soul-destroying land of socialism and made strange alliances through which we have become involved in almost continuous hot and cold wars over the whole of the earth. In this retreat from freedom the voices of protesting citizens have been drowned by raucous shouts of intolerance and abuse from those who led the retreat and their millions of gullible youth, who are marching merrily to their doom, carrying banners on which are emblazoned such intriguing and misapplied labels as social justice, equality, reform, patriotism, social welfare. . . ." (*Gospel Ideals,* p. 273.)

It is significant that the Prophet Joseph Smith, after attending lectures on socialism, made this official entry in Church history: "I said I did not believe the doctrine." (*Documentary History of the Church,* vol. 6, p. 33.)

No true Latter-day Saint and no true American can be

a socialist or a communist or support programs leading in that direction. These evil philosophies are incompatible with Mormonism, the true gospel of Jesus Christ.

What can priesthood holders do? There are many things we can do to meet the challenge of the adversary in our day.

First, we should become informed about communism, about socialism, and about Americanism. What better way can one become informed than by first studying the inspired words of the prophets and using that as a foundation against which to test all other material? This is in keeping with the Prophet Joseph Smith's motto, "When the Lord commands, do it." (*DHC,* vol. 2, p. 170.)

The Foundation for Economic Education at Irvington-on-Hudson, New York, on which President J. Reuben Clark, Jr., served as a board member, continues to supply sound freedom literature. We should know enough about American free enterprise to be able to defend it. We should know what makes it possible for six percent of humanity—living under our free economy—to produce about one-half of the earth's developed wealth each year.

We should know why paternalism, collectivism, or unnecessary federal supervision will hold down our standard of living and reduce productivity just as it has in every country where it has been tried. We should also know why the communist leaders consider socialism the highroad to communism.

Second, we should accept the command of the Lord and treat socialistic communism as the tool of Satan. We should follow the counsel of the President of the Church and resist the influence and policies of the socialist-communist conspiracy wherever they are found—in the schools, in the churches, in governments, in unions, in businesses, in agriculture.

Third, we should help those who have been deceived

or who are misinformed to find the truth. Unless each person who knows the truth will "stand up and speak up," it is difficult for the deceived or confused citizen to find his way back.

Fourth, we should not make the mistake of calling people "communist" just because they happen to be helping the communist cause. Thousands of patriotic Americans, including a few Latter-day Saints, have helped the communists without realizing it. Others have knowingly helped without joining the party. The remedy is to avoid name-calling, but point out clearly and persuasively how they are helping the communists.

Fifth, each priesthood holder should use his influence in the community to resist the erosion process which is taking place in our political and economic life. He should use the political party of his choice to express his evaluation of important issues. He should see that his party is working to preserve freedom, not destroy it. He should join responsible local groups interested in promoting freedom and free competitive enterprise, in studying political issues, appraising the voting records and proposed programs, and writing to members of Congress, promoting good men in public office, and scrutinizing local, state, and federal agencies to see that the will of the people is being carried out. He should not wait for the Lord's servants to give instruction for every detail once they have announced the direction in which the priesthood should go. Each member should exercise prayerful judgment and then act.

Sixth, and most important of all, each member of the priesthood should set his own house in order. This should include:

1. Regular family prayer, remembering especially our government leaders.

2. Getting out of debt.

3. Seeing that each member of the family under-

stands the importance of keeping the commandments.

4. Seeing that the truth is shared with members of the family, with neighbors, and with associates.

5. Seeing that each member is performing his duties in the priesthood, in the auxiliary organizations, in the temple, and in the civic life of the community.

6. Seeing that every wage earner in the home is a full tithe-payer and fulfilling other obligations in financial support of the kingdom.

7. Providing a one-year supply of essentials.

In doing these things a member of the Church is not only making himself an opponent of the adversary, but a *proponent* of the Lord.

In the prophecies there is no promise except to the obedient. To a modern prophet the Lord said:

> Therefore, what I say unto one, I say unto all: Watch, for the adversary spreadeth his dominions, and darkness reigneth;
> And the anger of God kindleth against the inhabitants of the earth;
> . . . I give unto you directions how you may act before me, that it may turn to you for your salvation.
> I, the Lord, am bound when ye do what I say; but when ye do not what I say, ye have no promise. (D&C 82:5-6, 9-10.)

May God give us the wisdom to recognize the threat to our freedom and the strength to meet this danger courageously. Yes, perilous times are ahead, but if we do our duty in all things, God will give us inner peace and overrule all things for our good. God grant it may be so.

36

Watchman, Warn the Wicked

The prophet Ezekiel declared:

> Son of man, I have made thee a watchman unto the house of Israel: therefore hear the word at my mouth, and give them warning from me.
>
> When I say unto the wicked, Thou shalt surely die; and thou givest him not warning, nor speakest to warn the wicked from his wicked way, to save his life; the same wicked man shall die in his iniquity; but his blood will I require at thine hand.
>
> Yet if thou warn the wicked, and he turn not from his wickedness, nor from his wicked way, he shall die in his iniquity; but thou hast delivered thy soul. (Ezekiel 3:17-19.)

The inspired Book of Mormon prophets saw our day and warned us of the strategy of the adversary:

> For behold, at that day shall he rage in the hearts of the children of men, and stir them up to anger against that which is good.
>
> And others will he pacify, and lull them away into carnal security, that they will say: All is well in Zion; yea, Zion prospereth, all is well—and thus the devil cheateth their souls, and leadeth them away carefully down to hell.
>
> Yea, wo be unto him that hearkeneth unto the precepts of men, and denieth the power of God, and the gift of the Holy Ghost! (2 Nephi 28:20-21, 26.)

Through a modern prophet, Joseph Smith, the Lord has also given us warning:

> Wherefore the voice of the Lord is unto the ends of the earth, that all that will hear may hear:
> And the arm of the Lord shall be revealed; and the day cometh that they who will not hear the voice of the Lord, neither the voice of his servants, neither give heed to the words of the prophets and apostles, shall be cut off from among the people;
> For they have strayed from mine ordinances, and have broken mine everlasting covenant;
> They seek not the Lord to establish his righteousness, but every man walketh in his own way, and after the image of his own God, whose image is in the likeness of the world, and whose substance is that of an idol, which waxeth old and shall perish in Babylon, even Babylon the great, which shall fall.
> What I the Lord have spoken, I have spoken, and I excuse not myself; and though the heavens and the earth pass away, my word shall not pass away, but shall all be fulfilled, whether by mine own voice or by the voice of my servants, it is the same. (D&C 1:11, 14-16, 38.)

These warnings were given more than 140 years ago. The fulfillment is now. We are living witnesses, unless we are blinded by our own complacency and the craftiness of evil men.

As watchmen on the tower of Zion, it is our obligation and right as leaders to speak out against current evils— evils that strike at the very foundation of all we hold dear as the true church of Christ and as members of Christian nations.

As one of these watchmen, with a love for humanity, I accept humbly this obligation and challenge and gratefully strive to do my duty without fear. In times as serious as these, we must not permit fear of criticism to keep us from doing our duty, even at the risk of our counsel being tabbed as political, as government becomes more and more entwined in our daily lives.

In the crisis through which we are now passing, we

have been fully warned. This has brought forth some criticism. There are some of us who do not want to hear the message. It embarrasses us. The things which are threatening our lives, our welfare, our freedoms are the very things some of us have been condoning. Many do not want to be disturbed as they continue to enjoy their comfortable complacency.

The Church is founded on eternal truth. We do not compromise principle. We do not surrender our standards regardless of current trends or pressures. As a church, our allegiance to truth is unwavering. Speaking out against immoral or unjust actions has been the burden of prophets and disciples of God from time immemorial. It was for this very reason that many of them were persecuted. Nevertheless, it was their God-given task, as watchmen on the tower, to warn the people.

We live in an age of appeasement—the sacrificing of principle. Appeasement is not the answer. It is never the right answer.

One of the modern Church watchmen has given this sound warning:

A milk-and-water allegiance kills; while a passionate devotion gives life and soul to any cause and its adherents. The troubles of the world may largely be laid at the doors of those who are neither hot nor cold; who always follow the line of least resistance; whose timid hearts flutter at taking sides for truth. As in the great Council in the heavens, so in the Church of Christ on earth, there can be no neutrality. We are, or we are not, on the side of the Lord. An unrelenting faith, contemptuous of all compromise, will lead the Church and every member of it, to triumph and the achievement of our high destiny.

The final conquerors of the world will be the men and women, few or many matters not, who fearlessly and unflinchingly cling to truth, and who are able to say no, as well as yes, on whose lofty banner is inscribed: No compromise with error. . . .

Tolerance is not conformity to the world's view and practices. We must not surrender our beliefs to get along with people, however beloved or influential they may be. Too high a price may be paid for social standing or even for harmony. . . . The Gospel rests upon eternal truth; and truth can never be deserted safely. (John A. Widtsoe, *Conference Report*, April 1941, pp. 115-16.)

It has been well said that "our greatest national problem is erosion. Not erosion of the soil, but erosion of the national morality."

The United States of America has been great because it has been free. It has been free because it has trusted in God and was founded upon the principles of freedom set forth in the word of God. This nation has a spiritual foundation. To me, this land has a prophetic history.

In the year 1831 Alexis de Tocqueville, the famous French historian, came to our country at the request of the French government to study our penal institutions. He also made a close study of our political and social institutions. In less than ten years, de Tocqueville had become world-famous as the result of the four-volume work that he wrote, entitled *Democracy in America.* Here is his own stirring explanation of the greatness of America:

I sought for the greatness and genius of America in her commodious harbors and her ample rivers, and it was not there; in her fertile fields and boundless prairies, and it was not there; in her rich mines and her vast world commerce, and it was not there. Not until I went to the churches of America and heard her pulpits aflame with righteousness did I understand the secret of her genius and power. *America is great because she is good, and if America ever ceases to be good, America will cease to be great.*

How strong is our will to remain free, to be good? False thinking and false ideologies, dressed in the most pleasing forms, quietly—almost without our knowing it—seek to reduce our moral defenses and to captivate our minds. They entice with bright promises of security, cradle-to-grave guarantees of many kinds. They masquerade under various names, but all may be recognized by one thing that they all have in common: to erode away character and man's freedom to think and act for himself.

Effort will be made to lull us away into a false security. Proposals will be and are being offered and programs sponsored that have wide appeal. Attractive labels are usually attached to the most dangerous programs, often in the name of public welfare and personal security. Again, let us not be misled.

Freedom can be killed by neglect as well as by direct attack.

Too long have too many Americans, and people of the free world generally, stood by as silent accessories to the crimes of assault against freedom—assault against basic economic and spiritual principles and traditions that have made nations strong.

Let us strive for progress down the road of goodness and freedom. With the help and blessings of the Lord, the free people of the United States and the free world can and will face tomorrow without fear, without doubt, and with full confidence. We do not fear the phony population explosion, nor do we fear a shortage of food, if we can be free and good. The Lord has declared, ". . . the earth is full, and there is enough and to spare. . . ." (D&C 104:17.) We can accept this promise with confidence.

President Calvin Coolidge pinpointed the problem some years ago with these words:

> We do not need more material development, we need more spiritual development. We do not need more intellectual power, we need more moral power. We do not need more knowledge, we need more character. We do not need more government, we need more culture. We do not need more law, we need more religion. We do not need more of the things that are seen, we need more of the things that are unseen. It is on that side of life that it is desirable to put the emphasis at the present time. If that side is strengthened, the other side will take care of itself. It is that side which is the foundation of all else. If the foun-

dation be firm, the superstructure will stand. (*The Price of Freedom*, Charles Scribner's Sons, 1924, p. 390.)

As a free people, we are following very closely in many respects the pattern which led to the downfall of the great Roman Empire. A group of well-known historians has summarized those conditions leading to the downfall of Rome in these words:

. . . Rome had known a pioneer beginning not unlike our own pioneer heritage, and then entered into two centuries of greatness, reaching its pinnacle in the second of those centuries, going into the decline and collapse in the third. Yet, the sins of decay were becoming apparent in the latter years of that second century.

It is written that there were vast increases in the number of the idle rich, and the idle poor. The latter [the idle poor] were put on a permanent dole, a welfare system not unlike our own. As this system became permanent, the recipients of public largesse [welfare] increased in number. They organized into a political block with sizable power. They were not hesitant about making their demands known. Nor was the government hesitant about agreeing to their demands . . . and with ever-increasing frequency. Would-be emperors catered to them. The great, solid middle class—Rome's strength then as ours is today—was taxed more and more to support a bureaucracy that kept growing larger, and even more powerful. Surtaxes were imposed upon incomes to meet emergencies. The government engaged in deficit spending. The denarius, a silver coin similar to our half dollar, began to lose its silvery hue. It took on a copper color as the government reduced the silver content.

Even then, Gresham's law was at work, because the real silver coin soon disappeared. It went into hiding.

Military service was an obligation highly honored by the Romans. Indeed, a foreigner could win Roman citizenship simply by volunteering for service in the legions of Rome. But, with increasing affluence and opulence, the young men of Rome began avoiding this service, finding excuses to remain in the soft and sordid life of the city. They took to using cosmetics and wearing feminine-like hairdo's and garments, until it became difficult, the historians tell us, to tell the sexes apart.

Among the teachers and scholars was a group called the Cynics whose number let their hair and beards grow, and who wore slovenly clothes, and professed indifference to worldly goods as they heaped scorn on what they called "middle class values."

The morals declined. It became unsafe to walk in the countryside or the city streets. Rioting was commonplace and sometimes whole sections of towns and cities were burned.

And, all the time, the twin diseases of confiscatory taxation and creeping inflation were waiting to deliver the death blow.

Then finally, all these forces overcome the energy and ambition of the middle class.

Rome fell.

We are now approaching the end of our second century. (Address by Governor Ronald Reagan of California at Eisenhower College, New York, 1969.)

In 1787 Edward Gibbon completed his noble work *The Decline and Fall of the Roman Empire*. Here is the way he accounted for the fall.

1. The undermining of the dignity and sanctity of the home, which is the basis of human society.

2. Higher and higher taxes and the spending of public monies for free bread and circuses for the populace.

3. The mad craze for pleasure, sports becoming every year more and more exciting and brutal.

4. The building of gigantic armaments when the real enemy was within the decadence of the people.

5. The decay of religion—faith fading into mere form, losing touch with life, and becoming impotent to warn and guide the people.

Is there a parallel for us in America today? Could the same reasons that destroyed Rome destroy America and possibly other countries of the free world?

For eight years in Washington I had this prayerful statement on my desk: "O God, give us men with a mandate higher than the ballot box."

The lessons of history, many of them very sobering, ought to be turned to during this hour of our great achievements, because during the hour of our success is our greatest danger. Even during the hour of our great prosperity, a nation may sow the seeds of its own destruction. History reveals that rarely is a great civilization conquered from without unless it has weakened or destroyed itself within.

The lessons of history stand as guideposts to help us safely chart the course for the future.

As American citizens, as citizens of the nations of the free world, we need to rouse ourselves to the problems which confront us as great Christian nations. We must recognize that these fundamental, basic principles—moral and spiritual—lay at the very foundation of our past achievements. To continue to enjoy present blessings, we must return to these basic and fundamental principles. Economics and morals are both part of one inseparable body of truth. They must be in harmony. We need to square our actions with these eternal verities.

The Church of Jesus Christ of Latter-day Saints stands firm in support of the great spiritual and moral principles which have been the basic traditions of the free world. We oppose every evil effort to downgrade or challenge the eternal verities which have undergirded civilization from the beginning.

We will use every honorable means to strengthen the home and family; to encourage obedience to the first and great commandment, to multiply and replenish the earth through noble parenthood; and to strengthen character through adherence to high spiritual and moral principles.

In The Church of Jesus Christ of Latter-day Saints chastity will never be out of date. We have one standard for men and women, and that standard is moral purity. We oppose and abhor the damnable practice of wholesale abortion and every other unholy and impure act which strikes at the very foundation of the home and family, our most basic institutions.

A continuation of these immoral practices will surely bring down the wrath and judgments of the Almighty.

In our concentration upon materialism and material acquisitions, are we forgetting the spiritual basis upon which our prosperity, security, and freedom rest? God help us to repent of our evil ways and humble ourselves before the offended power.

There is great safety in a nation on its knees.

What assurance it would give of the much-needed blessings of the Lord if the American people, and people everywhere, could all be found daily—night and morning—on their knees expressing gratitude for blessings already received, acknowledging our dependence upon God, and seeking his divine guidance.

The spectacle of a nation praying is more awe-inspiring, more powerful, than the explosion of an atomic bomb. The force of prayer is greater than any possible combination of man-controlled powers, because "prayer is man's greatest means of tapping the resources of God." The founding fathers accept this eternal verity. Do we? Will we?

Yes, it is in our own enlightened self-interest to engage in this simple practice, this powerful practice of prayer. Roger Babson said many years ago: "What this country needs more than anything else is old-fashioned family prayer." Yes, our greatest need is a return to the old-fashioned, time-tested verities.

God help us, as free men, to recognize the source of our blessings, the threat to our freedom and our moral and spiritual standards, and the need for humble, yet courageous, action to preserve these priceless, time-tested blessings.

37

America's Challenge

Near Boston, Massachusetts, rests a large boulder on Lexington Green. Inscribed on this rock are the words that Captain John Parker gave to his Minute Men on April 19, 1775:

> Stand your ground.
> Don't fire unless fired upon;
> but if they mean to have a war,
> let it begin here!

Said Webster, "They poured out their generous blood like water before they knew whether it would fertilize the land of freedom or of bondage."

But they aroused their fellow Americans. Within one year John Adams faced the body of men who were deliberating on whether to adopt the Declaration of Independence. With the inspiration of heaven resting upon him, Adams was said to have declared:

Sink or swim, live or die, survive or perish, I give my hand and my heart to this vote. It is true, indeed, that in the beginning we aimed not at independence. But there's a Divinity which shapes our ends. The injustice of England has driven us to arms; and blinded to her own interest for our good, she has obstinately persisted, till independence is now within our grasp. We have but to reach forth to it, and it is ours.

Why, then, should we defer the Declaration? Is any man so weak as now to hope for a reconciliation with England? . . .

You and I, indeed, may rue it. We may not live to the time when this Declaration shall be made good. We may die; die Colonists; die slaves, die, it may be, ignominiously and on the scaffold.

Be it so. Be it so.

If it be the pleasure of Heaven that my country shall require the poor offering of my life, the victim shall be ready. . . . But while I do live, let me have a country, or at least the hope of a country, and that a free country.

But whatever may be our fate, be assured . . . that this Declaration will stand. It may cost treasure, and it may cost blood; but it will stand, and it will richly compensate for both.

Through the thick gloom of the present, I see the brightness of the future, as the sun in heaven. We shall make this a glorious, an immortal day. When we are in our graves, our children will honor it. They will celebrate it with thanksgiving, with festivity, with bonfires, and illuminations. On its annual return they will shed tears, copious, gushing tears, not of subjection and slavery, not of agony and distress, but of exultation, of gratitude and of joy.

Sir, before God, I believe the hour is come. My judgment approves this measure, and my whole heart is in it. All that I have, and all that I am, and all that I hope, in this life, I am now ready here to stake upon it; and I leave off as I began, that live or die, survive or perish, I am for the Declaration. It is my living sentiment, and by the blessing of God it shall be my dying sentiment, Independence now, and Independence forever. (Daniel Webster Discourse on "Adams and Jefferson," August 2, 1826.)

I recently read the great volume *Quest of a Hemisphere* by Donzella Cross Boyle, published by Western Islands, Boston. I am grateful we have a textbook for our children, grandchildren, and their parents that restores that which has in many cases been removed by wolves in sheep's clothing—one-worlders who would surrender all we hold dear as true Americans. Chapter 8 is worth the price of the book.

Here we read again, as some of us are old enough to

remember, the courageous and stirring words against the Navigation Acts, the Stamp Act of 1765, and taxation without representation. In this real American history we have the record of Washington, Jefferson, and the record of Samuel Adams of Boston, who organized Committees of Correspondence and groups of young men banded together as Sons of Liberty. We read again the words of James Otis that a law was void if it violated the human rights of men and "a man who is quiet, is as secure in his house as a prince in his castle. . . ."

Here we read:

The colonists fought the threat of aggression as much as agres- sion itself. . . .

With grim determination, they opposed every attempt to rob them of any liberty they had gained.

[To the colonists—our benefactors—] it was not so much the amount as the *principle* of taxation (without representation) that the colonists opposed. (Pp. 105-106.)

Here again in this new history are also the fiery words "Give me liberty" of Patrick Henry of Virginia, as well as his words: "If this be treason, make the most of it." We find John Hancock, George Mason, Paul Revere, John Dickinson and his *Letters from a Farmer:* "We cannot be happy without being free. . . ."

Here are the words of the closing paragraph of chapter 8:

The British colonies were largely settled by people who had revolted against their living conditions in other lands. They were rebels, in a sense, who had the courage to flee from want and perse- cution, and face the perils of a wilderness to seek a better form of life. When they found a better way, they fought to keep it. Their children, grandchildren, and great-grandchildren did not want any monarch to change their way of life. They had plowed their own lands, built their own homes, and made their own clothes. They had hunted in the forests, fished in the streams, and slept under the stars. Who was their master? (*Quest of a Hemisphere,* p. 113.)

Chapter 7 closes with a discussion of freedom of the press and these stirring words inspired by Peter Zenger: "The right to print the truth is a necessary part of political liberty," and these by the famous lawyer Andrew Hamilton of Philadelphia: "The loss of liberty to a generous mind is worse than death. . . . The man who loves his country, prefers its liberty to all other considerations, well knowing that without liberty, life is a misery." (Ibid., p. 84.)

And this is the closing paragraph:

> Thus, in colonial days, did the people of the colonies stand firmly against any form of dictatorship. Thousands of immigrants came to the settlements along the Atlantic seaboard, with only a vague idea of the freedoms they were seeking, because they had not known many of them. They were pursuing a vision. Freedoms sprouted in a wilderness like flowers on a vacant lot, because each person who came had broken the pattern of life in his old country and he was starting all over again. "Something new" began to grow in the New World— a mere idea. People began to question the right of government to interfere with their freedom to come and go, to buy and sell, to own or lease, to talk or listen, to vote and elect. In other words, people began to think they had the right to govern themselves. Yet, a new nation had to rise in the Western Hemisphere before this idea gained a force of law. (Ibid., p. 84.)

Reading and promoting the book *Quest of a Hemisphere* will give you, as it has me, a warm, satisfying feeling. This excellent book of American history should be in every school and in every home to be read by young and old. We need more works of like quality in the days ahead.

And so today on Lexington Green, you will see a sacred old monument nearing two hundred years of age that covers the remains of those patriotic Minute Men and on this monument are inscribed these words:

Sacred to liberty and the rights of mankind!
The freedom and independence of America
Sealed and defended with the blood of her sons.

This monument is erected
By the inhabitants of Lexington,
Under the patronage, and at the expense, of
The Commonwealth of Massachusetts,
To the memory of their fellow citizens,
Ensign Robert Monroe, Messrs. Jonas Parker,
Samuel Hadley, Jonathan Harrington, Jr.,
Isaac Muzzy, Caleb Harrington and John Brown
Of Lexington, and Ashael Porter of Woburn,
Who fell on this field, the first victims to the
Sword of British tyranny and oppression,
On the morning of the ever memorable
19th of April, An. Dom. 1775.
The die was cast!

The blood of these martyrs
In the cause of God and their country,
Was the cement of the Union of these states, then
Colonies; and gave the spring to the spirit, firmness
And resolution of their fellow citizens.
They rose as one man, to revenge their brethren's
Blood and at the point of the sword, to assert and
Defend their native rights.
They nobly dared to be free!
The contest was long, bloody and affecting.
Righteous heaven approved the solemn appeal;
Victory crowned their arms; and
The peace, liberty and independence of the United
States of America was their glorious reward.

Built in the year 1799.

With independence won, another body of men assembled; and under the inspiration of heaven, they too drafted a document, probably the greatest instrument ever struck off at a given time by the mind of man: the Constitution of the United States.

Said President J. Reuben Clark, Jr., a great constitutional lawyer:

> The framers [of the Constitution] were not political tyros flying a political kite to keep in order the henyard, that is, the colonists. They were men widely experienced in affairs of government. . . .
>
> The Constitution was not the work of cloistered, fanatical theorists, but of sober, seasoned, distinguished men of affairs, drawn from various walks of life. They included students of wide reading and great learning in all matters of government. . . .
>
> The Constitution was born, not only of the wisdom and experience of the generations that had gone before and which had been transmitted to them through tradition and the pages of history. . . .
>
> These were the horse and buggy days as they have been called in derision; these were the men who traveled in the horsedrawn buggies and on horseback; but these were the men who carried under their hats, as they rode in the buggies and on their horses, a political wisdom garnered from the ages. As giants to pygmies are they when placed alongside our political emigres and their fellow travelers of today, who now traduce them with slighting and contemptuous phrase. (*Stand Fast by Our Constitution*, pp. 134-37.)

Those two documents—the Declaration of Independence and the Constitution of the United States—resting on the bedrock of the love of the Lord and of liberty, became the foundation of our republic. And from this foundation has come the greatest civilization on the face of the earth.

But for every righteous principle the devil seems to design a counterfeit. And so while our Constitution was being established in the land of America—a land choice above all others—the forces of evil across the world were laying the foundation of modern-day godless communism. Marx wanted to dethrone God and to destroy capitalism. In the Communist Manifesto, he called for "the forcible overthrow of all existing social conditions." Lenin demanded "a small tight kernel consisting of reliable, experienced, and steeled workers with responsible agents in the chief districts, and connected by all the rules of strict conspiracy." (*Lenin on Organization*, New York: International Publishers, 1:74.)

And from this foundation of communism has come the greatest tyranny ever imposed on mankind in recorded history. Today communism represents the greatest threat to peace, prosperity, and the spread of God's work on the earth.

Recently there was published a series of articles based on the observations of a number of historians: Spengler, de Reincourt, Ferraro, Gibbons, and others. The author told how Rome had known a pioneer beginning not unlike our own pioneer heritage, and then entered into two centuries of greatness, reaching its pinnacle in the second of those centuries, going into the decline and collapse in the third. Yet the sins of decay were becoming apparent in the latter years of that second century. We are now approaching the end of *our* second century.

Some time ago I spent two weeks in war-torn Asia. While there I held six meetings with Mormon servicemen in Vietnam. In combat dress—sometimes with guns stacked in the corner of the chapel—these faithful Latter-day Saints, bearers of the priesthood, strained to hear the gospel messages above the roar of helicopters and jet fighters leaving or returning from bombing missions, with the background of gunfire heard in the distance.

After shaking hands with more than eight hundred of these battle-hardened, brave, and patriotic men, men hard as nails physically and filled with faith and testimony, my right hand ached and my heart was filled with mingled feelings of gratitude and sadness.

I thought of the thousands of sons, brothers, and husbands who gave their lives in this, the strangest war in our nation's history. I made side trips by helicopter to visit others critically wounded in hospitals. I thought of those who were reported missing or captured, and those who had died from noncombat causes, whose loved ones also mourned the loss caused by this strange war.

A few days later at an Asia-wide Mormon Servicemen's Conference at Mt. Fuji, Japan, I listened to testimonies of faith and love of country that brought lumps to throats and tears to many eyes. These men, all American citizens, came to the conference from Thailand, Taiwan, Korea, Japan, Okinawa, the Philippines, Hong Kong, Guam, and other points. Some had traveled 3,000 miles to get there.

These were men who were ready to give their all in defense of freedom. These American servicemen worried about reports from home of rioters, draft-card burners, and other citizens—many times more numerous—who seemed oblivious to the threats to our freedom as they continued to enjoy their comfortable complacency. They worried about those many complacent citizens at home, some in high places, who talk—some gullibly, others they fear deceptively—of peaceful coexistence with the greatest, most destructive and insidious evil in the world. They knew that as college campus riots spread, so does the communist's role in the disturbances.

And yet we have men, including some in high places, who declare that communism is not the principal threat to the United States of America. People who make such statements are either uninformed, sadly naive, or else they are deliberately helping the communist conspiracy, the greatest evil in this world and the greatest threat to all we hold dear.

No, most of these servicemen—especially the officers— were not deceived. They would hope that their fellow citizens at home would get one thing straight at the very beginning: international communism is the self-avowed enemy of every loyal American. It has declared war against us and fully intends to win. The war in which we are engaged is total. Although its main battlefields are psychological, political, and economic, it also encompasses revolution, violence, terror, and limited military skirmishes.

One of the greatest tragedies of all time—and a fact that an increasing number of us are gradually coming to realize—is this: The growth and increasing success of communism around the world has been primarily the result of the support—yes, increasing support—that it has received from right within the United States, and particularly from our own government.

May I commend to you the book by Werner Keller entitled *East Minus West Equals Zero,* in order that you might see the documentation as to how we deliberately established Russia's industrial and war-making power. May I also commend to you the filmstrip *The Great Pretense— How to Finance Communism While Ostensibly Opposing It,* a documentary on how the free world finances communism.

Now, some people may feel that this has just been stupidity on our part and the mistakes of mortal men who really meant well but did not realize what they were doing. I agree that there has been some stupidity on the part of some people, but consistence has never been a hallmark of stupidity. I believe it was Forrestal who said that if it were just stupidity, then we would have made a few more mistakes on our side now and then, because stupidity is not consistent.

Sometimes we have appeared to take a step forward toward freedom, but it has inevitably been followed by two steps backward toward communism. Not only has this been true in our foisting communism onto other countries, but it also holds true regarding the increasing socialistic-communistic trends in America.

President Clark said:

> And do not think that all these usurpations, intimidations, and impositions are being done to us through inadvertence or mistakes; the whole course is deliberately planned and carried out; its purpose is

to destroy the Constitution and our constitutional government; then to bring chaos, out of which the new Statism, with its slavery, is to arise, with a cruel, relentless, selfish, ambitious crew in the saddle, riding hard with whip and spur, a red-shrouded band of night riders for despotism. . . .

If we do not vigorously fight for our liberties, we shall go clear through to the end of the road and become another Russia, or worse. . . . (*Church News,* September 25, 1949.)

Thomas Jefferson said:

Single acts of tyranny may be ascribed to the accidental opinion of a day; but a series of oppressions, begun at a distinguished period, and pursued unalterably through every change of ministers, too plainly prove a deliberate, systematical plan of reducing us to slavery. (*A Summary View of the Rights of British America,* 1774.)

Do you think we could have defeated Hitler in World War II if we had trained his pilots for him, built his steel mills, sent him billions in aid, traded with him, and let his men run for office in our country, work in our defense plants, teach our children? Yet this is exactly what we did for the communists, and our trade with them was in practically all the essentials that they needed to kill our men in Vietnam.

Quoting again from President Clark:

I have wished to bring together and call to your attention a number of matters, the close relationship of which it is easy to miss, and to indicate to you that, so assembled, they make a pattern which cannot be accounted for except on the theory that some group of minds is working out a diabolical plan for the destruction of our liberties and freedom, our divinely inspired Constitution and the Government our fathers set up thereunder, and the wiping out of our constitutional guarantees and the free lives, the security, the happiness, and the blessings we have enjoyed thereunder. (Address given to the Utah Wool Growers Association, January 24, 1945.)

Of the objectives for which the communists are presently pressing, how many can you name where they are not presently succeeding in this country? The communist party line is for increased East-West trade, peaceful co-existence, disarmament talks, reduction in military spending, etc. Are they succeeding?

Even back in the FBI Annual Report for 1964, J. Edgar Hoover reported: "The signing of the partial nuclear test-ban treaty was interpreted by the Communist Party, USA, as resulting from a shift in the world balance of forces in favor of communism and as a turning away from capitalism toward 'socialism.'"

Now what are we going to do about it? Said John Greenleaf Whittier:

> . . . Where's the manly spirit
> Of the true-hearted and the unshackled gone?
> Sons of old freemen, do we but inherit their names
>   alone?
> Is the old Pilgrim spirit quench'd within us?
> Stoops the proud manhood of our souls so low
> That Mammon's lure or Party's wile can win us to
>   silence now?
> Now, when our land to ruin's brink is verging,
> In God's name let us speak while there is time;
> Now, when the padlock for our lips is forging,
> Silence is a Crime.
> —"A Summons"

So let's speak up. James Russell Lowell was right when he said, "Our American Republic will endure only as long as the ideas of the men who founded it continue dominant."

What were those ideas? Well, they were in part incorporated in our Declaration of Independence and our Constitution. And George Washington covered them well when he said:

> Of all the dispositions and habits which lead to political prosperity, religion and morality are indispensable supports . . . reason

and experience both forbid us to expect that national morality can prevail in exclusion of religious principle. It is substantially true that virtue or morality is a necessary spring of popular government. . . . (Farewell Address, September 17, 1796.)

Only a moral and religious people deserve or will defend their freedom. Edmund Burke stated it well when he said:

Men are qualified for civil liberty in exact proportion to their disposition to put moral chains upon their own appetites—in proportion as their love of justice is above their rapacity;—in proportion as their soundness and sobriety of understanding is above their vanity and presumption;—in proportion as they are more disposed to listen to the counsels of the wise and good, in preference to the flattery of knaves. Society cannot exist, unless a controlling power upon the will and appetite is placed somewhere; and the less of it there is within, the more there must be without. It is ordained in the eternal constitution of things, that men of intemperate minds cannot be free. Their passions forge their fetters. (*Works*, 1888 ed., vol. 4, pp. 51-52.)

Elder Albert E. Bowen said, "Self-government involves self-control, self-discipline, an acceptance of and the most unremitting obedience to correct principles. . . . No other form of government requires so high a degree of individual morality." (*Improvement Era*, vol. 41 [1938], p. 266.)

And how are we to accomplish this?

We cannot accomplish this and be like the young man who lived with his parents in a public housing development, rode the free school bus, and participated in the free school lunch program. He obtained his degree at the state university, working part-time in the state capitol to supplement his GI education check.

Upon graduation, he married a public health nurse and obtained an RFC loan to go into business. He then bought a ranch with an FHA loan and obtained emergency feed from the government. He later put part of his land into the soil bank, and the payments soon took care of the loan on his ranch.

The government helped to clear his land, and the county agent showed him how to terrace it. Then the government built him a fish pond and stocked it with many fish. The government guaranteed him a sale for his farm products at highest prices.

His children grew up, entered public schools, ate free lunches, rode free school buses, and swam in public pools.

He signed a petition seeking federal assistance in developing a doubtful industrial project to help the economy of his area. He was the leader in obtaining the new post office and federal building and went to Washington with a group to ask the government to build a great dam costing millions so that his community could get the benefit of a temporary payroll.

He petitioned the government to give the local airbase to the county. He was also a leader in the movement to get special tax write-offs and exemptions for his specific type farming.

Then, one day, after calculating his taxes, he wrote his congressman, "I wish to protest the excessive government expenditures and attendant high taxes. I believe in rugged individualism. I think people should stand on their own two feet without expecting handouts. I am opposed to all socialistic trends, and I demand a return to the principles of our Constitution and the policies of states' rights."

Too many of us are like this young man.

We must be devoted to sound principles in word and deed: principle above party, principle above pocketbook, principle above popularity.

After we are soundly grounded in principle, the next two steps should follow automatically:

1. We must be well informed from sources that are consistently accurate on the things of greatest consequence.

2. We must take action after we have done our homework.

"My people are destroyed from lack of knowledge," said the prophet Hosea. Let's not let it happen to us. First, let's do our homework, because action without the proper education can lead to fanaticism. But after we have done our homework, then let's take action, because education without action can only lead to frustration and failure.

Said Lenin:

The Party is the conscious, advanced section of a class, its advance guard. The power of this advance guard is ten, a hundred times greater than its number. Is that possible? Can the power of a hundred exceed the power of thousands? It can exceed it when the hundreds are organized. Organization increases power by tenfold. (Quoted in *Political Education: The Communist Party*, Part III, New York: International Publishers, 1935, p. 6.)

He was right, and an organized Gideon's army in the fight for freedom can defeat this godless communist conspiracy. And so, I commend and salute all those patriots who have banded together to work in an effective and honorable manner to accomplish the objective of less government, more individual responsibility, and, with God's help, a better world.

May God bless America and preserve our divine Constitution and the republic that he established thereunder.

38

Not Commanded in All Things

In 1831 the Lord said this to his church:

> For behold, it is not meet that I should command in all things; for he that is compelled in all things, the same is a slothful and not a wise servant; wherefore he receiveth no reward.
>
> Verily I say, men should be anxiously engaged in a good cause, and do many things of their own free will, and bring to pass much righteousness.
>
> For the power is in them, wherein they are agents unto themselves. And inasmuch as men do good they shall in nowise lose their reward.
>
> But he that doeth not anything until he is commanded, and receiveth a commandment with doubtful heart, and keepeth it with slothfulness, the same is damned. (D&C 58:26-29.)

The purposes of the Lord—the great objectives—continue the same: the salvation and exaltation of his children.

Usually the Lord gives us the overall objectives to be accomplished and some guidelines to follow, but he expects us to work out most of the details and methods. The methods and procedures are usually developed through study and prayer and by living so that we can obtain and follow the promptings of the Spirit. Less spiritually advanced people, such as those in the days of Moses, had to be commanded in many things. Today those who are spiritually alert look at the objectives, check the guidelines laid down by the Lord and his prophets, and then prayerfully act—without having to be commanded "in all things." This attitude prepares men for godhood.

The overall objective to be accomplished in missionary work, temple work, providing for the needy, and bringing up our children in righteousness has always been the same; only our methods to accomplish these objectives have varied. Any faithful member in this dispensation, no matter when he lived, could have found righteous methods to have carried out these objectives without having to wait for the latest, specific churchwide program.

Sometimes the Lord hopefully waits on his children to act on their own, and when they do not, they lose the greater prize, and the Lord will either drop the entire matter and let them suffer the consequences or else he will have to spell it out in greater detail. Usually, I fear, the more he has to spell it out, the smaller is our reward.

Often, because of circumstances, the Lord, through revelation to his prophets or through inspired programs designed by faithful members that later become adopted on a churchwide basis, will give to all the membership a righteous means to help accomplish the objective; for instance, any member of the Church a century ago who studied Church doctrine would have known that he had the prime responsibility to see that his children had spiritualized family recreation and were taught in the home lessons in character building and gospel principles. But some did not do it.

Then, in 1915 President Joseph F. Smith introduced, churchwide, the "weekly home evening program" with promised blessings to all who faithfully adopted it. Many refused and lost the promised blessings. Today we have the

home evening manual and other helps. Yet some still refuse to bring up their children in righteousness.

However, there are some today who complain that
the home evening manual should have been issued years
ago. If this is true, then the Lord will hold his servants
accountable; but no one can say that from the inception
of the Church up to the present day the Lord, through his
Spirit to the individual members and through his spokes-
men, the prophets, has not given us the objectives and
plenty of guidelines and counsel. The fact that some of us
have not done much about it even when it is spelled out
in detail is not the Lord's fault.

For years we have been counseled to have on hand a
year's supply of food. Yet there are some today who will
not start storing until the Church comes out with a de-
tailed monthly home storage program. Now suppose
that never happens. We still cannot say we have not been
warned.

Should the Lord decide at this time to cleanse the
Church—and the need for that cleansing seems to be
increasing—a famine in this land of one year's duration
could wipe out a large percentage of slothful members, including some ward and stake officers. Yet we cannot say we
have not been warned.

Another warning: you and I sustain one man on this
earth as God's mouthpiece. We do not need a prophet—we
have one; what we desperately need is a listening ear.

Should it be of concern to us when the mouthpiece
of the Lord keeps constantly and consistently raising his
voice of warning about the loss of our freedom? There are
two unrighteous ways to deal with his prophetic words
of warning: you can fight them or you can ignore them.
Either course will bring you disaster in the long run.

Hear the words of President David O. McKay: "No

greater immediate responsibility rests upon members of the Church, upon all citizens of this Republic and of neighboring Republics than to protect the freedom vouchsafed by the Constitution of the United States." (*Man May Know for Himself*, 1967, p. 377.)

As important as are all other principles of the gospel, it was the freedom issue that determined whether you received a body. To have been on the wrong side of the freedom issue during the war in heaven meant eternal damnation. How then can Latter-day Saints expect to be on the wrong side in this life and escape the eternal consequences? The war in heaven is raging on earth today. The issues are the same: Shall men be compelled to do what others claim is for their best welfare or will they heed the counsel of the prophets and preserve their freedom?

Satan argued that men given their freedom would not choose correctly; therefore, he would compel them to do right and save us all. Today Satan argues that men given their freedom do not choose wisely; therefore a so-called brilliant, benevolent few must establish the welfare government and force us into a greater socialistic society. We are assured of being led into the promised land as long as we let them put a golden ring in our noses. In the end we lose our freedom and the promised land also. No matter what you call it—communism, socialism, or the welfare state— our freedom is sacrificed. We believe that the gospel is the greatest thing in the world; why then do we not force people to join the Church if they are not smart enough to see it on their own? Because this is Satan's way, not the Lord's plan. The Lord uses persuasion and love.

President McKay also said:

Today two mighty forces are battling for the supremacy of the world. The destiny of mankind is in the balance. It is a question of God and liberty, or atheism and slavery. . . . (*Church News,* July 18, 1953, p. 3.)

Those forces are known and have been designated by Satan on the one hand, and Christ on the other.

In Joshua's time they were called "gods of the Amorites," for one, and "the Lord" on the other. . . . In these days, they are called "domination by the state," on one hand, "personal liberty," on the other; communism on one, free agency on the other. (Speech at Brigham Young University, May 18, 1960, p. 2.)

Now, the Lord knew that before the gospel could flourish there must first be an atmosphere of freedom. This is why he first established the Constitution of this land through gentiles whom he raised up before he restored the gospel. In how many communist countries today are we doing missionary work, building chapels, etc.? And yet practically every one of those countries has been pushed into communism and kept under communism with the great assistance of evil forces which have been and are operating within our own country and neighboring lands. Yes, were it not for the tragic policies of governments—including our own—tens of millions of people murdered and hundreds of millions enslaved since World War II would be alive and free today to receive the restored gospel.

President J. Reuben Clark, Jr., put it clearly and courageously when he said:

Reduced to its lowest terms, the great struggle which now rocks the whole earth more and more takes on the character of a struggle of the individual versus the state. . . .

This gigantic world-wide struggle, more and more takes on the form of a war to the death. We shall do well and wisely so to face and so to enter it. And we must all take part. Indeed, we all are taking part in that struggle, whether we will or not. Upon its final issue, liberty lives or dies. . . . The plain and simple issue now facing us in America is freedom or slavery. . . . We have largely lost the conflict so far waged. But there is time to win the final victory, if we sense our danger, and fight. (*Vital Speeches,* vol. 5 [1939], pp. 174-75.)

Now where do we stand in this struggle, and what are we doing about it?

The devil knows that if the elders of Israel should ever

wake up, they could step forth and help preserve freedom and extend the gospel. Therefore the devil has concentrated, and to a large extent successfully, on neutralizing much of the priesthood. He has reduced them to sleeping giants. His arguments are clever. Here are a few samples.

First: "We really haven't received much instruction about freedom," the devil says. This is a lie, for we have been warned time and again. No prophet of the Lord has ever issued more solemn warning than President David O. McKay.

Second: "You're too involved in other church work," says the devil. But freedom is a weighty matter of the law; the lesser principles of the gospel you should keep, but not leave this one undone. We may have to balance and manage our time better. Your other church work will be limited once you lose your freedom, as our Saints have found out in Czechoslovakia, Poland, and many other nations.

Third: "You want to be loved by everyone," says the devil, "and this freedom battle is so controversial you might be accused of engaging in politics." Of course, the government has penetrated so much of our lives that one can hardly speak for freedom without being accused of being political. Some might even call the war in heaven a political struggle—certainly it was controversial. Yet the valiant entered it with Michael. Those who support only the popular principles of the gospel have their reward. And those who want to lead the quiet, retiring life but still expect to do their full duty can't have it both ways.

Said Elder John A. Widtsoe:

> The troubles of the world may largely be laid at the doors of those who are neither hot nor cold; who always follow the line of least resistance; whose timid hearts flutter at taking sides for truth. As in the great Council in the heavens, so in the Church of Christ on earth, there can be no neutrality. (*Conference Report,* April 1941, pp. 16-17.)

Fourth: "Wait until it becomes popular to do," says the devil, "or, at least, until everybody in the Church agrees on what should be done." But this fight for freedom might never become popular in our day. And if you wait until everybody agrees in this church, you will be waiting through the second coming of the Lord. Would you have hesitated to follow the inspired counsel of the Prophet Joseph Smith simply because some weak men disagreed with him? God's living mouthpiece has spoken to us—are we for him or against him? In spite of our prophets' opposition to increased federal aid and compulsory unionism, some Church members still champion these freedom-destroying programs. Where do you stand?

Fifth: "It might hurt your business or your family," says the devil, "and besides, why not let the gentiles save the country? They aren't as busy as you are." Well, there were many businessmen who went along with Hitler because it supposedly helped their business. They lost everything. Many of us are here today because our forefathers loved truth enough that they fought at Valley Forge or crossed the plains in spite of the price it cost them or their families. We had better take our small pain now than our greater loss later. There were souls who wished afterwards that they had stood and fought with Washington and the founding fathers, but they waited too long—they passed up eternal glory. There has never been a greater time than now to stand up against entrenched evil. And while the gentiles established the Constitution, we have a divine mandate to preserve it. But unfortunately, today in this freedom struggle, many gentiles are showing greater wisdom in their generation than the children of light.

Sixth: "Don't worry," says the devil; "the Lord will protect you, and besides, the world is so corrupt and heading toward destruction at such a pace that you can't stop it, so why try?" Well, to begin with, the Lord will not protect us unless we do our part. This devilish tactic of persuading people not to get concerned because the Lord will protect them no matter what they do is exposed by the Book of Mormon. Referring to the devil, it says: "And others will he pacify, and lull them away into carnal security, and they will say: All is well in Zion; yea, Zion prospereth, all is well—and thus the devil cheateth their souls, and leadeth them away carefully down to hell." (2 Nephi 28:21.)

I like that word *carefully*. In other words, don't shake them—you might wake them. But the Book of Mormon warns us that when we see these murderous conspiracies in our midst, we should awaken to our awful situation. Now, why should we awaken if the Lord is going to take care of us anyway? Let us suppose that it is too late to save freedom. It is still accounted unto us for righteousness' sake to stand up and fight. Some Book of Mormon prophets knew of the final desolate end of their nations, but they still fought on, and they saved some souls, including their own, by so doing. For, after all, the purpose of life is to prove ourselves, and the final victory will be for freedom.

But many of the prophecies referring to America's preservation are conditional. That is, if we do our duty we can be preserved, and if not, then we shall be destroyed. This means that a good deal of the responsibility lies with the priesthood of this church as to what happens to America and as to how much tragedy can be avoided if we do act now.

And now as to the last neutralizer that the devil used most effectively—it is simply this: "Don't do anything in the fight for freedom until the Church sets up its own specific program to save the Constitution." This brings us right back to the scripture about the slothful servants who will not do anything until they are "compelled in all things."

Maybe the Lord will never set up a specific Church program for the purpose of saving the Constitution. Perhaps if he set one up at this time it might split the Church asunder, and perhaps he does not want that to happen yet, for not all the wheat and tares are fully ripe.

The Prophet Joseph Smith declared that it will be the elders of Israel, not the Church, who will step forward to help save the Constitution. And have the elders been warned? Yes, they have. And besides, if the Church should ever inaugurate a program, who do you think would be in the forefront to get it moving? It would not be those who were sitting on the sidelines prior to that time or those who were appeasing the enemy. It would be those choice spirits who, not waiting to be "commanded in all things," will use their own free will, the counsel of the prophets, and the Spirit of the Lord as guidelines and who enter the battle "in a good cause" and bring to pass much righteousness in freedom's cause.

If we had done our homework and were faithful, we could step forward at this time and help save this country. The fact that most of us are unprepared to do it is an indictment we will have to bear. The longer we wait, the heavier the chains, the deeper the blood, the more the persecution, and the less we can carry out our God-given mandate and worldwide mission. The war in heaven is raging on the earth today. Are you being neutralized in the battle?

"Verily I say, men should be anxiously engaged in a good cause, and do many things of their own free will, and bring to pass much righteousness;

"For the power is in them, wherein they are agents unto themselves. . . ."

39

Righteousness Exalteth a Nation

"Righteousness exalteth a nation." This statement of eternal truth from Proverbs appeared on the flyleaf and the last page of a booklet at each plate at the President's Prayer Breakfast in the Grand Ballroom of the Mayflower Hotel in Washington, D.C., on February 7, 1963.

As I listened to the prayers, readings from the Old and New Testaments, and messages from government and nongovernment leaders, I reviewed hurriedly our spiritual background as a nation and today's spiritual needs. For truly, "Righteousness exalteth a nation: but sin is a reproach to any people." (Proverbs 14:34.)

The beautiful old print that hangs in Carpenter's Hall, Philadelphia, came to mind. It is captioned "The First Prayer in Congress, September 1774." It depicts most of the members of that Congress on their knees with George Washington, our first President, as leader.

I recalled the terrible winter at Valley Forge and Washington on his knees in the snow, praying for divine aid. I thought of the words of Abraham Lincoln during another time of crisis as he said humbly: "I have been driven many times to my knees by the overwhelming conviction that I had nowhere else to go."

Washington acknowledged God's direction and stated, "Of all the dispositions and habits which lead to political prosperity, religion and morality are indispensable supports. . . . Reason and experience both forbid us to expect that national morality can prevail in exclusion of religious principles." (Farewell address.)

Lincoln knew that God rules in the affairs of men and nations. He solemnly declared: "God rules this world. It is the duty of nations as well as men to own their dependence upon the overruling power of God, to confess their sins and transgressions in humble sorrow . . . and to recognize the sublime truth that those nations only are blessed whose God is the Lord."

The founding fathers knew that "where the Spirit of the Lord is, there is liberty." (2 Corinthians 3:17.) The United States of America began and lives as a result of faith in God. The Bible has been and is the foundation for this faith.

"It is impossible to govern the world without the Bible," said George Washington.

"The Bible is the rock on which this Republic rests," Andrew Jackson proclaimed.

The fathers of our country had to turn to religion in order that their new experiment would make sense.

As I left the prayer breakfast, bidding goodbye to many warm friends, I thought of the greatness of America, the world's greatest power. During World War II she outproduced both her enemies and her allies—"the American miracle."

But I also recalled FBI reports that revealed an ever-increasing crime record. I recalled our shockingly defiant record of drunkenness and immorality and the fact that we have become a nation of pleasure-seeking Sabbath breakers.

My thoughts turned to our homes and families, our

ever-increasing divorce rate, the alarming increase in sexual sin, infidelity, yes, even adultery. We live in a day of slick, quiet, and clever sins. It is made easy to cover up.

I recalled the solidarity of the homes of long past when family prayer, daily devotion, the reading of scriptures, and the singing of hymns were common practices in American homes—practices that, I am sorry to say, have all but disappeared today.

I became saddened as I reviewed evidence of a lessening of moral stability, honor, integrity, love of country; a seeking for the honors of men, of something for nothing; the tendency to lean more and more on government; the result of our ever-increasing demands, even though often economically, socially, and spiritually unsound.

There has been a nationwide erosion of individual character. Jefferson's words still ring true: "Material abundance without character is the surest way to destruction." I recalled how proudly in generations past we spoke of the "American way of life."

Then I saw thirty million doorknob hangers being distributed by Scouts, setting forth our political and economic rights in an effort to stimulate patriotism in this choice land. As I read the message from the Freedom Foundation and the Scouts, I thought of our basic American concepts, our constitutional government, based on a fundamental belief in God.

I became alarmed as I reviewed what has happened in our schools under so-called progressive education. What about the loss of patriotism, faith in God, and the teachings of character-building principles once so much a part of our education? We have all but "forced Americanism out of the classroom to make way for temporary trivialities." (De Love.)

I remember President Joseph F. Smith's warning of

the three dangers to the Church from within, viz., the flattery of prominent men, sexual impurity, and false educational ideas. (*Gospel Doctrine,* p. 312.)

Then there came to me the words of that courageous American patriot, J. Edgar Hoover:

> Today as never before, America has need for men and women who possess the moral strength and courage of our forefathers—modern-day patriots, with pride in our country and faith in freedom....
>
> Too often in recent years, patriotic symbols have been shunted aside. Our national heroes have been maligned, our history distorted. Has it become a disgrace to pledge allegiance to our flag—or sign a loyalty oath, or pay tribute to our national anthem? Is it shameful to encourage our children to memorize the stirring words of the men of '76? Is it becoming opprobrious to state "In God we trust" when proclaiming our love of country?
>
> What we desperately need today is patriotism founded on a real understanding of the American ideal—a dedicated belief in our principles of freedom, and a determination to perpetuate America's heritage. (*FBI Law Enforcement Bulletin,* April 1962, p. 3.)

Are we slipping from our moorings, becoming soft, carelessly drawing away from the course that has brought us such priceless blessings in days past?

David Lawrence, editor of *U.S. News and World Report,* wrote: "The destiny of the world is in the hands of those statesmen who can interpret faithfully the commands of the Almighty."

Can our national leaders do this? Can they interpret faithfully the commands of the Almighty? Can we as citizens of this blessed land? Can we as people of the free world? Do we believe that "righteousness exalteth a nation," that there is safety only in righteous living?

Fortunately, today we are not left in darkness. We have guides—not only the Holy Bible, but added modern scriptures. And of the utmost importance for us today, we have the counsel and direction of living oracles. This counsel, this direction—in fact, the message of the fulness of the restored gospel—is being carried to the world by our missionaries, ambassadors of the Lord Jesus Christ.

And what is this message? It is a world message of the utmost importance. It is that God has again spoken from the heavens. The priesthood and authority to act in his name have been restored again to men on the earth, following centuries of darkness. The fulness of the everlasting gospel is here with all of its saving principles. To these facts I bear humble witness.

The prophets of a new gospel dispensation have counsel for us today—counsel on matters that concerned the founding fathers: freedom, liberty, righteousness which "exalteth a nation."

Do we believe and accept their counsel, or have we drifted away from those basic concepts and principles, without adherence to which, no nation can be exalted? Elder Albert E. Bowen said:

> That which is right does not become wrong merely because it may be deserted by the majority, neither does that which is wrong today become right tomorrow by the chance circumstance that it has won the approval or been adopted by overwhelmingly predominant numbers. Principles cannot be changed by nor accommodate themselves to the vagaries of popular sentiment. (*Conference Report*, April 1941, p. 85.)

Modern-day prophets have said much by way of counsel and warning for our guidance. I turn to one who was called "a seer in the area of government" and who stood closest to the prophet of the Lord—the president of the Church—longer than any other man in Church history. I speak of President J. Reuben Clark, Jr.:

> There always comes a time when unpleasant truths must be retold, even though the retelling disturbs the ease and quiet of a luxurious error. Today seems to be such a time. On such occasions, the criticism, slander, misrepresentation that one gets, are of no consequence. (Address to Utah Wool Growers Association, January 24, 1945.)

. . . today government has touched our lives so intimately in all their relationships and all these governmental touchings have been so tabbed as political, that we cannot discuss anything relating to our material welfare and existence without laying ourselves liable to the charge that we are talking politics. (*Church News,* June 16, 1945, p. 4.)

I have been preaching against Communism for twenty years. I still warn you against it, and I tell you that we are drifting toward it more rapidly than some of us understand, and I tell you that when Communism comes, the ownership of the things which are necessary to feed your families is going to be taken away from us. I tell you freedom of speech will go, freedom of the press will go, and freedom of religion will go.

I have warned you against propaganda and hate. We are in the midst of the greatest exhibition of propaganda that the world has ever seen, and all directed toward one end. Just do not believe all you read. (*Conference Report,* October 3, 1941, p. 16.)

The plain and simple issue now facing us in America is freedom or slavery. . . .

Our real enemies are *communism* and its running mate, *socialism.* . . .

And never forget for one moment that communism and socialism are state slavery. . . .

. . . one thing seems sure, we will not get out of our present difficulties without trouble, serious trouble. Indeed, it may well be that our government and its free institutions will not be preserved except at the price of life and blood. . . .

. . . the paths we are following, if we move forward thereon, will inevitably lead us to socialism or communism, and these two are as like as two peas in a pod in their ultimate effect upon our liberties. . . .

We may first observe that communism and socialism—which we shall hereafter group together and dub Statism—cannot live with Christianity, nor with any religion that postulates a Creator such as the Declaration of Independence recognizes. The slaves of Statism must know no power, no authority, no source of blessing, no God, but the State. . . .

This country faces ahead enough trouble to bring us to our knees in humble honest prayer to God for the help which He alone can give, to save us. . . .

Do not think that all these usurpations, intimidations, and impositions are being done to us through inadvertency or mistake; the whole course is deliberately planned and carried out; its purpose is to destroy the Constitution and our Constitutional government. . . .

We have largely lost the conflict so far waged. But there is time to win the final victory, if we can sense our danger, and fight. (*Church News,* September 25, 1949, pp. 2, 15.)

Thus spoke the very forthright and courageous President J. Reuben Clark, Jr.

President David O. McKay said:

During the first half of the twentieth century we have traveled far into the soul-destroying land of socialism and made strange alliances through which we have become involved in almost continuous hot and cold wars over the whole of the earth. In this retreat from freedom the voices of protesting citizens have been drowned by raucous shouts of intolerance and abuse from those who led the retreat and their millions of gullible youth, who are marching merrily to their doom, carrying banners on which are emblazoned such intriguing and misapplied labels as social justice, equality, reform, patriotism, social welfare. (*Church News,* October 18, 1952, p. 2.)

The fostering of full economic freedom lies at the base of our liberties. Only in perpetuating economic freedom can our social, political, and religious liberties be preserved. . . . We must not let complacency blind our eyes to the real dangers threatening to destroy us. (*Gospel Ideals,* p. 433.)

Communism is antagonistic to the American way of life. Its avowed purpose is to destroy belief in God and free enterprise. In education for citizenship, therefore, why should we not see to it that every child in America is taught the superiority of our way of life, of our Constitution and the sacredness of the freedom of the individual. Such definite instruction is not in violation of either the federal or the state constitution. . . .

I love the Stars and Stripes, and the American Way of Life. I have faith in the Constitution of the United States. I believe that only through a truly educated citizenry can the ideals that inspired the Founding Fathers of our Nation be preserved. (*Treasures of Life,* pp. 501-503.)

Then President McKay listed as one of the four fundamental elements in such an education the "open and forceful teaching of facts regarding communism as an enemy to God and to individual freedom." (Ibid.)

At the opening session of the October 1961 semiannual

general conference, President McKay gave a stirring address on our American way of life and the communist threat. He expressed grief and shock over a Supreme Court decision and stated that the enemies to our republican form of government are becoming more blatant.

At the close of the general conference in April 1962, President McKay emphasized that "men are rapidly classifying themselves into two groups: believers and nonbelievers." Then he quoted J. Edgar Hoover's warning:

> This nation is face to face with the greatest danger ever to confront it, a sinister and deadly conspiracy, which can be conquered only by an alert, informed citizenry. It is indeed appalling that some members of our society continue to deplore and criticize those who stress the communist danger. Public indifference to this threat is tantamount to national suicide. Lethargy leads only to disaster. Knowledge of the enemy, alertness to the danger, everyday patriotism are the brick and mortar with which we can build an impregnable fortress against communism. (*Conference Report,* April 1962, p. 125.)

In October 1962 President McKay said:

> In these days of uncertainty and unrest, liberty-loving people's greatest responsibility and paramount duty is to preserve and proclaim the freedom of the individual, his relationships to Deity, and the necessity of obedience to the principles of the gospel of Jesus Christ. *Only thus will mankind find peace and happiness.*

He concluded by urging Church members to "support good and conscientious candidates of *either party* who are aware of the great dangers inherent in communism, and who are truly dedicated to the Constitution in the tradition of the founding fathers." (*Conference Report,* October 1962, p. 8.)

We cannot say that the prophets of the Lord have not warned us. Do we heed their counsel? Are we in harmony? Every Latter-day Saint has spiritual obligations in four basic areas: his home, his church, his job, and his citizenship. Each of these areas should receive consistent attention, although not necessarily equal time. Are we doing our duty in these important fields? What about our citizenship responsibility—our obligation to safeguard our freedom and preserve the Constitution?

The Prophet Joseph Smith said the time would come when the Constitution would hang, as it were, by a thread. Modern-day prophets for the past several decades have been warning us that we have been rapidly moving in that direction. Fortunately, the Prophet Joseph Smith saw the part the elders of Israel would play in this crisis. Will there be some of us who won't care about saving the Constitution, others who will be blinded by the craftiness of men, and some who will knowingly be working to destroy it? He who has ears to hear and eyes to see can discern by the Spirit and through the words of God's mouthpiece that our liberties are being taken.

The enemy is amongst and upon us. Zion must awake and arouse herself. We, the elders of Israel, can be and should be the leaven in the loaf for freedom.

Years ago President Brigham Young stated:

> We all believe that the Lord will fight our battles; but how? Will he do it while we are unconcerned and make no effort whatever for our own safety when the enemy is upon us? . . . it would be quite as reasonable to expect remission of sins without baptism, as to expect the Lord to fight our battles without our taking every precaution to be prepared to defend ourselves. The Lord requires us to be quite as willing to fight our own battles as to have Him fight them for us. If we are not ready for the enemy when he comes upon us, we have not lived up to the requirements of Him who guides the ship of Zion, or who dictates the affairs of His kingdom. (*Journal of Discourses*, vol. 11, p. 121.)

May we as a free people face courageously the challenging responsibility that faces us. "All that is necessary for the triumph of evil is that good men do nothing." (Edmund Burke.) We are not here to sit by complacently while our birthright of freedom is exchanged for a mess of socialist-communist pottage.

I love this great land—the Lord's latter-day base of operations. I love the free world. I love our Father's children everywhere.

God bless us in our stewardship. May we be at least as valiant for freedom and righteousness, here and now, as we were when we fought for these principles in the preexistence. There is no other safe way, for "righteousness exalteth a nation."

40

God, Family, and Country

While attending the Fairfax Christian School in Virginia, my grandson Ezra Taft was introduced to the historical character Israel Putnam. Israel Putnam was one of the Revolutionary War farmers who left his plow in the field and gave up his comfort in order to protect his family, defend his inalienable God-given rights, and help establish this great, free country. It is heartening to know that today there are still those who answer to the rallying cry of God, family, and country.

Recently it was my privilege to walk across a part of that sacred soil where some of the best blood of Israel Putnam's generation was shed for freedom and the redemption of this land. Those noble souls did not initiate freedom, and one of the privileges of mortal life is the opportunity to rise in freedom's defense during the time when Lucifer is permitted to tempt and test men with his satanic schemes of slavery. This is part of our mission today. The same sun that shone on Israel Putnam during his mortal probation shines on us. And the same issues of light and darkness, force and freedom, right and wrong, that provided men a chance to prove themselves in his day continue to sift the souls of men today.

The thing that concerns so many of us today is not that wickedness is new, but that never before in our history has it been so well organized or so insidiously successful. Now, in view of this fact, and with a final showdown approaching between the powers of good and evil, may I be so bold as to make a few personal observations and express my convictions regarding God, family, and country.

I know, as I know that I live, that there is a God in heaven; that he is perfect and all powerful; that we are his children; that he loves us; and that we are eternal beings. I also know that life is a testing time in man's eternal existence, during which he is given his free agency—the right to choose between right and wrong—and that on those choices hang great consequences, not only in this life, but, even more important, in the life to come. There are boundaries beyond which Satan cannot go. Within those bounds, he is presently being permitted to offer an unrighteous alternative to God's righteous principles, thus allowing men to choose between good and evil and thereby determine the station they shall occupy in the next life. Said the poet:

> Know this, that every soul is free
> To choose his life and what he'll be,
> For this eternal truth is given
> That God will force no man to heaven.

> He'll call, persuade, direct aright,
> Bless with wisdom, love, and light;
> In nameless ways be good and kind,
> But never force the human mind.

God has not left man alone. He sends prophets, gives scripture, whispers counsel, answers righteous prayers, and in innumerable ways blesses his children. And he would more richly bless them if they were willing to obey the commands on which those blessings are predicated. I know that truth will eventually triumph and freedom will ultimately and finally prevail.

That fact alone should lift the spirit and hope of those who have an eternal view of things. Some of you will recall that during World War II, many of the British children were sent into rural areas for protection. One night, one of the small children, saying her prayers while the Battle of Britain raged over London, asked the Lord to bless the members of her family who were absent, including her father who was serving in the Royal Air Force. And as she was about to close her prayer, she said: "And dear God, please take care of yourself—because if anything happens to you, we're *all* sunk!"

Now, the great consolation and hope of every patriot should be that God is in his heaven; that he is the same yesterday, today, and forever; that this is his earth; that he is in charge; that his word will not fail; that in due time every wrong shall be righted, every virtue justified, every evil punished, and every good rewarded. But for the immediate future, we face times and calamities that will test the spiritual fibre of the best of us.

Now, with that knowledge, what is our responsibility? Why, what it has always been: to keep God's commandments. No more and no less. And that includes the declaration of Moses, inscribed on the Liberty Bell in Constitution Hall in Philadelphia, where the Declaration of Independence was signed: "Proclaim liberty throughout all the land, unto all the inhabitants thereof." (Leviticus 25:10.)

It is my conviction that despite the serious trials and tribulations we will have to face before Jehovah's triumphal return, the forces of freedom and righteousness, which have never been better organized than they are today, shall not be destroyed. The number who are dedicated to, and will preserve, our inspired Constitution are on the increase, and God watches over the faithful no matter what is going on in the world.

It is our duty to be faithful, and a man cannot be counted among the fully faithful unless he is an active fighter for freedom. Resistance to tyranny is still obedience to God. How to resist in the most effective manner will require careful and prayerful thought on the part of all of us. To be fully effective in the fight for freedom, a man must be in tune with the greatest champion and leader of free men—the Lord our God. And to be in tune with him, we must be in step with him; we must walk in his way.

Now, that divine duty to be a faithful fighter for freedom requires that those of us who have been warned do our duty to warn our neighbor, for our neighbor's involvement in this struggle can bless his soul, strengthen his family, and protect him from pitfalls while he helps his country. The blessings far outweigh the burden when we stand up for freedom. With gall comes glory; with a cross comes a crown; with thorns comes a throne, if we will persevere in righteousness. There are still more victories to be won in this fight for freedom, the most important of which is to save our own souls by taking a stand for liberty with the Lord. For amid the encircling gloom, the kindly light of the Lord can lead us on—can help expose and stop evil in some places, slow it down in others, give the forces of freedom the chance to become better entrenched, provide righteous alternatives, and develop faith and hope to keep on keeping on in the divine assurance that in the brightness of the Lord's coming, the darkness of Satan's conspiracy will eventually be fully exposed and destroyed.

Now, in preparation for the showdown, may I encourage each of us to strengthen our families. The communists are determined to destroy the three great loyalties—loyalty to God, loyalty to family, and loyalty to country. Some of our patriots are losing their children. In our attempt to save our country, we must not let our own homes crumble. Don't neglect your own. You can't delegate that divine duty nor neglect it without tragic consequences. Be careful in sending them away from your hearth for additional education. There are worse things that can happen to a young person today than not getting a liberal college degree.

We must multiply our influence by raising up God-fearing patriots at our own fireside. We need more than one generation of patriots in a family line. We need more men like John Adams, who took time amid all the demands of the revolution and the building of this republic to teach and train a future president, his own son, John Quincy Adams. We must stay close to our children.

Not only should we have strong spiritual homes, but we should have strong temporal homes. We should avoid bondage by getting out of debt as soon as we can, pay as we go, and live within our incomes. There is wisdom in having on hand a year's supply of food, clothing, and fuel, if possible, and in being prepared to defend our families and our possessions and to take care of ourselves. I believe a man should prepare for the worst while working for the best. Some people prepare and don't work, while others work but don't prepare. Both are needed if we would be of maximum service to our God, our family, and our country.

It is a part of my religious belief that America is a land choice above all others, that we are not just another of the family of nations, but that we have been singled out to perform a divine mission for liberty-loving people everywhere. Those who founded this republic were wise men raised up by our Father in heaven to perform that very task, and the Constitution of this land was inspired by God. We have a divine duty—even a destiny—to preserve that Constitution from destruction and hold it aloft to the world.

A book that I accept as scripture tells of two ancient

American civilizations that were destroyed as a result of murderous conspiracies lusting for power and seeking to overthrow freedom. That book warned that when we should see a similar situation developing in our land in our day, we would be under commandment of the Lord to awake to our awful situation. That day is upon us, and those of us who are awake to our situation have a moral obligation to do all we can to awaken our fellow citizens.

The Book of Mormon states that America will remain a free land as long as the people worship the God of the land. It also assures us that "unto the righteous" this land "shall be blessed forever."

I remember a number of years ago when Cecil B. DeMille, the great producer of such films as *The Ten Commandments,* was invited to accept an honorary degree from Brigham Young University. In his address to the student body, Mr. DeMille made an interesting observation. He said that men and nations cannot really break the Ten Commandments; they can only break themselves upon them. How true!

And so, in talking about our country as well as our families, we return again to God, because this whole basic struggle revolves around the spiritual and moral fitness of our people. Nineveh was saved because the people repented while there was still time. But Sodom was destroyed because God couldn't find even ten worthy souls. As the wicked become more wicked and more numerous, the righteous will need to increase in spiritual strength and numbers to offset them. One of the great blessings of the last few years is that the patriotic movement in America has become organized and strengthened to an unprecedented degree.

A while ago some lonely American must have felt like Elijah, who fled into the wilderness thinking that he was alone in rejecting false gods. But God knew differently and told Elijah of some 7,000 who had not bent their knees to the idols. This lifted Elijah's heart and he went back to the battle with Baal. We know that we are not alone in this freedom fight. Many have helped lift other hearts, but there are many more who feel alone whose knees have not bent or who might be wobbly. There may be some who, with our help, understanding, and encouragement, might get off their knees to the idol of socialism and acquit themselves like men.

We must have an even greater determination to reach and influence those who, with our help, understanding, and encouragement, might themselves join us in the battle. God is counting on us to follow through. If we do it well, then we will have done our job. Like the watchman on the tower referred to in the Bible, it is our task to warn others of the darkness. Some will not listen, and they will be held accountable. But if we who have the word fail to issue the warning, then God will hold *us* accountable.

May we pledge anew that the divine principles embodied in the divinely inspired documents that govern our country be written on the tablets of our own hearts. I pray that our eyes might be single to the will of God, that we might thereby bless our families and our country, and that we shall, with increased devotion, work for less government, more individual responsibility, and, with God's help, a better world.

APPENDIX
Sources of Material Used

The chapters in this book have been adapted from the following sources:

1. "In His Steps." General conference address, April 10, 1966.

2. "Our Lord and Master." Address delivered at the Church Office Building employees Christmas program, December 22, 1967, Salt Lake City, Utah.

3. "Life Is Eternal." General conference address, April 3, 1971.

4. "Joseph Smith—Man of Destiny." Address delivered at the Joseph Smith memorial program, LDS Institute of Religion, Logan, Utah, December 3, 1967.

5. "Missionary Work—A Major Responsibility." General conference address, April 7, 1974.

6. "Missionary Memories." Article in the *Friend,* August 1971, p. 14.

7. "Essentials for Missionary Success." Remarks to missionaries of the Andes Mission in Lima, Peru, November 2, 1960.

8. "A Love for the Work." Remarks at the quarterly temple meeting of the Council of the Twelve, April 1, 1973.

9. "The Things That Endure." Address delivered at the Sunday afternoon session of the Mutual Improvement Association June Conference, June 14, 1959.

10. "The Latter-day Saints and the World." Address at the area general conference held in Mexico City, August 27, 1972.

11. "Keeping the Sabbath Day Holy." Remarks at the general priesthood board meeting, February 10, 1971.

12. "The Power of Prayer." Article in the *Reader's Digest,* November 1954.

13. "How to Improve Prayers, Public and Private." Address delivered to the General Authorities at the general priesthood board meeting, March 26, 1969.

14. "How to Delegate Wisely." Address delivered to the General Authorities at the general priesthood board meeting, November 1, 1967.

15. "Suggestions on Making Decisions." Address delivered at the general priesthood board meeting, February 11, 1970.

16. "Listen to a Prophet's Voice." General conference address, October 6, 1972.

17. "The Family—A Sacred Institution." General conference address, October 4, 1953.

18. "Family Joys." Article in the *New Era,* January 1973.

19. "Putting Father at the Head of the Family." Address at the general priesthood board meeting, November 21, 1973.

20. "A Challenge to Youth." Address delivered at the Washington, D.C. Stake M-Man and Gleaner fireside, March 28, 1954.

21. "Receive All Things with Thankfulness." Address delivered at the annual leadership assembly at Ricks College, Rexburg, Idaho, November 17, 1961.

22. "Scouting—Builder of Men." Address delivered at the Eagle recognition banquet, Utah State University Center, Logan, Utah, March 22, 1974.

23. "Fitness—A Total Concept." Address delivered before the second annual meeting of the President's Council on Youth Fitness, Camp Ritchie, Cascade, Maryland, September 8, 1958.

24. "Strengthening the Family." General conference address, October 2, 1970.

25. "Three Threatening Dangers." General conference address, October 3, 1964.

26. "Satan's Thrust—Youth." General conference address, October 1, 1971.

27. "Destructive Precepts of Men." General conference address, April 4, 1969.

28. "Prepare Ye." General conference address, October 6, 1973.

29. "The Twelfth Article of Faith." Article in the *Instructor,* December 1955, pp. 332-33.

30. "The Proper Role of Government." Address delivered at the Utah Forum, Salt Lake City, Utah, February 29, 1968.

31. "Survival of the American Way of Life," *Improvement Era,* June 1948, p. 362.

32. "Civic Standards for the Faithful Saints." General conference address, April 6, 1972.

33. "Christ and the Constitution." General conference address, April 8, 1967.

34. "Be Not Deceived." General conference address, October 1963.

35. "The American Heritage of Freedom." General conference address, September 30, 1961.

36. "Watchman, Warn the Wicked." General conference address, April 6, 1973.

37. "America's Challenge." Address delivered at the New England Rally for God, Family, and Country, Boston, Massachusetts, July 4, 1970.

38. "Not Commanded in All Things." General conference address, April 5, 1965.

39. "Righteousness Exalteth a Nation." General conference address, April 7, 1963.

40. "God, Family, and Country." Address delivered at the New England Rally for God, Family, and Country honor banquet, Boston, Massachusetts, July 4, 1972.

Index

-A-
Abomination of desolation, 346
Abortion, 224
Accountability, 132
Actions on decisions, 151
Adams, John, 405; quotation by, 367-68
Adams, John Quincy, 405
Adams, Samuel, 369
Adversary, strategy of, 357
Aid to other nations, 376
Alabama Constitution, 287
Allegiance, 359
America
    land of promise, 95
    foundation pillars of, 298-99
    industrialization in, 308-309
    discovery of, 343
    established by God as land of liberty,
      344, 345
    what is greatness of, 360
    warnings on preservation of, 388
    to be free if people worship God, 406
"America on Its Knees," 114
American independence, 344
American Revolution, 302, 367-71
American Tradition, The, 319
American way of life, 195, 305-315, 397
Americans, challenges for, 302-303
Amussen, Barbara S., 31
Andersen, H. Verlan, 321
Anderson, Tom, 11
Anthon, Don K., 83
Anti-Christ sign, 229
Apathy, 214
Apostasy, 238
Apostate, 254; doctrines, 253-63
Appeasement, 359
Article of Faith, twelfth, 277-80
Asia Servicemen's conference, 374
Associates, influence of, 241
Authority, keys of, 135; in Church, 135;
    of priesthood, 158

-B-
Baal, 407

Babbel, Fred, 71
Babson, Roger, 365
Balance needed in life, 328
Baptist Church in Russia, 13-16
Bastiat, Frederick, quotations by, 283,
    285, 286, 291-92
Battle of Britain, 403
Beecher, Henry Ward, 99
Behavior, influence of music on, 250
Belgium, King of, 85
Ben-Gurion, David, 90
Benson, Beth, 175
Benson, Beverly, 175
Benson, Bonnie, 175
Benson, Ezra Taft (grandfather), 335
Benson, Ezra Taft (grandson), 401
Benson, Flora, 70
Benson, Mark, 133, 175, 177
Benson, Reed, 77, 175, 176
Beverly Hills Hilton Hotel, 85
Bill of Rights, 300, 307
Birth control, 224, 257, 258
Blessings of priesthood, 192
Boise, Idaho, experience with father in,
    186-88
Bok, Edward W., 6
Book of Mormon
    mission of, 158
    how to test truth of, 159
    testifies of conspiracy in latter days,
      161
    predictions in about evil conspiracies,
      321-22
    warnings of, 388
Bowen, Albert E., 282, 378, 395
Boyle, Donzella Cross, 368
Bradford, William, 115
Brainwashing, 260
Brainwashing in the High Schools, 236
Brigham Young University, 226, 406
Brimhall, George H., 128
Broadmindedness, 220
Brother of Jared, 117, 119
Burke, Edmund, 378, 399
Butz, Earl, 127
Byrd, Admiral Richard, 210-11

-C-

Calamities, warnings of, 265-67
Cannon, George Q., 256, 262, 336
Cardozo, Benjamin Nathan, 150
Carnegie Fund hero medal, 213
Carpenter's Hall, 391
Carson, Clarence, 319
CCC camp, experience at, 62-63
Celestial marriage, 161
Challenge, America's, 367-80
Changeless verities of life, 234-35
Character, importance of, 2
Chase, Daryl, 36
Chastity, 5, 196, 259, 364; parents to
    teach children about, 240
Children, blessings of having, 198;
    commandment to have, 257
Church, and state, separation of, 283-84;
    man's duty to, 328; work,
    involvement in, 386
Church Education System, 258
Church of Jesus Christ of Latter-day
    Saints
    mission of, 40-41
    is world church, 89-95
    importance of programs of, for youth,
        251
    distinction between church and
        members, 253-54
    no division in, 253-54
    apostates in, 254
    civic standards for members of, 317-24
    early leaders excommunicated
        from, 355-56
Church Welfare Committee, 268
Citizenship, necessity for, 194
Civil rights movement, 256
Clark, J. Reuben, Jr., quotations by
    on Joseph Smith, 38-39
    on responsibilities of parents, 225
    on culture in the home, 229
    on propaganda, 238
    on "ravening wolves" in Church, 255
    on sex education, 259
    on modern art, etc., 261-62
    on current magazines, 262
    on welfare program, 267, 271
    on allegiance on citizens, 320
    on dangers of losing liberties, 323
    on Holy Ghost, 341
    on freedom and liberty, 342
    on framers of U.S. Constitution, 372
    on conspiracy to destroy
        Constitution, 375-76

    on freedom versus slavery, 385
    warnings of, on communism and
        socialism, 395-97
Coleridge, Samuel Taylor, 99
Collectivism, 354
Collectivism on the Campus, 236
Collectivized socialism, 351
College student, note by, on examination
    paper, 237
Colleges, false teachings at, 236-37
Colonies in colonial America, 369
Columbus, Christopher, 210, 343
"Come, Listen to a Prophet's Voice,"
    162
Commandments, 156; promises given in,
    266; importance of keeping, 356
Committees of Correspondence, 369
Communism
    war against, 300
    socialistic, 346-56
    godless, 347
    no alternate system to, 351
    is tool of Satan, 354
    thrust of, 373
Communist Manifesto, 372
Communist, The Naked, 347
Competition, benefits of, 310
Compromise, 359
Confession of individuals, 260
Confidence given by Savior, 137
Conspiracy, secret, 345
Constitution Hall, 403
Constitution, U.S., 299
    Preamble to, 284
    outlines laws, 288-89
    guarantees of freedom in, 307-308
    divinely inspired, 319-21, 325-26, 344,
        405
    Saints to protect, 384
Conversion to church, 41-42
Coolidge, Calvin, statement by, 361-62
Cornelius, 156
Council of the Twelve, 69
Country, duty to, 329
Courage, 329-30
Courts, role of, 287
Cyrus the Great, 317

-D-

Dallas Morning News, 303
Dalley, Brother, 52
Danforth, William H., 220
Darwin, Charles, 225
Dealey, Ted, 303

Dean, William F., 261
Death, story about, 23
Debt, 271, 355, 415; warnings against, 267, 268
Decision making
    suggestions on, 143-53
    fundamental steps in, 145-46
    based on correct principles, 146-47
    should be timely, 147
    postponing decisions in, 148
    comes after prayerful consideration, 149
    diagnosing problems in, 150
    prayer and fasting in, 150
    how to evaluate, 151
    action on, 151
    ten points for consideration, 152-53
Decisions for Successful Living, 153
Declaration of beliefs on government, 299-302
Declaration of Independence, 115, 222, 284, 299, 307, 367-68
Decline and Fall of the Roman Empire, The, 363
Delegation, 129-41
    prayerful preparation for, 131
    principles of, 131-32
    reasons for failure of, 132
    of responsibility, 133
    of authority, 133-34
    of Jesus by the Father, 134
    examples of from life of Jesus Christ, 135-40
    loyalty in, 138
    feedback in, 139
DeMille, Cecil B., 406
Democracy in America, 360
Depression days of 1930s, 296
Devotion in the home, 170
Dewey, John, 225
Dickinson, John, 369
Dirksen, Everett, 20-21
Divine Origin of Rights, 298
Divorce, 169
Doctrine and Covenants, section 1, 48-49, 57-58
Doctrines, counterfeit, 335-42
Doniphan, General, 318
Douglas, Stephen A., 35
Drugs, 247, 248
Duty
    to Church, 328
    to home, 328
    to country, 329

    to work, 329
    members to perform, 356
Duties of youth, 218-19

-E-
Eagle Scout, sons become, 175
East Minus West Equals Zero, 375
Economic security, 294-95; loss of in Europe, 313; freedom, 298; system in America, 311
Edison, Thomas, 221-22
Education, 330; adult, 312; and action, 380
Educational ideas, false, 225, 235-39
Egan, Howard, 102
Eisenhower, Dwight D., 69-70
Elders of Israel and the Constitution, The, 321
Elijah, 406-407
Emerson, Ralph Waldo, 99
England, socialism in, 295
Entertaining in home in Washington, 85-86
Equality, through governmental intervention, 313-14
"Ere You Left Your Room This Morning," 115-16
Erosion of national morality, 360
Eternal life, 19-26; marriage, 167; verities, 364
Europe, welfare relief activities in, 110-12; Saints in, after World War II, 204; after World War II, 272
Evans, James R., 292-93
Evans, Richard L., 82
Evil forces in media, 243-51
Exaltation, 195-96, 381
Exemplary lives, Latter-day Saints who lead, 79-81
Expo '70 in Japan, 89

-F-
Fairfax Christian School, 401
Faith in God, 7; in Church leaders, 335-42
Faithful, duty to be, 404
False security, 361
Family
    is sacred institution, 167-72
    vacations, 171
    prayer, 170, 175, 355, example of, 184

recreation, need for, 171
personal experiences in author's, 173-78
council, example of, 174
putting father at head of, 179-88
sealed in Salt Lake Temple, 180-81
reunions, 182
spiritual development of, 184
ways to strengthen, 223-32
need for solidarity in, 230
poem by Edgar A. Guest on, 230-31
poem by Charles Sprague on, 232
dangers to, 233
plea to strengthen, 404-405
Family home evening, 160, 174, 177, 228, 251, 328, 382-83
Famine, 258
Fanaticism, 380
Farewell address of George Washington, 289
Farm subsidies, 292-93
Farmer who lost crop, experience of, 203
Farmers, 305
Fasting, 150
Father
responsibilities as head of family, 179-88
cannot be released from responsibility, 184
in Boise who became priesthood leader, 186-88
FBI Annual Report for 1964, 377
Federal Bureau of Investigation reports, 392
Federal supervision, 354
Feedback in delegation, 139
Figures of the Past, 34
Financial obligations of Saints, 356
First inaugural address of Thomas Jefferson, 289, 294
First Presidency statements, 195, 228, 256, 259, 319, 321, 349, 351
First Prayer in Congress, 391
Fitness, physical, mental, and moral, 209; preparing youth for, 217-22; spiritual, 218
Flattery of prominent men, 233-35
Food storage, 268-69, 356, 383, 405
Forgiveness, 196
Foundation for Economic Education, 354
Founding Fathers, 319, 325-26, 344, 392
France, fall of in 1940, 309
Francis, J. A., 12

Frankfurt, Germany, 73
Free agency, 246-47, 306-308, 326-27, 337-38, 384, 402
Free enterprise, 306-315, 352, example of, 378-79
Freedom
how to achieve, 7
guidelines to safeguard, 282
individual, 296
guaranteed by Constitution, 308
heritage of, 343-56
Saints warned to preserve, 357-65
gospel thrives on, 385
economic, 397
Freedom Foundation, 393
Freud, Sigmund, 225
Funerals, 182

-G-

Gadiantons, 348
General Motors Building, 114
Gentiles, promises to, 345; warnings to, 348
Germany, inflation in 1920s in, 272
Gibbon, Edward, 363
Gladstone, 307
Glorious Quest, The, 292
Glory of God is intelligence, 81
God, growing in favor with, 7-8
God and Man at Yale, 236
Gold standard, 301
Golden Rule, 6
Government
ways to determine rightness of, 279-80
proper role of, 281-303
guidelines for functions of, 282
derives powers from the governed, 286-87
defensive roles in, 287
best achieved in smaller group, 289-90
rights of states in, 290
welfare programs in, 290
protective role of, 290-91
special interests in, 292-93
welfare state programs of, 297-98
limited, 298
declaration of beliefs on, 299-302
constitutional, 299-302
to provide military protection, 301-302
nationalized, 306-307
planned economy of, 312

subsidies, 314
evil infiltration in, 348
Grant, Heber J., 12, 193; calling of to
be apostle, 31-32
Grant, Jedediah M., 32
Gratitude, 199-206
Gray, Elbert, 213
*Great Pretense—How to Finance Communism
While Ostensibly Opposing It, The,* 375
Guest, Edgar A., 231

-H-
Hamilton, Andrew, 370
Hancock, John, 369
Happiness, 191-92; pursuit of, 298
Harris, Martin, 119
Harris, William, 109
Health, 4-5; need for, 330
Henry, Patrick, 237, 369
Hilton, Conrad, 115
Hinckley, Gordon B., 181
History, lessons of, 363-64
Hitler, Adolph, 376, 387
Hodge, A. A., 226
Holy Ghost, testifies to truth, 340-41
Holy Land, 90
Holy Roman Empire, 343
Holy Spirit, follow promptings of,
323-24
Home
is cornerstone of salvation, 5
prayer in, 116
is greatest educational institution,
167
forces threatening, 168-69
parents need to spend more time in,
169-70
devotion needed in, 170
parents to instruct children in,
170-71
divinely ordained, 173
is eternal unit, 182
threatening dangers to, 233
man's duty to, 328
solidarity of in past, 393
Home teaching, 140, 149
Hoover, J. Edgar, 169, 377, 394, 398
Horowitz, Jerome, 321
Humanitarianism, 7
Humility, 61
Hyde, Orson, 90, 268

-I-
I Dare You (book), 220-21

Immodesty in dress, 262
Immorality, 247; sexual, 239-41; how
to avoid, 240-41; evils of, 364-65
Incentive, individual, 294-95
Indolence, 329
Inflation, 272
Intelligence, 4
Intentions, following through on, 148
"Intimations of Immortality," 19
Ishmael, sons of, 249
Israel, visit to, 90

-J-
Jackson, Andrew, 392
Jefferson, Thomas, 222, 289, 290, 369,
393
quotations by, 283, 284, 294, 312,
319, 376
Jesus Christ
resurrection of, 1, 16
divinity of, 11-17
written characterization of, 12-13
appeared to Nephites, 16
life and ministry of, 20-21
crucifixion of, 24
appeared to Joseph Smith and
Sidney Rigdon, 25
delegation of by the Father, 134
example of in delegation, 135-40
example of, 155-56
for blessings, 199
early life of, described by Luke, 209
teachings of concerning constitution
and government, 325-33
second coming of, 349-50
Jethro, 138
Jewish people, 90
Job, 21
Joel, 148
Joshua, 147
June Conference, 77

-K-
Kane, Thomas L., 318
Keats, John, 221
Keller, Werner, 375
Keynes, John, 225
Keynes at Harvard, 236
Keys of authority given to Joseph Smith,
135
Kimball, Heber C., 337, 340
Kimball, Spencer W., 159, 262
Knight, Joseph, Jr., 120

"Know this, that every soul is free" (poem), 402
Knowledge, 2-4
Korean War, 260, 261

-L-
Labor Socialist Party, British, 353
Law, of Moses, 101; moral, 300
Lawrence, David, 394
Laws
    binding upon Saints, 277-80
    of God, 278
    established to protect freedom, 288
    to protect rights of free men, 344
Leadership
    need for courageous, 9
    guides for decision making in, 149-50
    in youth, 213
    needed for youth, 214-15
Lee, Harold B., 153, 186, 223, 269, 272, 341
Legal tender, 301
Lehi's prophecy on Joseph Smith, 33
Lenin, 380
Letter, of father to son on Christmas, 171-72; to David O. McKay from serviceman, 190; in newspaper concerning sex education, 227
Letters from a Farmer, 369
Lexington Green, 367, 370
Liahona, the Elders' Journal, 98
Liberties, Saints to safeguard, 278-79; individual, 299
Liberty, danger of loss of, 313; proclaim throughout land, 403
Liberty Bell, 403
Liberty Jail, 140, 204
Life, basic purpose of, 332
Lincoln, Abraham, 8, 115, 391, 392
Lindbergh, Charles, 221
Listen, article on Mormons in, 82-84
Literature, freedom, 354
Locke, John, 286, 288
Long and Short Range Arrows, 128
Longfellow, Henry Wadsworth, 99
Los Angeles Temple, 85
Louvre in Paris, 78
Lowell, James Russell, 28
Loyalty in leadership, 138
Lucifer, satanical priestcraft of, 347

-M-
Madison, James, 285, 289

Maeser, Karl G., 225
Mainspring of Human Progress, 296
Man, His Origin and Destiny, 227
Management principles on delegation, 131-33
Manifesto, by Karl Marx, 225-26
Many Are Called But Few Are Chosen, 321
Marriage, temple, 161, 192-93; is sacred institution, 167; eternal, 167
Marshall, Peter, 23
Martin, William A., 64
Marx, Karl, 225, 372
Marxism, 293
Mary, mother of Jesus, 12
Mason, George, 369
Material wealth, 21
McCormick, Cyrus, 221
McKay, David O., 64, 69-70, 321
    picture of in Listen, 82
    on strengthening the home, 223
    on public schools and Supreme Court, 226
    on persecution of Church, 255, 336
    on suppressing anger, 261
    on fad dances, 262
    on socialism and communism, 340, 397
    on Constitution of the United States, 341, 383-84
    on threat of communism, 347, 353, 398
    on secret combinations, 350
    on freedom of men, 351
    on God and liberty, 384-85
McNarney, General, 73, 74
Media, evils in, 240, 243-51; criticisms of, 262
Men, learning of, 258
Mental striving of men, 2-3
Minute Men, 367, 370
Military protection, need for, 301-302
Missionaries
    message of, 26
    responsibilities of, 43-50
    number of, 44
    message of from days of Adam, 45-46
    earliest in Church, 46-47
    to warn the world, 47-48
    to teach salvation, 49
    influence of an author, 51-52
    in Benson family, 54-55
    advice to, 57-67
    to preach salvation, 58

should heed counsel of mission president, 59
to keep healthy, 60
need testimonies, 60-61
need to be humble, 61
need to love people, 62
to live exemplary lives, 62-63
example set by, 64
in Ireland, 64
to support companions, 65
returned, 79-80
prayers of, answered, 109-110
approach of, to families, 179
Missionary call of author's parents, 53-54
Missionary work, sections in Doctrine and Covenants on, 66
Models, need for, 191
Modesty in dress, 240-41
Monetary system, 287
Monument to Minute Men, inscription on, 370-71
Moral
    cleanliness, 196
    law, 300
    principles, 364
    purity, 364
Morality, 5, 239-41
Mormon Miracle pageant, 244
Mormonism, predictions concerning, 189-90
Mortality, purpose of, 326-27
Moses, 138
Motherhood, 5
Mothers, 170; responsibilities of, 183; working, 197
Mozart, 222
Mt. Fuji, Japan, 374
Mullendore, W. C., 353
Murrow, Edward R., 176-77
Music, rock, 228, 244, 248, 249, 250, 262

-N-
Name-calling, Saints to avoid, 355
Navigation Acts, 369
Necking and petting, 241
New England Rally for God, Family, and Country, 11
New York *Times,* 306
Newquist, Jerreld L., 321
Newton, Isaac, 221
Nibley, Hugh, 243
Nibley, Richard, 244, 248, 249, 250

Nineveh, 406

-O-
Obedience, 21; to God's laws, 327
Objectives of God, 381-82
Obscenity, 247
Oneida Stake, 200
Otis, James, 369

-P-
Page, John E., 335
Paine, Thomas, 283, 302
Parable of wheat and tares, 91-92
Parent-child relationships, 171
Parenthood, 5; blessings of, 193; postponing, 197-98
Parents
    obedience to, 168
    to be models for youth, 191
    responsibilities of, 224
    to train children, 238-39
    duties of, 328-29
Parker, John, 367
Pasteur, Louis, 212-13
Paternalism, 354
Patriarchal blessing, 52; order, 223
Patriotism, 320
Peace movement, 229
Penn, William, 127
Persia, king of, 317
Person to Person, 176-77
Personal freedom, 298
Peter, calling of by Jesus, 136
Philadelphia, experience of missionaries in, 65
Physical fitness, 217-18; exercise, need for, 241
Pilgrims, 115
Poland, meeting with members in, 71-73
Police, 288
Political responsibilities of priesthood holders, 355
Popular thing, theme of Satan, 387
Population control, 257
Pornography, 247
Post office, missionaries preaching at, 65
Pratt, Parley P., 317
Prayer, 8, 241
    parents' belief in, 109
    of missionaries answered, 109-110
    of children, 110
    for help in direction of European relief, 110-12
    poems on, 113

how to improve, 113-28
on building in New York, 114
America founded on, 115
family, 116, 170
and brother of Jared, 117
counsel from ancient prophets on,
    117-19
admonished to have frequent, 120
personal preparation for, 120
talk directly to the Father in, 120
should be meaningful, 120-22, 126
in groups, 123-24
language of, 124
be spiritually in tune in, 124-25
length of, 125
blessings from, 126
in U.S. Department of Agriculture,
    127
for inspiration in delegation, 150
personal memories of, 174
great power of, 365
early U.S. presidents believed in,
    391-92
of child whose father was in RAF, 403
Preamble to U.S. Constitution, 284
Preparedness, need for, 265-73; spiritual
    and physical, 331
"Present Crisis, The," 28-29
President of Church, following counsel
    of, 339-40
President's Prayer Breakfast, 391
Price supports, 292
Priesthood
    responsibility in, 137
    feedback in, 139-40
    authority, 158
    ordination to, 180-82
    fathers exercising, 186
    citizenship responsibility of, 186
    responsibility of, to job, 186
    blessings of, 192
    duty of holders to understand Lord's
        plan, 343-56
    holders of to become informed about
        communism, 354
Principles, discerning correctness of,
    281-82; moral, 364
Private enterprise, 306-316
Private property, protection of, 300
Programs of Church, inspiration for,
    382-83
Property, right to own, 286
Prophecies, on conditions in last days,
    265-73, 343-56; on discovery of America,

343; on preservation of America, 388
Prophets
    role of, 157-63
    need for, 160
    Lord speaks to, 266
    following counsel of, 323
    latter-day, 339-40
    counsel of, 395
Prophets, Principles, and National Survival,
    321
Putnam, Israel, 401
Purdue University, experience at, 81-82
Purity, 5; moral, 364

-Q-
Quest of a Hemisphere, 368, 369, 370
Quorum, priesthood, responsibilities of, 183

-R-
Rafferty, Max, 236
Randall, Clarence B., 150
Reagan, Ronald, speech by, 362-63
Recreation, 330
Relief for Saints in Europe after war, 272
Religion, and science, 3; freedom of, 311;
    practiced by founding fathers, 391-92
Repentance, 196
Responsibility, delegating, 133
Resurrection, 19-26; of Jesus Christ, 16
Revelations, 256; publication of, 48;
    through prophets, 159
Revere, Paul, 369
Revolution, American, 302, 367-71
Revolutionary War, 401
Richards, LeGrand, 54
Rigdon, Sidney, 25
Righteous people to be saved, 94
Righteousness in America, 345; America
    to be preserved by, 391-400
Rights of individuals, 282-87, 301
Rock music, 228, 244, 248, 249, 250, 262
Roman Empire, 362
Rome, reasons for downfall of, 362-63
Romney, Marion G., 337
Roosevelt, Theodore, 133, 217-18, 302,
    320
Root, E. Merrill, 236
Russia, attending Baptist Church in,
    13-16
Russians, philosophies of, 293-94

-S-
Sabbath Day, 97-107
    article in Liahona on, 98

poem in *Improvement Era* on, 98-99
quotations on, 99
experiment to hold every twenty-one
  days, 99
in ancient times, 100-101
in latter days, 101-103
in Salt Lake Valley, 103
purpose of, 103-104
activities on, 104-105
First Presidency statement on, 105-106
ways to keep sacred, 106
closing business on, 106-107
consequences of disobedience to, 107
Sacrament meeting in Whitney, Idaho, 202
Salt Lake Temple, families sealed in,
  180-81
Salvation, 381
Satan, plan of, 384, 386; uses tactic
  of persuasion, 387-88
Saul, conversion of, 134; on road to
  Damascus, 155
Savoy Hilton Hotel, 114
School books, false ideas in, 226-27
Schools, prayers in, 226
Science and religion, 3
Scout program, 207-215; Oath, 208; Law,
  209-210
Scouting, emphasizes ideals of America,
  210; needs good leadership, 214-15
Scoutmaster in Idaho, 207
Scouts, doorknob hangers distributed by,
  393
Scriptures, warnings in, of evil
  conspiracies, 321-22; importance of
  studying, 330, 338-39; guide to
  Americans today, 394-95
Second century, end of, 373
Second coming of Christ, 349-50
Secret combinations, 349; conspiracy,
  350
Secretary of Agriculture, experience in
  Russia while serving as, 14-16; family
  experiences while author was, 176-77
Security, 298
Selbongen, East Prussia, 71
Self-control, 261
Self-government, 289, 301
Self-sufficiency, 270-71
Sensitivity training, 260-61
Separation of Church and state, 283-84
Service to others, 5-7
Serviceman, stationed in Salt Lake City,
  experience with, 201
Servicemen in southeast Asia, 373-74

Seventy, called by Jesus in ancient
  times, 136
Sex education, 171-72, 227, 259-60
Sex Information and Education Council
  of the United States (SIECUS), 259-60
Sexual immorality, 239-41; impurity, 259
Skilled labor, developing, 270
Skousen, W. Cleon, 347
Smith, Adam, 295
Smith, George A., 271
Smith, George Albert, 107
Smith, Hyrum, 29, 320
Smith, Joseph
  testifies of Jesus Christ, 25, 26
  message and mission of, 27-41
  martyrdom of, 29, 38
  in premortal council, 30
  prophecy of Lehi on, 33
  instructions to regarding duties,
    33-34
  described by Josiah Quincy, 34-35
  described in New York *Times*, 35
  comment about by Stephen A.
    Douglas, 35
  described in *Weekly Bostonian*, 35-36
  described by John Greenleaf Whittier,
    36
  translates scriptures, 36
  described by John Henry Evans, 37
  described by J. Reuben Clark, Jr.,
    38-39
  describes first vision, 39-40
  receives revelations on missionary
    work, 46
  keys of authority given to, 135
  in Liberty Jail, 140, 204-205
  followed admonition of James, 144
  first vision of, 157
  receives revelation on being prepared,
    265
  outlined Articles of Faith, 277
  described by Parley P. Pratt, 317
  on citizenship responsibilities, 320-21
  on when a prophet is a prophet, 323
  testifies to sermon of Brigham Young,
    339
  said Constitution would hang by a
    thread, 345, 399
  did not believe doctrine of socialism,
    353
  said elders to save Constitution, 389
Smith, Joseph F., 107, 200, 223, 225, 233,
  258, 382, 393-94
Smith, Joseph Fielding, 92, 93, 102, 104,

105, 223, 226, 227, 270, 321
Smith, Samuel Harrison, 43
Smoot, Dan, 295
Social sciences, errors in, 258
Socialism
   in England, 295
   evils of, 296-97, 300, 384
   collectivized, 351
   definition of, 352
Socialistic communism, 346
Sodom, 406
Sons of Liberty, 369
Sorensen, W. A., 107
Sovereignty of states, 301
Soviet philosophy, 293
Spending in government, example of,
   379-80
Spirit, men to follow promptings of,
   381-89
Spirit world, 22
Spirituality, 327-28
Sprague, Charles, 232
St. George Temple, 193
Stamp Act of 1765, 369
Standard works, 338
Standards
   of Church, 62-63
   examples of living, 77-87
   living gospel, 194-95
   for youth, 229
   threats to, 243-51
   upholding, 359
States' rights, 290, 301, 379
Stature, Jesus increased in, 405
Storage, plan, 331; home, 383
Strachey, John, 353
Strengthen home and family, need to, 364
Subsidies, governmental, 314
Success in chosen profession, 193-94
Suffer Little Children, 236
"Summons, A" (poem), 377
Sunday School class, experience in, 51
Supply, food, 405
Supreme Court, U.S., 226, 398

-T-
Tabernacle Choir, on ship to Europe,
   83-84
Talmage, James E., 100, 101, 137
Taxation without representation, 369
Taxes, 287, 301
Taylor, John, 139
Tel Aviv, 90
Temple marriage, 161, 192-93

Temple work, 146
Ten Commandments, 406
Ten Commandments, The, 406
Testimony, 9, 12; anchor of, 192
Textbooks, false ideas in, 227, 236-37
Thanksgiving, 199
Theory and Practice of Socialism, The, 353
"Things That Are More Excellent, The"
   (poem), 77-78
This Week magazine, 237
Thoreau, Henry D., 294
"Though in the Outward Church Below,"
   254-55
Thoughts, influence of, 241
Threat to U.S., secret conspiracy is, 345
Three witnesses to Book of Mormon,
   335
Thurmond, Strom, letter to editor from,
   351-52
Tithing, 356; blessings from paying, 267
Tokyo, experience in conference in,
   181-82
Tolerance, 214, 359
Toqueville, Alexis de, 360
Translations of scriptures by Joseph
   Smith, 36
Truth, 40
   eternal nature of, 3-4
   is eternal, 332
   to be shared with all, 356
   Church founded on, 359

-U-
Unchastity, 196
United Religious Organization, 317
United States Department of Agriculture,
   127
United States Supreme Court, 226, 398

-V-
Vacations, family, 171
Valley Forge, 332, 387, 391
Veritas Foundation, 236
Verities, changeless, 234-35
Vietnam, meeting with servicemen in,
   373-74
Virtue of Saints, 234
Von Blomberg, Baron, 317

-W-
War, of 1870, 99; planes in World War
   II, 309; in heaven, 337, 347, 389
Wars fought by America, 306
Warnings, given to Saints, 358; of God

to man, 381-89

Warsaw, Poland, 71-73, 111

Washington, George, 8, 288, 289, 350, 369, 377-78, 391, 392

Wealth, equalizing, 292-93

Wealth of Nations, 295

Weaver, Henry Grady, 296

Webster, Daniel, 367

Weekly Bostonian, 35

Welfare
    supplies distributed to Saints in Europe, 74
    relief activities in Europe, 110-12
    plan, 146, 161-62, 266-69, 272-73, 331, 356, 383
    state, 297
    supplies, 405

Well, baby caught in, 213

Wesley, John, 229

West, law in early, 285-86

"What Is a Family?" (pamphlet), 182-83

What They Are Doing to Your Children, 236

Wheat, Saints admonished to store, 268

White House, 69

Whitmer, John, 75

Whitmer, Peter, Jr., 75

Whitney, Eli, 221

Whitney, Idaho, 200, 202; ward in, 51

Whitney, Orson F., 64, 104, 318

Whittier, John Greenleaf, 36, 377

Wickedness in world, 90-95

Widtsoe, John A., statements by, 359-60, 389

Winter Quarters, 102

Wisdom, 2-4

Word of Wisdom, 63, 83-84, 86, 269-70

Wordsworth, William, poem by, 19

Work, 6; week, shortening of, 309; duty to, 329

Woodruff, Wilford, 93, 270, 317, 339

World, acceptance of, 233-34

Worldliness in Church, 256

-Y-

Yale University, 236

Young, Brigham, 34, 93, 127, 260, 271, 323, 335, 336, 338, 339, 399

Youth
    challenge to, 189-98
    letter of, to David O. McKay, 190
    need good leaders, 214-15
    compared to savings bank, 218-19
    to be taught duties, 218-19
    examples of successful, 221-22
    needs of, 222
    Satan's thrust against, 243-51

-Z-

Zenger, Peter, 370